广西职业教育铁道信号自动控制专业及专业群发展研究基地研究成果

铁道信号自动控制专业课程标准

（中英双语）

莫振栋　黄　聪
赵　宁　吴雄升　著

西南交通大学出版社
·成　都·

图书在版编目（CIP）数据

铁道信号自动控制专业课程标准：汉英对照 / 莫振栋等著. —成都：西南交通大学出版社，2020.10
ISBN 978-7-5643-7804-2

Ⅰ. ①铁… Ⅱ. ①莫… Ⅲ. ①铁路信号－自动控制－高等学校－教学参考资料－汉、英 Ⅳ. ①U284.3

中国版本图书馆 CIP 数据核字（2020）第 210513 号

Tiedao Xinhao Zidong Kongzhi Zhuanye Kecheng Biaozhun

铁道信号自动控制专业课程标准

（中英双语）

莫振栋　黄　聪　赵　宁　吴雄升　著

责任编辑　孟　媛
封面设计　何东琳设计工作室

出版发行　西南交通大学出版社
（四川省成都市金牛区二环路北一段 111 号
西南交通大学创新大厦 21 楼）
邮政编码　610031
发行部电话　028-87600564　028-87600533
网址　http://www.xnjdcbs.com
印刷　四川煤田地质制图印刷厂

成品尺寸　210 mm × 285 mm
印张　10.25
字数　402 千
版次　2020 年 10 月第 1 版
印次　2020 年 10 月第 1 次
定价　88.00 元
书号　ISBN 978-7-5643-7804-2

课件咨询电话：028-81435775

前言

PREFACE

在“一带一路”倡议下，中国轨道交通企业的海外市场不断扩展，为整个轨道交通行业带来新的发展与机遇。中国轨道交通企业在东南亚地区有众多在建项目，东盟各国对轨道交通专业技术人才存在巨大需求，人才培养和技术输出势在必行。我校是全国铁道通信信号专业教学指导委员会主任单位，为了更好地服务“一带一路”沿线国家的人才培养，我校牵头组建了中国—东盟轨道交通职业教育集团，面向东盟开发具有中国行业特色的教学项目，助力东盟国家铁路人才的培养。

2018年，我校铁道信号自动控制专业及专业群发展研究基地入选广西职业教育第一批专业发展研究基地，在开展教育部交通运输大类国家示范专业点的建设过程中，始终坚持响应国家“一带一路”倡议和广西创新驱动发展战略“九张名片”，紧跟国家高速铁路新技术和自动控制新技术的发展理念，全面实施“国际引领，多措并举，内涵升级，建设全国行业特色鲜明高水平专业”的发展战略。针对高职院校服务东盟国家轨道交通控制类行业企业人才需求，与中国铁路南宁局集团有限公司柳州电务段、南宁电务段等行业企业深度合作，以教育部发布的职业教育专业教学标准为引领，编写了本书，着力推进国际职业教育标准本土化，服务“中国高铁走出去”，为“一带一路”沿线国家培训铁路运营人才，推动中国职业教育标准的国际输出。

“铁道信号自动控制专业中英文课程标准”是广西职业教育第一批专业发展研究基地项目研究成果，具有鲜明的中国轨道交通行业特色；进一步增强了铁道信号自动控制专业核心竞争力，为建设国内高水平专业打下坚实的基础，进一步提高学校的知名度和社会影响力。

本书由广西职业教育第一批专业发展研究基地——铁道信号自动控制专业项目组成员编写和审定，莫振栋、黄聪、赵宁、吴雄升著，吴建军、吴昕慧、唐匀生、冯云智、陶汉卿几位老师也参与了编写。在编写过程中，得到了中国铁路南宁局集团有限公司柳州电务段、南宁电务段等企业高级技术人员的大力支持，在此表示衷心的感谢!

由于编写时间和编者水平有限，本书还有许多需要完善之处，恳请广大读者批评和指正。

作者

2020.6

目 录

CONTENTS

第一章 专业基础课程 Basic Courses

第一节 “电路分析基础”课程标准

Curriculum Standard for the Basis of Circuit Analysis

一、课程性质 Nature of the Course

1. 课程类型、课程功能 Types and Functions

本课程是高职轨道交通控制类专业的专业基础课，课程共计 72 学时、4.5 学分。本课程旨在使学生掌握电类技术人员必须具备的电路基础理论、基本分析方法，掌握各种常用电工仪器、仪表的使用及简单的电工测量方法，初步学习一些电工常用工具的使用及布线工艺，为后续专业课的学习和今后踏入社会后的工程实际应用打下一定的基础。同时，使学习者通过本课程的学习提高自身的思维能力、逻辑推理能力、理论联系实际的能力。

This course is a specialized basic course for rail transportation control major in higher vocational education, including 72 lessons and 4.5 credits. Students are required to learn the basic theories and analysis method of the circuit to be an electrician, to master the use of various common electrical instruments, meters and simple electrical measurement methods, to learn the use of some common tools and wiring technique, therefore lay a certain foundation for the study of subsequent courses prefessional and the practical application of engineering after entering the society in the future. Meanwhile it enables the learners to improve their thinking ability, logical reasoning ability and the ability of integrate theory with practice.

2. 课程功能定位 Orientation of the Function

表 1 课程功能定位分析

Table 1 Analysis of the Orientation of the Function

对接的工作岗位 Jobs	对接培养的职业岗位能力 Abilities
电工仪器仪表、电工工具管理生产岗位 Positions as electrician for instrument and meter, electrician for tool management and production	1. 熟悉电工仪器仪表的使用方法 Familiar with the use of electrical instruments
	2. 掌握常用电工工具的使用方法 Master the use of common electrical tools
	3. 了解电工仪器仪表、电工工具的维护、维修方法 Understand the maintenance and repairs of electrical instruments and tools
电气产品组装、装配岗位 Positions on electrical production assembly	1. 熟悉电气原理图、电气布置图和电气安装接线图的阅读方法 Familiar with the interpretation methods of electrical schematic diagram, electric layout diagram and electric installation wiring diagram
	2. 有较强的电路分析能力 Strong circuit analysis abilities

对接的工作岗位 Jobs	对接培养的职业岗位能力 Abilities
电气产品组装、装配岗位 Positions on electrical production assembly	3. 掌握常用电气元件的识别方法、技术参数和装配要求 Master the identification methods, technical parameters and assembly requirements of common electrical components
	4. 掌握常用电子元件的安装与焊接工艺 Master the installation and soldering technique of common electronic components
	5. 掌握电子产品的调试技术 Master the debugging technology of electronic products
仿真电路设计岗位 Simulation circuit design	1. 会使用常见的电路仿真软件 Be able to use common circuit simulation software
	2. 理解电路原理，并能用仿真软件进行简单的电路设计 Understand circuit principle and use simulation software to design simple circuit
电气设备检测、调试与维修岗位 Electrical equipment testing, debugging and maintenance	1. 能分解整个大电路为小电路，并分析小电路的功能 Be able to decompose the entire large circuit into small circuits, and analyze their functions
	2. 会用电工仪器仪表检测电气设备故障 Be able to use electrical instruments to detect electrical equipment failures
	3. 能对电气设备进行调试和简单维修 Be able to debug and maintain electrical equipment

二、课程目标与内容 Objectives and Contents

1. 课程总目标 General Objectives

本课程的总目标是使学生掌握基本电路分析方面的基本理论、基本知识和基本技能，培养学生具备电气工程人员应具备的基本的电路组装、调试能力，使其初步具备工程计算和实验研究的能力，并为学习后续课程打好基础。

The general objective of the course is to enable students to acquire basic theories, knowledge, and skills of basic circuit analysis, to equip the students with basic circuit assembly and debugging ability as electricians, to have the basic engineering calculation and experimental research capabilities, and lay a good foundation for the study of follow-up courses.

2. 课程具体目标 Specific Objectives

表 2 课程教学目标与内容 1

Table 2 Teaching Objectives and Contents 1

序号 NO.	毕业要求指标点 Index point of graduation requirement	知识目标 Knowledge goals	技能目标 Ability goals	素质目标 Quality goals	教学内容 Teaching contents
1	掌握电路的基本概念和基本定律 Master the basic concepts and laws of circuits	了解电路和电路模型的基本概念，掌握电路主要物理量的定义及测量，熟悉电阻、电压源、电流源等电气元件的功能，掌握基尔霍夫定律 Know the basic concepts of circuits and circuit models; master the definition and measurement of the main physical quantities of circuits; be familiar with the functions of electrical components, such as resisters, voltage sources, and current sources; and master the Kirchhoff's law	掌握电路的基本组成和原理，掌握电路物理量的测量方法和常见电气元件的参数，具有一定的查阅电子元器件、集成电路手册和其他资料的能力 Master the basic composition and principles of the circuit; master the measurement methods of circuit physical quantities and the parameters of common electrical components, and have the ability to consult electronic components, integrated circuit manuals and other materials	培养学生对元器件、仪器仪表及其操作的职业素质感情和职业道德 Cultivate students' vocational quality feelings and professional ethics on components, instruments and their operation	电路的基本概念和基本定律 Basic concepts and laws of circuits

续表

序号 NO.	毕业要求指标点 Index point of graduation requirement	知识目标 Knowledge goals	技能目标 Ability goals	素质目标 Quality goals	教学内容 Teaching contents
2	掌握线性电路的分析方法 Master the analysis method of linear circuit	掌握电阻串联和并联的计算方法，掌握直流电路的基本分析方法 Master the calculation method of series and parallel resistors, master the basic analysis method of direct current (DC) circuit	会分析电阻的串联和并联，并能用串、并联电阻解决电路问题，能利用叠加定理、戴维南定理等解决实际问题 Be bale to analyze the series and parallel resistor, and use series and parallel resistor to solve circuit problems, to use the superposition theorem, Thevenin's theorem, etc. to solve practical problems	养成认真细致、实事求是、积极探索的科学态度和工作作风，形成理论联系实际、自主学习和探索创新的良好习惯 Develop a scientific attitude and work style that is conscientious, meticulous, realistic, and active exploration, and form a good habit of integrating theory with practice, independent learning, and exploration and innovation	线性电路的分析方法 The analysis method of linear circuit
3	掌握正弦交流电路及其应用 Master sinusoidal alternating current (AC) circuit and its application	理解正弦交流电的基本概念，掌握单一元件在正弦交流电路的应用，掌握RLC交流电路的分析方法，掌握正弦交流电的功率及功率因数的计算方法 Understand the basic concepts of sinusoidal AC current, master the application of single components in sinusoidal AC circuits, master the analysis methods of RLC AC circuits, and master the calculation methods of sinusoidal AC power and power factor	会分析正弦交流电的使用和分析方法，会用万用表测量交流电的物理量，会用功率表测量交流电功率 Be able to analyze the use and analysis method of sinusoidal AC, to use a multimeter to measure the physical quantity of alternating current, and use a power meter to measure the power of AC	提高学生分析问题和解决问题的能力 Improve students' ability to analyze and solve problems	正弦交流电路及应用 The sinusoidal AC circuit and its application
4	掌握三相交流电路的分析和应用 Master the analysis and application of three-phase AC circuits	掌握三相交流电的产生和连接方法，熟悉三相负载的连接和分析方法，了解三相电路的功率计算 Master the generation and connection method of three-phase AC, familiar with the connection and analysis method of three-phase load, understand the power calculation of three-phase circuit	能够根据三相负载的额定电压选择三相负载的正确连接方式 Be able to choose the correct connection method of three-phase load according to the rated voltage of three-phase load	提高学生分析问题和解决问题的能力 Improve students' ability to analyze and solve problems	三相交流电路 Three-phase AC circuits
5	了解互感耦合电路的分析方法和应用 Know the analysis method and application of mutual inductance coupling circuit	熟悉自感、互感的基本概念，掌握同名端的测量方法，掌握互感耦合电路的分析方法，掌握理想变压器的分析方法 Familiar with the basic concepts of self-inductance and mutual inductance, master the measurement method of the dotted terminals, master the analysis method of the mutual inductance coupling circuit, and master the analysis method of the ideal transformer	掌握用万用表测量同名端的方法，会自感、互感电路的分析方法 Master the method of measuring the dotted terminals with a multimeter, and master the analy sis method of self-inductance and mutual inductance circuits	培养学生对元器件、仪器仪表及其操作的职业素质感情和职业道德 Cultivate students' professional quality feelings and professional ethics on components, instruments and their operation	互感耦合电路 The mutual inductance coupling circuit

续表

序号 NO.	毕业要求指标点 Index point of graduation requirement	知识目标 Knowledge goals	技能目标 Ability goals	素质目标 Quality goals	教学内容 Teaching contents
6	掌握线性电路的瞬态过程分析方法 Master the analysis method of transient process in linear circuit	掌握瞬态过程及换路定律的计算方法，了解 RC 电路、RL 电路的瞬态过程，会用一阶电路的三要素法分析和解决一阶电路的计算 Master the calculation of the transient process and the switching law, understand the transient process of the RC circuit and the RL circuit, and use the three-factors method of the first-order circuit to analyze and solve the calculation of the first-order circuit	能用示波器观察一阶电路的瞬态过程，会用一阶电路三要素发解决一阶电路的计算问题 Observe the transient process of the first-order circuit with an oscilloscope, and use the three elements of the first-order circuit to solve the calculation problem of the first-order circuit	通过对问题的分析，体验分析的乐趣，提高学生对生活和学习的积极性 Experience the joy of andysis through problem andysis and improve students' enthusiasm for life and learning	线性电路的瞬态过程 Transient processes of linear circuits

表 3　课程教学目标与内容 2

Table 3　Teaching Objectives and Contents 2

序号 NO.	项目（模块） Items	任务（单元） Tasks	教学内容 Teaching contents	重点、难点 Key points and difficulties	学时 Hours
1	项目 1：电路的基本概念和基本定律 Item 1: basic concepts and laws of circuits	1.1 电路和电路模型 Circuits and circuit models	电路的组成及作用；理想元件和电路模型；电路的工作状态 The composition and function of the circuit; ideal components and circuit models; the working status of the circuit	重点：理想元件和电路模型 Key points: ideal components and circuit models 难点：理想元件的物理含义 Difficulties: the physical meaning of ideal components	2
		1.2 电路的主要物理量 The main physical quantity of the circuit	电流及参考方向；电位、电压及电动势；电功率及电能 Current and reference direction; electric potential, voltage and electromotive force; electrical power and electrical energy	重点：各电路参数的方向 Key points: the direction of each circuit parameter 难点：各电路参数的参考方向 Difficulties: the reference direction of each circuit parameter	4
		1.3 电阻元件 Resistance elements	电阻元件及伏安特性；电阻元件的功率 Resistance elements and voltammety characteristics; power of resistance element	重点：电阻元件的伏安特性 Key points: voltammety characteristics of resistance elements 难点：参考方向对欧姆定律中正负符号的影响 Difficulties: the influence of the reference direction on the sign of Ohm's law	2

续表

序号 NO.	项目（模块） Items	任务（单元） Tasks	教学内容 Teaching contents	重点、难点 Key points and difficulties	学时 Hours
1	项目 1：电路的基本概念和基本定律 Item 1: basic concepts and laws of circuits	1.4 电压源与电流源 Voltage source and current source	理想电压源与实际电压源；理想电流源与实际电流源；实际电源模型的等效变换 Ideal voltage source and actual voltage source; ideal current source and actual current source; equivalent transformation of actual power supply model	重点：实际电压源和实际电流源的模型 Key points: models of actual voltage source and actual current source 难点：实际电源模型的等效变换 Difficulties: equivalent transformation of actual power model	2
		1.5 基尔霍夫定律 Kirchhoff's Law	电路的几个常用名词；基尔霍夫电流定律；基尔霍夫电压定律 The common terms of circuit; Kirchhoff's current law; Kirchhoff's voltage law	重点：基尔霍夫电流、电压定律 Key points: Kirchhoff's current and voltage laws 难点：用基尔霍夫定律解决实际问题 Difficulties: use Kirchhoff's law to solve practical problems	4
		1.6 电路中电位的计算 Calculation of potential in the circuit	电路中电位的计算 Calculation of potential in the circuit	重点：电位的计算 Key points: calculation of potential 难点：用电位的计算方法解决实际问题 Difficulties: solve practical problems with potential calculation methods	2
2	项目 2：线性电路的分析方法 Item 2: linear circuit's analysis method	2.1 电阻电路的等效变换 Equivalent transformation of resistance circuit	二端网络等效的概念；电阻的串联及等效；电阻的并联及等效；电阻的混连及等效 The concept of two-terminal network equivalence; series resistance and equivalence; parallel connection and equivalence; mixed connection and equivalence	重点：电阻串、并联等效的计算 Key points: the calculation of equivalence for the series and parallel resistance 难点：串联、并联电阻的实际应用 Difficulties: the application of resistance in series and parallel	2
		2.2 星形电阻网络与三角形电阻网络的等效变换 Equivalent transformation between star resistance network and triangle resistance network	电阻星形连接与电阻的三角形连接；等效变换的方法 Resistance star connection and resistance triangle connection; equivalent transformation method	重点：等效变换的方法 Key points: equivalent transformation method 难点：等效变换的实际应用 Difficulties: practical application of equivalent transformation	2

序号 NO.	项目（模块） Items	任务（单元） Tasks	教学内容 Teaching contents	重点、难点 Key points and difficulties	学时 Hours
2	项目 2：线性电路的分析方法 Item 2: linear circuit's analysis method	2.3 直流电路的基本分析方法 Basic analysis method of DC circuit	支路电流法；网孔电流法；节点电压法；弥尔曼定理 Branch current method; mesh current method; node voltage method; Millman's theorem	重点：支路电流法 Key points: branch current method 难点：支路电流法解决电路问题 Difficulties: solves circuit problems with branch current method	4
		2.4 叠加定理 Superposition theorem	叠加定理 Superposition theorem	重点：叠加定理 Key points: superposition theorem 难点：叠加定理的实际应用 Difficulties: the practical application of superposition theorem	2
		2.5 戴维南定理 Thevenin's theorem	戴维南定理 Thevenin's theorem	重点：戴维南定理 Key points: Thevenin's theorem 难点：戴维南定理的实际应用 Difficulties: the practical application of Thevenam's theorem	2
3	项目 3：正弦交流电路及应用 Item 3: sinusoidal AC circuit and its application	3.1 正弦交流电的基本概念 Basic concepts of sinusoidal AC	正弦交流电的基本概念 Basic concepts of sinusoidal AC	重点：正弦交流电三要素 Key points: Three factors of sinusoidal AC 难点：振幅、有效值的计算；周期、频率、角频率之间的转换；相位差的计算 Difficulties: calculation of amplitude and effective value; conversion between period, frequency and angular frequency; calculation of phase difference	4
		3.2 正弦交流电的相量表示法 Phasor representation of sinusoidal alternating current	复数；正弦量的相量表示法 plural; phasor representation of sine	重点：正弦量的相量表示法 Key points: phasor representation of sine 难点：正弦量和相量之间的转化及计算方法 Difficulties: method of conversion and calculation between sine and phasor	4
		3.3 单一元件的正弦交流电路 Single element sinusoidal AC circuit	纯电阻、电感、电容元件的正弦交流电路 Sine AC circuit of pure resistance, inductance and capacitance	重点：电感、电容元件的正弦交流电路 Key points: sinusoidal AC circuit of inductance and capacitance element 难点：用相量计算的方式计算电感、电容正弦交流电路 Difficulties: calculate the inductance and capacitance in sinusoidal AC circuit on phasor calculation	4
		3.4 RLC 交流电路的分析 Analysis of RLC AC circuit	RLC 串联交流电路的分析；并联交流电路的分析 Analysis of RLC series AC circuit RLC analysis of RLC parallel AC circuit	重点：RLC 串联、并联交流电路的分析 Key points: analysis of RLC series and parallel AC circuits 难点：用相量方法计算 RLC 串并联电路 Difficulties: calculate RLC series and parallel circuit on phasor method	4

续表

序号 NO.	项目（模块） Items	任务（单元） Tasks	教学内容 Teaching contents	重点、难点 Key points and difficulties	学时 Hours
3	项目 3：正弦交流电路及应用 Item 3: sinusoidal AC circuit and its application	3.5 RLC 谐振电路的分析 Analysis of RLC resonant circuit	串联电路的谐振；并联电路的谐振 Resonance of series circuit; resonance of parallel circuit	重点：串联、并联电路的谐振 Key points: resonance of series and parallel circuits 难点：串联谐振的分析 Difficulties: analysis of series resonance	4
		3.6 正弦交流电路中的功率及功率因数 Power and power factors in sinusoidal AC circuit	正弦交流电路的功率因数；无功功率、视在功率和功率三角形；功率因数的提高 Power factors of sinusoidal AC circuit;reactive power, apparent power and delta power; power factor improvement	重点：正弦交流电路有功功率、无功功率、视在功率的计算 Key points: calculation of active power, reactive power and apparent power in sinusoidal AC circuit 难点：功率三角形的计算 Difficulties: calculation of delta power	4
4	项目 4：三相交流电路 Item 4: three-phase AC circuit	4.1 三相电源 Three-phase power	三相交流电的产生；三相电源的连接 Three-phase alternating current generation; three-phase power connection	重点：三相电源的连接 Key points: three-phase power connection 难点：三相电源星形连接时，线电压和相电压的计算 Difficulties: calculation of line voltage and phase voltage of three phase power in star connection	2
		4.2 三相负载 Three-phase load	负载的星形连接；负载的三角形连接 Star connection of load; delta connection of load	重点：三相负载的连接 Key points: three-phase load connection 难点：负载三角形连接时，线电流和相电流的计算 Difficulties: calculation of line current and phase current when the load is delta connected	2
		4.3 三相电路的功率 Three-phase circuit power	三相电路的功率 Three-phase circuit power	重点：三相电路的功率计算 Key points: calculation of three-phase circuitpouer 难点：三相电路的功率计算 Difficulties: calculation of three-phase circuit power	4
5	项目 5：互感耦合电路 Item 5: mutual inductance coupling circuit	5.1 自感与互感 Self-inductance and mutual inductance	自感与自感电压；互感与互感电压；同名端 Self-inductance and self-inductance voltage; mutual inductance and mutual inductance voltage; dotted terminal	重点：互感与互感电压的相量计算；同名端的判断 Key points: phasor calculation of mutual inductance and mutual inductance voltage; judgment at the end of the same name 难点：用万用表判断同名端 Difficulties: use a multimeter to determine the end of the same name	2

续表

序号 NO.	项目（模块） Items	任务（单元） Tasks	教学内容 Teaching contents	重点、难点 Key points and difficulties	学时 Hours
5	项目 5：互感耦合电路 Item 5: mutual inductance coupling circuit	5.2 互感耦合电路的分析 Analysis of mutual inductance coupling circuit	互感线圈的串联； 互感线圈的并联； 互感线圈的T型等效 Series connection of mutual inductance coils; parallel connection of mutual inductance coils; T-type equivalent of mutual inductance coils	重点：互感线圈的串并联等效变换 Key points: series-parallel equivalent transformation of mutual inductance coil 难点：互感线圈的 T 型等效 Difficulties: T-shaped equivalent of mutual inductance coil	4
		5.4 理想变压器 Ideal transformer	理想变压器的条件；理想变压器的主要性能 Condition of the ideal transformer; the main performance of the ideal transformer	重点：理想变压器的主要性能 Key points: the main performance of ideal transformer 难点：理想变压器的阻抗变换 Difficulties: impedance transformation of ideal transformer	2
6	项目 6：线性电路的瞬态过程 Item 6: transient processes of linear circuits	6.1 瞬态过程及换路定律 Transient process and the law of switching	瞬态过程的基本概念；换路定律；电压、电流初始值的计算 Basic concepts of transient process; law of switching; calculation of initial values of voltage and current	重点：换路定律；电压、电流初始值的计算 Key points: law of switching; calculation of initial values of voltage and current 难点：电压、电流初始值的计算 Difficulties: calculation of initial values of voltage and current	2
		6.2 RC 电路的瞬态过程 Transient process of RC circuit	RC 电路的充电过程；RC 电路的放电过程 charging of RC circuit; discharging of RC circuit	重点：RC 电路的充放电过程 Key points: the charging and discharging of RC circuit 难点：RC 电路的充放电过程 Difficulties: the charging and discharging of RC circuit	2
		6.3 RL 电路的瞬态过程 Transient process of RL circuit	RL 电路接通直流电源；RL 电路短接 RL circuit is connected to DC power supply; RL circuit is shorted	重点：RL 电路接通直流电源、RL 电路短接 Key points: RL circuit is connected to DC power supply, RL circuit is shorted 难点：RL 电路接通直流电源、RL 电路短接 Difficulties: RL circuit is connected to DC power supply, RL circuit is shorted	2
		6.4 一阶电路的三要素法 Three-factor law in the first-order circuit	一阶电路过渡过程的一般规律；一阶电路的三要素法的应用 The general law of the transition process in the first-order circuit; the application of the three-factor law in the first-order circuit	重点：一阶电路的三要素法的应用 Key points: application of the three-factor law in the first-order circuits 难点：一阶电路的三要素法的应用 Difficulties: the application of the three-factor law in the first-order circuits	4

说明：本课程标准适用于 72～78 学时的“电路分析基础”课程的教学，表 3 中的学时为建议和参考学时，实际教学内容和课时可结合课程标准，根据教学的专业和课时进行选择和调整。

Notes: This curriculum standard applies to the teaching of The Basis of Circuit Analysis, accounting for 72—78 teaching periods. The teaching hours in table 3 are arranged for reference, the actual teaching contents and periods can be adjusted according to the major and practical teaching hours.

三、课程考核 Course Assessment

（1）课程考核分为总结性评价和过程性评价，关注学生个体差异。

Course assessment consists of summative evaluation and process evaluation, focusing on students' individual difference.

（2）总结性评价包括标准化试题的闭卷考试。

The summative evaluation includes standardized test.

（3）过程性评价指使用铁道信号自动控制专业教学资源库开展线上、线下混合式教学，由线上成绩、线下成绩、线上作业和线上考试组成。对项目中的平时作业、基本实践技能进行考核。考核内容可以根据实践教学设备的变化进行相应的调整。

Process evaluation is composed of online and off-line performance, online assignment and online test by using the online and off-line blended teaching through teaching resources database of railway signaling automatic control major. The usual performance and awareness in different modules are also evaluated. Assessment contents can be adjusted according to the practical situation.

（4）课程考核比例：过程性评价占 30%，总结性评价占 70%。

The proportion of course assessment: process evaluation accounts for 30%, summative assessment aceounts for 70%.

四、实施要求 Implementation Requirements

1. 授课教师基本要求 Basic Requirements for Teachers

具有高等学校教师资格证，电工电子技术理论知识扎实，有较强的理论教学能力，熟悉电子仪器仪表操作，有较强的实践操作能力和实践教学管理经验。

With the teacher certificate of higher education; solid theoretical knowledge of electrical and electronic technology; strong theory-teaching ability; familiar with electronic instrument operation; strong ability and experience in practical operations and teaching management.

2. 教学方法和策略 Teaching Methods and Strategies

（1）教学方法 Teaching methods。

本着"淡化理论、够用为度、培养技能、重在应用"的原则，课程注重培养学生分析和解决问题的能力以及对所学知识进行应用的能力。本课程主要推荐采用讲授教学法、讨论教学法、实验教学法、案例教学法、指导自学法等。

In line with the principle of "weaken theory teaching to be adequate for using, and emphasize application when cultivate skills", the course focuses on cultivating students' ability to analyze and solve problems and to apply the knowledge they have learned. This course mainly recommends the use of lecture teaching method, discussion teaching method, experimental teaching method, case teaching method, self-study teaching method, etc.

（2）教学策略 Teaching strategies。

教学过程中采用铁道信号自动控制专业教学资源库实现混合式教学，使学生了解电路的基本概念及电路分析的相关知识，熟悉直流、交流电路结构和工作原理，具备进行简单电路设计与应用的能力。

Blended teaching is realized by the implement of the teaching resource database for railway signal automatic control major during the process. This course aims to help students to learn the relevant knowledge of basic electronic components and integrated circuits, to be familiar with the structure and working principle of DC or AC electronic circuits, to have the ability to carry out simple circuit design and application.

在实践教学环节，采用企业实地考察，请企业专家、技术能手给学生授课，让学生清楚企业的工作流程、岗位职责要求和企业岗位工作的其他纪律规定。

As to the practical teaching aspect, field investigation is adopted. Enterpise experts and technical experts are invited to lecture in order to make students be clear about the workflows, requirements of job description and work disciplines and rules of posts.

第二节　“电子技术基础”课程标准

Curriculum Standard for the Basis of Electronic Technology

一、课程性质 Nature of the Course

1. 课程类型、课程功能 Types and Functions

本课程是轨道交通控制类专业的一门专业基础课，共计 84 课时、5 学分。本课程是学生在学习了“电路分析基础”“高等数学”“电路认知与焊接实训”等课程，具备了基本电路分析、计算、焊接、调试能力的基础上，开设的一门理论加实践的课程，其功能是使学生获得电子技术方面的基本理论、基本知识和基本技能，初步具备工程计算和实验研究的能力，并为学习后续课程和电子技术在专业中的应用打好基础。

This course is a specialized basic course for the rail transportation control major, including 86 hours and 5 credits. It is a integration of theoretical and practical, opened to the students who have already learned the courses such as The Basis of Circuit Analysis, Advanced Maths, Recognition of Circuit and Solder Training, etc., and have certain circuit knowledge of analysis, calculation, soldering and debugging. Its function is to equip the students with basic theories, knowledge, skills in electronic technology, to enable students to carry out the engineering calculation and experimental research, therefore lay a solid foundation for the follow-up study of specialized courses and the application of the electronic techniques on the subject.

2. 课程功能定位 Orientation of the Function

表 1　课程功能定位分析

Table 1　Analysis for the Orientation of the Function

对接的工作岗位 Jobs	对接培养的职业岗位能力 Abilities
电子产品一线生产、质量检验、调试、管理生产岗位 Work in electronic production, quality inspection, debugging, and management	1. 熟悉电子线路基本理论 Familiar with the basic theory of electronic circuits
	2. 掌握常用电子元器件的技术性能和装配要求 Master the technical performance and assembly requirements of common electronic components

续表

对接的工作岗位 Jobs	对接培养的职业岗位能力 Abilities
电子产品一线生产、质量检验、调试、管理生产岗位 Work in electronic production, quality inspection, debugging, and management	3. 能熟练使用电子仪器仪表，正确测量电路参数，具备一定的分析、调试能力 Be proficient in using electronic instruments and meters, correctly measure circuit parameters, and have certain analysis and debugging capabilities
	4. 具有熟练使用电子设计与分析辅助软件的能力 Be able to use electronic design and analyze auxiliary software proficiently
	5. 具有对电子信息产品设计、开发、管理的能力 Be able to design, develop and manage electronic products
	6. 具有学习和跟踪电子信息新技术的能力 Be able to learn and track new electronic technologies
电子产品装配岗位 In Electronic product assembly line	1. 熟悉电子线路基本理论及电子产品的装配工艺 Familiar with the basic theory of electronic circuit and the assembly process of electronic products
	2. 有较强的电子线路识图能力 Has a strong ability to interpret electronic circuit diagrams
	3. 掌握常用电子元件的识别方法、技术参数和装配要求 Master the identification, technical parameters and assembly requirements of common electronic components
	4. 掌握电子元件的安装与焊接工艺 Master the installing and soldering of electronic components
	5. 掌握电子产品的调试技术 Master the debugging technology of electronic products
电子产品安装和维护岗位 In electronic product installation and maintenance	1. 熟悉电子线路基本理论，能熟练分析电子产品的工作原理 Familiar with the basic theory of electronic circuits, proficient in analyzing the working principle of electronic products
	2. 掌握常用电子元器件的技术参数和使用要求 Master the technical parameters and use requirements of common electronic components
	3. 能运用常用的电子测量仪器测量、分析与判断电路故障 Use common electronic measuring instruments to measure, analyze and judge circuit failures
	4. 具有电子信息产品安装、调试、使用和维护的能力 Have the ability to install, debug, use and maintain electronic products

二、课程目标与内容 Objectives and Contents

1. 课程总目标 General Objectives

本课程的总目标是使学生掌握电子技术方面的基本理论、基本知识和基本技能，培养学生具备电子工程人员应具备的基本的电路组装、调试能力，使其初步具备工程计算和实验研究的能力，并为学习后续课程打好基础。

The general objective of this course is to enable students to acquire basic theories, basic knowledge and basic skills of electronic technology, to train students to have the basic circuit assembly and debugging capabilities that the electrician should have, and to have preliminary engineering calculation and experimental research capabilities, and to lay a good foundation for the study of follow-up courses.

2. 课程具体目标 Specific Objectives

表 2 课程教学目标与内容 1

Table 2 Teaching Objectives and Contents 1

序号 NO.	毕业要求指标点 Index point of graduation requirement	知识目标 Knowledge goals	技能目标 Ability goals	素质目标 Quality goals	教学内容 Teaching contents
1	能够正确识别、检测和选择合适的半导体器件 Able to identify, detect and select the appropriate semiconductor device correctly	理解常用半导体器件(如二极管、三极管、场效应管)的基本结构和工作原理，掌握它们的外特性、主要参数及其合理选用的方法，了解新型电子元器件的工作原理、性能特点及使用方法 Understand the basic structure and working principle of common semiconductor (such as diodes, transistors, field effect transistors), master their external characteristics, main parameters and their reasonable selection methods, understand the working principle, performance characteristics and use of new electronic components	掌握常用电子元器件主要参数和基本电路主要技术指标的测量方法，具有一定的查阅电子元器件、集成电路手册和其他资料的能力 Master the measures of the main parameters of common electronic components and the main technical indicators of basic circuits, and have the ability to consult electronic components, integrated circuit manuals and other materials	培养学生对元器件、仪器仪表及其操作的职业素质感情和职业道德 Cultivate students' professional quality feelings and professional ethics on components, instruments and their operation	半导体基础及常用电子元器件 Basis of semiconductor and common electronic components
2	熟悉放大电路的结构、特点、工作原理及分析调试方法 Familiar with the structure, characteristics, working principle, analysis and debugging method of the amplifier circuit	掌握三种组态放大电路、多级放大电路、功率放大电路的结构和特点，理解放大电路的静态及动态工作原理 Master the structure and characteristics of three configuration amplifier circuits, multi-stage amplifier circuits, power amplifier circuits, and understand the static and dynamic working principles of amplifier circuits	掌握三种组态放大电路、多级放大电路、差动放大电路、功率放大电路的分析计算方法和实际应用，能正确测量放大电路的参数并对电路进行调试 Master the analysis and calculation and practical applications of three configuration amplifier circuits, multi-stage amplifier circuits, differential amplifier circuits, power amplifier circuits; correctly measure the parameters of the amplifier circuit and debug the circuit	养成认真细致、实事求是、积极探索的科学态度和工作作风，形成理论联系实际、自主学习和探索创新的良好习惯 Develop a scientific attitude and work style that is conscientious, meticulous, realistic, and active exploration, and form a good habit of integrating theory with practice, independent learning, and exploration and innovation	三极管放大电路 Transistor amplifier circuit
3	能合理使用反馈调节放大电路性能 Able to use feedback to adjust the performance of the amp properly	理解反馈的概念、类型和基本电路形式，掌握负反馈对放大电路的影响 Understand the concept, type and basic circuit form of feedback, and grasp the influence of negative feedback on the amplifier circuit	能够判断反馈的类型，并能分析负反馈对放大电路的影响，熟练运用负反馈放大电路 Be able to judge the type of feedback and analyze the influence of negative feedback on the amplifier circuit, be proficient in the use of negative feedback amplifier circuit	提高学生分析问题和解决问题的能力 Improve students'ability to analyze and solve problems	放大电路的反馈 Amplifier feedback

序号 NO.	毕业要求指标点 Index point of graduation requirement	知识目标 Knowledge goals	技能目标 Ability goals	素质目标 Quality goals	教学内容 Teaching contents
4	能熟练运用正弦波振荡电路 To use sine wave oscillation circuit skillfully	掌握正弦波振荡电路的组成及类型，理解自激振荡的条件，能够识读LC、RC及石英晶体振荡器的电路图，了解振荡电路工作原理，能估算振荡频率 Master the composition and types of sine wave oscillation circuit, understand the conditions of self-excited oscillation; be able to interpret the circuit diagrams of LC, RC and quartz crystal oscillators; understand the working principle of oscillation circuit, and estimate the oscillation frequency	能判断电路是否起振，能排除振荡器的常见故障，能用示波器观测振荡波形，能用频率计测量振荡频率 To determine whether the circuit is oscillating, eliminate common faults of the oscillator, observe the oscillation waveform with an oscilloscope, measure the oscillation frequency with a frequency meter	提高学生分析问题和解决问题的能力 Improve students' ability to analyze and solve problems	正弦波振荡电路 Sine wave oscillation circuit
5	能正确分析和使用集成运算放大电路 Able to analyze and use integrated operational amplifier circuits correctly	熟悉集成运放的特点、主要技术指标和使用常识，理解并掌握集成运放典型电路 Familiar with the characteristics, main technical index and common sense of integrated op amp, master the typical circuit of integrated op amp	掌握集成运算放大器在线性和非线性应用时的分析方法，熟练使用集成运算放大器 Master the analysis method of integrated operational amplifier in linear and non-linear applications, be proficient in using integrated operational amplifier	培养学生对元器件、仪器仪表及其操作的职业素质感情和职业道德 Cultivate students' vocational quality senses and vocational ethics on components, instruments and their operation	集成运算放大电路 Integrated operational amplifier circuit
6	能设计、分析、制作、调试直流稳压电源 Able to design, analyze, build and debug DC stabilized power supply	理解直流稳压电源的作用和结构，掌握整流、滤波、稳压电路的电路特点、工作原理和应用，了解集成稳压器的种类、参数及典型应用 To know the function and structure of DC stabilized power supply, master the circuit characteristics, working principles and applications of rectification, filtering and voltage stabilization circuits; to know the types, parameters and typical applications of integrated voltage regulators	能设计、制作直流稳压电源，正确使用仪器仪表测量直流电源参数，掌握电路的排故和调试方法 Be able to design and build DC stabilized power; to use instruments and meters to measure DC power supply's parameters correltly, master circuit troubleshooting and debugging methods	通过对问题的分析，体验逻辑分析的乐趣，提高学生对生活和学习的积极性 Experience the joy of analysis through problem analysis and improve students' enthusiasm for life and learning	直流稳压电源 DC power supply

序号 NO.	毕业要求指标点 Index point of graduation requirement	知识目标 Knowledge goals	技能目标 Ability goals	素质目标 Quality goals	教学内容 Teaching contents
7	熟悉数字电路的特点及其基础知识 Familiar with the characteristics and basic knowledge of digital circuits	理解常用数制及码值的特点、表示、转换方法；掌握逻辑代数的基本公式、定律及化简方法；掌握逻辑电路的表示方法，并能相互转换 Understand the characteristics, representation and conversion methods of common number systems and code values; master the basic formulas, laws and simplification methods of logical algebra; master the representation methods of logical circuits and be able to convert each other	具有小型逻辑电路的分析及设计能力，能将工作中的一些实例用逻辑函数的思维分析和设计 Capable of analyzing and designing small logic circuits, able to analyze and design some examples in work with logic function thinking	提高逻辑思维分析能力，提升学习能力 Improve logical thinking and analysis ability, improve learning ability	数字电路基础 Basis of digital circuit
8	能分析、设计组合逻辑电路 Analyze and design combined logic circuits	理解组合逻辑电路的特点及典型电路的工作原理，掌握组合逻辑电路的分析、设计方法 Understand the characteristics of combined logic circuits and the working principle of typical circuits, and master the analysis and design methods of combined logic circuits	通过学生自主实验和电路制作，培养学生观察、动手、自主探究性学习及创造性思维的能力，通过查阅电子元件手册与实际电路对比，培养学生分析、解决问题的能力 Cultivate students' abilities of observation, operation, independent exploratory learning and creative thinking through students' independent experiments and circuit making, and cultivate students' ability to analyze and solve problems by referring to manuals of electronic component and comparing with actual circuits	激发学习电子技术的浓厚兴趣，形成主动学习的态度，培养协作学习能力和团队精神 Stimulate a strong interest in learning electronic technology, foster an active learning attitude, and cultivate collaborative learning ability and team spirit	组合逻辑电路 Combined logic circuit
9	能分析、设计组合逻辑电路 Analyze and design combined logic circuits	熟悉触发器的逻辑功能，掌握时序逻辑电路的分析和设计方法，掌握寄存器和计数器的逻辑功能和应用 Familiar with the logic functions of triggers; master the analysis and design methods of sequential logic circuits; master the logic functions and application of registers and counters	会查阅集成电路手册，能按要求选用集成时序逻辑器件，会用万用表测试集成时序逻辑器件性能好坏，能利用实验箱验证时序逻辑电路的逻辑功能，具备一定的时序逻辑电路分析设计能力 Read the integrated circuit manual and choose the integrated sequential logic device according to the requirements, test the performance of the integrated sequential logic device with multimeter; verify the logic function of the sequential logic circuit with the experimental box, and have a certain ability to analyze and design the sequential logic circuit	培养严谨的学习态度和良好的学习习惯，养成爱岗敬业的职业操守，具有安全、质量、效率意识 Cultivate a rigorous learning attitude and good learning habits, cultivate professional ethics of dedication, equip with a sense of safety, quality and efficiency	时序逻辑电路 Sequential logic circuit

序号 NO.	毕业要求指标点 Index point of graduation requirement	知识目标 Knowledge goals	技能目标 Ability goals	素质目标 Quality goals	教学内容 Teaching contents
10	能分析、设计脉冲波形电路 Analyze and design pulse waveform circuits	理解施密特触发器、单稳态触发器、多谐振荡器的工作原理、波形及参数计算，熟悉555定时器的功能及应用 Understand the working principle, waveform and parameter calculation of Schmitt trigger, monostable trigger and multivibrator, familiar with the function and application of 555 timer	掌握脉冲波形电路的分析方法，能计算对应波形的脉冲周期、占空比等典型参数，能够根据要求分析、设计各种应用电路 Master the analysis method of pulse waveform circuit, can calculate typical parameters such as pulse period and duty ratio of corresponding waveform, and analyze and design various application circuits according to requirements	做事认真细致，敢于动手，具备良好的执行力和自主学习新知识的能力 Work carefully, and dare to start work, have good executive and self-directed learning ability	脉冲波形的产生和整形 The generation and shaping of pulse waveform
11	熟悉AD/DA的转换 Familiar with AD/DA conversion	熟悉AD/DA转换的基本概念和工作原理，了解常用AD/DA转换芯片的使用方法 Familiar with the basic concepts and working principles of AD/DA conversion, and know how to use common AD/DA conversion chips	通过AD/DA转换电路的测试，初步掌握AD/DA转换芯片的应用 Grasp the application of AD/DA conversion chip through the test of AD/DA conversion circuit	具有自主学习和终身学习的意识，有不断学习和适应发展的能力 Have the consciousness of independent and lifelong learning; and be able to learn continuously and adapt to development	模拟量和数字量的转换 Conversion of stimulation parameter and digital quantity

表3　课程教学目标与内容2

Table 3　Teaching Objectives and Contents 2

序号 No.	项目（模块） Items	任务（单元） Tasks	教学内容 Teaching contents	重点、难点 Key points and difficulties	学时 Hours
1	项目1:二极管及其应用 Item 1: diodes and its applications	1.1　二极管 Diode	半导体基本知识，PN结的单向导电性，二极管结构、功能和特性 Basic knowledge of semiconductors, unidirectional conductivity of PN junction, diode's structure, function and characteristics	重点：二极管的单向导电性 Key points: unidirectional conductivity of diodes 难点：单向导电性的原理 Difficulties: the principle of unidirectional conductivity	1
		1.2　二极管的应用 Diode application	二极管的伏安特性及其应用 The volt-ampere characteristic of diode and its application	重点：二极管的作用 Key points: the role of diodes 难点：二极管的应用电路的分析 Difficulties: analysis of the application circuit of the diode	1
		1.3　特殊二极管 Special diodes	特殊二极管的结构、符号、特性和作用 The volt-ampere characteristic of diode and its application	重点：特殊二极管的符号、特性和应用电路 Key points: symbols, characteristics and application circuits of special diodes 难点：特殊二极管应用电路的分析 Difficulties: analysis of the application circuit of special diode	1

续表

序号 No.	项目（模块） Items	任务（单元） Tasks	教学内容 Teaching contents	重点、难点 Key points and difficulties	学时 Hours
1	项目 1：二极管及其应用 Item 1: diodes and its applications	1.4 二极管的简易测试 Simple test of diode	二极管的测试方法 The testing method of diode	重点：二极管的测试方法 Key points: the testing method of diode 难点：二极管的质量判断方法 Difficulties: the quality judgment method diode	1
2	项目 2：三极管及放大电路 Item 2: triode and amplifying circuit	2.1 三极管 Triode	三极管的结构、符号及工作特性 Triode's structure, symbol and working features	重点：三极管的结构及特性 Key points: the structure and characteristics of triode. 难点：三极管工作状态判断 Difficulties: judging the working status of triode	4
		2.2 共射放大电路 Common-emitter amplifying circuit	共射放大电路的组成、工作原理、分析方法 Composition, working principle and analysis method of common-emitter amplifying circuit	重点：放大电路的工作原理 Key points: working principle of the amplifier circuit 难点：静态工作点的选择与波形失真 Difficulties: selection of static operating point and waveform distortion	2
		2.3 放大电路的图解分析法 Graphical analysis method of amplifying circuit	放大电路的图解分析法 Graphical analysis method of amplifying circuit	重点：会画直流负载线和交流负载线 Key points: able to draw DC load track and AC load track 难点：学会应用交、直流负载线分析问题 Difficulties: learn to analyse problems with AC and DC load lines	2
		2.4 放大电路的微变等效电路分析法 Micro-variable equivalent circuit analysis for amplifying circuit	放大电路的微变等效电路分析法 Micro-variable equivalent circuit analysis for amplifying circuit	重点：放大电路的微变等效电路分析法 Key points: micro-variable equivalent circuit analysis for amplifying circuit 难点：放大电路静态和动态参数的计算 Difficulties: calculation of static and dynamic parameters in the amplifying circuit	2
		2.5 静态工作点稳定电路 Stabilized circuit with static operating point	静态工作点稳定电路的组成、工作原理、分析方法 Composition, working principle and analysis method of stabilized circuit with static operating point	重点：电路的分析和计算 Key points: analysis and calculation of circuits 难点：稳定静态工作点的原理 Difficulties: the principle of stabilized and static operating point	2
		2.6 共集放大电路和共基放大电路 Common collector amplifier circuit and common-base amplifier circuit	共集放大、共基放大电路的电路结构，工作原理 The structure and working principle of common collector amplifier and common-base amplifier circuit	重点：共基放大电路、共集放大电路的结构、特性及应用 Key points: the structure, characteristics and application of common-base amplifier circuit and common collector amplifier circuit 难点：电阻折算方法 Difficulties: resistance calculation	1

续表

序号 No.	项目（模块） Items	任务（单元） Tasks	教学内容 Teaching contents	重点、难点 Key points and difficulties	学时 Hours
2	项目 2：三极管及放大电路 Item 2: triode and amplifying circuit	2.7 MOS 场效应管及放大电路 MOS field effect tube and amplifier circuit	MOS 管的结构及工作原理，MOS 管放大电路工作原理 MOS tube's structure and working principle, the working principle of MOS tube amplifier circuit	重点：三种组态放大器的分析方法 Key points: the analysis methods of three kinds of amplifier configurations 难点：MOS 管的结构和工作原理 Difficulties: MOS tube's structure and working principle	2
		2.8 多级放大电路 Multistage amplifier circuit	放大或多级放大电路的电路结构，工作原理 The structure and working principle of amplifier or multistage amplifier circuit	重点：多级放大器的耦合方式 Key points: coupling mode of multistage amplifier 难点：放大倍数的计算 Difficulties: calculation of magnification	1
		2.9 差动放大电路 Differential amplifier circuit	差动放大电路的组成、工作原理、静态工作情况的分析 Analysis of the composition, working principle and static working condition of the differential amplifier circuit	重点、难点：差动放大电路对差模信号的放大作用，对共模信号的抑制作用 Key points and difficulties: the amplification of differential mode signal by differential amplifier circuit, and suppression of common mode signal by differential amplifier	2
		2.10 功率放大电路 Power amplifying circuit	功率放大电路的特点及分类，OCL 功放电路的结构、工作原理、分析计算方法 The characteristics and classification of power amplifying circuit, the structure, working principle, analysis and calculation method of OCL power amplifying circuit	重点：OCL 电路的结构、工作原理 Key points: OCL circuit's structure and working principle 难点：OCL 电路的分析计算 Difficulties: analysis and calculation of OCL circuit	2
3	项目 3：集成运算放大器及其应用 Item 3: integrated operational amplifier (op amp) and its application	3.1 集成运算放大器 Integrated operational amplifier	集成运放电路的结构、符号、特点及传输特性 The structure, symbol, characteristics and transmission features of integrated op amp circuit	重点：集成运放的传输特性 Key points: transmission features of integrated op amps 难点：虚短和虚断 Difficulties: virtual short circuit and virtual opening	1
		3.2 集成运放的线性应用 Linear application of integrated op amps.	集成运放线性应用电路的分析和计算 Analysis and calculation of integrated operational amplifier in linear application circuit	重点：集成运放在线性区的特点和分析方法 Key points: the characteristics and analysis method of integrated op amp in the linear region 难点：运算放大电路的分析方法 Difficulties: the analysis method of the operational amplifier circuit	3

续表

序号 No.	项目（模块） Items	任务（单元） Tasks	教学内容 Teaching contents	重点、难点 Key points and difficulties	学时 Hours
3	项目3：集成运算放大器及其应用 Item 3: integrated operational amplifier (op amp) and its application	3.3 集成运放的非线性应用 Non-linear application of integrated op amps	集成运放非线性应用电路的分析和计算 Analysis and calculation of non-linear application circuit for integrated op amp	重点：集成运放在非线性区的特点和分析方法 Key points: the characteristics and analysis methods of the integrated op amp in the non-linear region 难点：运算放大电路的分析方法 Difficulties: the analysis method of operational amplifier circuit	1
		3.4 集成运放的使用常识 General knowledge of integrated op amp	集成运放的应用常识 Application of common sense of integrated op amp	重点：集成运放的应用常识 Key points: application knowledge of integrated op amp 难点：集成运放的使用 Difficulties: the use of integrated op amps	1
4	项目4：反馈与振荡 Item 4 : feedback and oscillation	4.1 反馈的基本概念 Basic concept of feedback	反馈的概念及反馈放大电路的组成 The concept of feedback and the composition of feedback amplifier circuit	重点：反馈的概念 Key points: the concept of feedback 难点：反馈的判断 Difficulties: check of feedback	1
		4.2 负反馈电路的类型 Types of negative feedback circuit	反馈的分类及判别方法 The classification and identification method of feedback	重点：反馈的分类 Key points: classification of feedback 难点：反馈的判别 Difficulties: identification of feedback	2
		4.3 负反馈对放大器性能的影响 Negative feedback's impact on amplifier's performance	理解负反馈对放大电路性能的影响 Understand negative feedback's impact on the performance of amplifier circuit	重点、难点：负反馈对放大器性能的影响 Key points and difficulties: negative feedback's impact on amplifier's performance	1
		4.4 自激振荡 Self-oscillation	理解自激振荡的定义及正弦波振荡器的组成，振荡器的起振条件 To know the definition of self-excited oscillation and the composition of sine wave oscillator, the oscillator start-up conditions	重点：正弦波振荡器的组成 Key points: the composition of sine wave oscillator 难点：振荡的平衡条件、起振条件 Difficulties: the conditions for oscillation equilibrium and start-up	1
		4.5 RC正弦波振荡器 RC sine wave oscillator	RC 串并联电路的选频特性，RC桥式振荡器 Frequency selection characteristics of RC series and parallel circuits, RC bridge oscillator	重点：RC桥式振荡器工作原理 Key points: how RC bridge oscillator works 难点：RC串并联电路的选频特性 Difficulties: frequency selection characteristics of RC series and parallel circuits	1

续表

序号 No.	项目（模块） Items	任务（单元） Tasks	教学内容 Teaching contents	重点、难点 Key points and difficulties	学时 Hours
4	项目 4：反馈与振荡 Item 4 : feedback and oscillation	4.6 LC 正弦波振荡器 LC sine wave oscillator	LC 正弦波振荡电路的工作原理、起振条件、稳幅原理及振荡频率的计算 The working principle, starting conditions, amplitude stabilization principle of LC sine wave oscillation circuit and the calculation of oscillation frequency	重点：LC 正弦波振荡器的工作原理、起振条件和振荡频率 Key points: the working principle, starting conditions and oscillation frequency of LC sine wave oscillator 难点：LC 正弦波振荡器的工作原理 Difficulties: the working principle of LC sine wave oscillator	1
		4.7 石英晶体振荡器 Quartz crystal oscillatorzx	石英晶体谐振器的特性及石英晶体振荡电路 Characteristics of quartz crystal resonator and quartz crystal oscillation circuit	重点：石英晶体振荡器的工作原理 Key points: working principle of quartz crystal oscillator 难点：晶振的特性 Difficulties: the characteristics of crystal oscillator	1
5	项目 5：直流稳压电源 Item 5: DC power supply	5.1 整流电路 Rectifier circuit	直流稳压电源的组成及作用，整流电路结构和工作原理 The composition and function of the DC power supply, the structure and working principle of the rectifier circuit	重点：单相半波、单相桥式整流电路的工作原理、波形、计算 Key points: the working principle, waveform, calculation of single-phase half-wave and single-phase bridge rectifier circuit 难点：单相桥式整流电路的工作原理 Difficulties: the working principle of single-phase bridge rectifier circuit	2
		5.2 滤波电路 Filter circuit	桥式整流电容滤波电路的结构、工作原理、波形以及输出的电压计算 The structure, working principle, waveform and output voltage calculation of bridge rectifier and capacitor filter circuit	重点：单相桥式整流电容滤波电路的结构、工作原理、波形、计算 Key points：the structure, working principle, waveform, calculation of single-phase bridge rectifier and capacitor filter circuit 难点：滤波电路的工作原理、波形 Difficulties: working principle and waveform of filter circuit	1
		5.3 稳压电路 Voltage regulator circuit	稳压电路的结构、类型及应用 The structure, type and application of voltage regulator circuit	重点：稳压电路的作用 Key points: the function of voltage regulator circuit 难点：稳压电路的工作原理 Difficulties: the working principle of voltage regulator circuit	1
6	项目 6：数字电路基础 Item 6: basis of digital circuit	6.1 数字电路概述 Overview of digital circuit	数字电路的有关概念 Related concept of digital circuit	重点、难点：数字电路的特点、分类 Key points and difficulties: characteristics and classification of digital circuit	1

序号 No.	项目（模块） Items	任务（单元） Tasks	教学内容 Teaching contents	重点、难点 Key points and difficulties	学时 Hours
6	项目6：数字电路基础 Item 6: basis of digital circuit	6.2 数制与码制 Number system and code system	常用的数制与码制，数制与数制、码制与数制之间的转换 Common number system and code system, the conversion of number systems, the conversion between code system and number system	重点：二进制数与十进制数的转换 Key points: conversion of binary number and decimal number 难点：数制及不同数制间数据的转换 Difficulties: data conversion in the same number system and different number system	1
		6.3 基本逻辑门 Basic logic gate	逻辑代数的基本运算，逻辑门电路符号 Basic operation of logic algebra, logic gate circuit symbol	重点：基本代数的基本运算 Key points: basic operation of basis algebra 难点：逻辑关系 Difficulties: logical relationship	2
		6.4 逻辑运算法则 Logic algorithm	逻辑代数的基本定律、公式以及逻辑函数的化简方法 Basic laws, formulas of logic algebra, and reduction methods of logic function	重点：逻辑代数的定律、公式和逻辑函数的化简方法 Key points: laws and formulas of logic algebra and reduction methods of logic function 难点：逻辑函数化简 Difficulties: reduction of the logic function	3
		6.5 集成与非门电路 Integrated and NAND circuit	CMOS和TTL集成门电路的逻辑功能和电气特性 The logic functions and electrical characteristics of CMOS and TTL integrated gate circuit	重点：集成门电路的逻辑功能 key points: logic function of integrated gate circuit 难点：集成门电路的电气特性 Difficulties: electrical characteristics of integrated gate circuit	1
7	项目7：组合逻辑电路 Item 7: combined logic circuit	7.1 组合逻辑电路的分析 The analysis of combined logic circuit	组合逻辑电路的特点、分析方法 Combined logic circuit's characteristics and analysis methods	重点、难点：组合逻辑电路的特点和分析 Key points and difficulties: characteristics and analysis of combined logic circuit	1
		7.2 组合逻辑电路的设计 The design of combined logic circuit	组合逻辑电路的设计 The design of combined logic circuit	重点：组合电路的设计方法，常用中规模集成器件的功能和应用 Key points: the method of design combined circuit, the function and application of common medium integrated devices 难点：组合电路的设计 Difficulties: the design of the combined circuit	1
		7.3 常用的组合逻辑电路 Common combined logic circuit	加法器、编码器、译码器的原理，集成芯片的使用方法 The principle of adder, encoder, decoder, and the use of integrated chip	重点：组合逻辑电路的分析设计方法 Key points: the analysis and design method of combined logic circuit 难点：组合逻辑电路的设计思路与步骤 Difficulties: the design ideas and steps of combined logic circuit	6

续表

序号 No.	项目（模块） Items	任务（单元） Tasks	教学内容 Teaching contents	重点、难点 Key points and difficulties	学时 Hours
7	项目 7：组合逻辑电路 Item 7: combined logic circuit	7.4 组合逻辑电路中的竞争与冒险 Competition and risk in combined logic circuit	组合逻辑电路中的竞争与冒险的原因、判断与消除 Cause, judgement and elimination of the competition and risk in combined logic circuit	重点：竞争与冒险的原因、判断与消除 Key points: cause, judgment and elimination of competition and risk 难点：竞争与冒险的判断与消除方法 Difficulties: the judge and elimination method of competition and risk	2
8	项目 8：触发器及时序逻辑电路 Item 8: trigger and sequential logic circuit	8.1 基本 RS 触发器 Basic RS trigger	时序逻辑电路的特点，RS 触发器的逻辑功能 Characteristics of sequential logic circuit, logic function of RS flip-flop	重点：RS 触发器的逻辑功能 Key points: the logic function of RS trigger 难点：RS 触发器的原理 Difficulties: the principle of RS trigger	2
		8.2 同步触发器 Synchronization trigger	同步 RS、JK、D 和 T 触发器的逻辑功能和符号 The logic function and symbol of synchronize in RS, JK, D and T triggers	重点：各触发器的功能 Key points: the function of each trigger 难点：画触发器的输出波形 Difficulties: draw the output waveform of the trigger	2
		8.3 触发器的分类及转换 Classification and conversion of trigger	触发器的类型、功能、相互转换及应用 The type, function, mutual conversion and application of trigger	重点：触发器的逻辑功能 Key point: the logic function of trigger 难点：触发器之间的相互转换及应用 Difficulties: the mutual conversion and application between triggers	2
		8.4 时序逻辑电路的分析 Analysis of sequential logic circuit	时序逻辑电路的特点、分析方法 Characteristics and analysis methods of sequential logic circuit	重点、难点：时序逻辑电路的分析方法 Key points and difficulties: the analysis method of sequential logic circuit	2
		8.5 计数器 Counter	计数器的电路组成、逻辑功能及原理 Counter's circuit composition, logic function and principle	重点：计数器的逻辑功能及工作原理，集成计数器的使用 Key points: counter's logic function and working principle, the use of integrated counter 难点：集成计数器的应用 Difficulties: the application of integrated counter	2
		8.6 寄存器 Register	寄存器的结构与逻辑功能 Register's structure and logic function	重点：寄存器的逻辑功能 Key points: logical function of register 难点：集成寄存器的应用 Difficulties: the application of integrated register	2
9	项目 9：脉冲波形的产生和整形 Item 9: pulse waveform generation and shaping	9.1 施密特触发器 Schmitt trigger	施密特触发器的电路结构和工作原理，555 定时器的原理及应用 Schmitt trigger's circuit structure and working principle, 555 timer's principle and application	重点、难点：施密特触发器的工作原理及应用 Key points and difficulties: the working principle and application of Schmitt trigger	2

续表

序号 No.	项目（模块） Items	任务（单元） Tasks	教学内容 Teaching contents	重点、难点 Key points and difficulties	学时 Hours
9	项目9：脉冲波形的产生和整形 Item 9: pulse waveform generation and shaping	9.2 单稳态触发器 Monostable trigger	单稳态触发器的电路结构和工作原理 The circuit structure and working principle of monostable trigger	重点、难点：单稳态触发器的工作原理及应用 Key points and difficulties: the working principle and application of monostable trigger	1
		9.3 多谐振荡器 Multivibrator	多谐振荡器的电路结构和工作原理 Circuit structure and working principle of multivibrator	重点、难点：多谐振荡器的工作原理及应用 Key points and difficulties: the working principle and application of multivibrator	1
10	项目10：模拟量和数字量的转换 Item 10: conversion of analog and digital quantities	10.1 A/D 转换器 A/D converter	A/D 转换的工作原理、技术参数，集成 A/D 转换芯片的应用 The working principle and technical parameters of A/D conversion, the application of integrated A/D conversion chip	重点：A/D 转换的工作原理及 A/D 转换的应用 Key points: the working principle of A/D conversion and the application of A/D conversion 难点：量化过程 Difficulties: quantification process	2
		10.2 D/A 转换器 D/A converter	D/A 转换的工作原理、技术参数，集成 D/A 转换芯片的应用 The working principle and technical parameters of D/A conversion, the application of integrated D/A conversion chip	重点：D/A 转换的过程 Key points: the process of D/A conversion 难点：集成 D/A 转换芯片的应用 Difficulties: the application of integrated D/A conversion chip	2
11	实验 Experiments	实验1：用万用表测试二极管、三极管 Experiment 1: test diode and transistor with a multimeter	二极管、三极管的识别与检测 Identification and detection of diode and transistor	重点：二极管、三极管的识别与检测方法 Key points: the identification and testing methods of diode and transistor 难点：三极管的判别 Difficulties: the identi-fication of transistor	2
		实验2：常用电子仪器的使用 Experiment 2: usage of common electronic instrument	示波器、函数信号发生器、直流稳压电源、数字万用表、交流毫伏表、频率计的正确使用 Correct use of oscilloscope, function signal generator, DC stabilized power supply, digital multimeter, AC millivoltmeter and frequency meter	重点：常用电子仪器的使用方法 Key points: the use of common electronic instrument 难点：示波器的使用 Difficulties: the use of oscilloscope	2
		实验3：单管共射放大电路 Experiment 3: single-tube common-emitter amplifier circuit	单管共射放大电路的调试和参数的测量 Debugging and parameter measurement of single-tube common-emitter amplifier circuit	重点：电路连接及参数测量 Key points: circuit connection and parameter measurement 难点：静态工作点的测量和放大倍数的测量 Difficulties: measurement of static operating point and of magnification	2

续表

序号 No.	项目（模块） Items	任务（单元） Tasks	教学内容 Teaching contents	重点、难点 Key points and difficulties	学时 Hours
11	实验 Experiments	实验 4：比例、求和运算电路 Experiment 4: the ratio and sum in mathematical operation of circuit	集成运算放大器组成比例，求和电路的特点、性能及参数测量 The composition ration of integrated operational amplifier, and the characteristic, performance and parameter measurement of summing circuit	重点：电路的连接与测量方法 Key points: the connection and measurement of circuit 难点：加法、减法电路的测试，实验数据分析 Difficulties: testing of addition and subtraction in circuits, analysis of experimental data	2
		实验 5：直流稳压电源 Experiment 5: DC stabilized power supply	稳压电源主要性能指标的测试 The test of main performance index of stabilized power supply	重点、难点：稳压电源主要性能指标的测试方法，实验数据分析 Key points and difficulties: the test method of the main performance indicator of stabilized power supply, the analysis of the experimental data	2
		实验 6：TTL 集成逻辑门的逻辑功能测试及逻辑变换 Experiment 6: logic function test and logic transformation of TTL integrated logic gate	TTL 集成门电路逻辑功能测试 Logic function test for TTL integrated gate	重点：TTL 集成门电路逻辑功能 Key points: the logic function of TTL integrated gate 难点：逻辑功能测试方法 Difficulties: the test method of logic function	2
		实验 7：译码器、译码显示电路 Experiment 7: decoder, decoding display circuit	集成译码器的逻辑功能和使用方法，七段数码管的使用 The logic function and instruction of integrated decoder, the use of seven-segment digital tube	重点：译码器的逻辑功能 Key points: the logical function of the decoder 难点：译码器的应用 Difficulties: the application of the decoder	2
		实验 8：触发器的功能测试及应用 Experiment 8: functional test and application of trigger	基本 RS、D、JK 触发器逻辑功能测试及应用 Logic function test and application of basic RS, D, JK trigger	重点：触发器逻辑功能 Key points: logic function of triggers 难点：触发器的应用 Difficulties: the application of trigger	2
		实验 9：集成计数器 Experiment 9: integrated counter	中规模集成计数器逻辑功能测试及应用 Logic function test and application of medium scale integrated counter	重点：计数器逻辑功能 Key points: logic function of counter 难点：计数器的应用 Difficulties: the application of counter	2
		实验 10：移位寄存器 Experiment 10: shift register	中规模四位双向移位寄存器逻辑功能测试及应用 Logic function test and application of medium four-bit bidirectional shift register	重点：寄存器逻辑功能 Key points: logic function of register 难点：寄存器的应用 Difficulties: the application of register	2

续表

序号 No.	项目（模块） Items	任务（单元） Tasks	教学内容 Teaching contents	重点、难点 Key points and difficulties	学时 Hours
11	实验 Experiments	实验 11:555 时基电路及其应用 Experiment 11: 555 time-base circuit and its application	555 时基电路逻辑功能测试及应用 Logic function test and application of 555 time-base circuit	重点：555 时基电路逻辑功能 Key points: logic function of 555 time-base circuit 难点：555 时基电路的应用 Difficulties: the application of 555 time base circuit	2

说明：本课程标准适用于 78～96 学时的“电子技术基础”课程的教学，表 3 中的学时为建议和参考学时，实际教学内容和课时可结合课程标准，根据教学的专业和课时进行选择和调整。

Notes: this curriculum standard applies to the teaching of The Basis of Electronic Technology, accounting for 78—96 teaching periods. The teaching hours in table 3 are arranged for reference, the actual teaching contents and periods can be adjusted according to the major and practical teaching hours.

三、课程考核 Course Assessment

（1）课程考核分为总结性评价和过程性评价，关注学生个体差异。

Course assessment consists of summative evaluation and process evaluation, focusing on students' individual difference.

（2）总结性评价包括标准化试题的闭卷考试。

The summative evaluation includes standardized test.

（3）过程性评价指使用铁道信号自动控制专业教学资源库开展线上、线下混合式教学，由线上成绩、线下成绩、线上作业和线上考试组成。对项目中的平时作业、基本实践技能进行考核。考核内容可以根据实践教学设备的变化进行相应的调整。

Process evaluation is composed of online and off-line performance, online assignment and online test by using the online and off-line blended teaching through teaching resources database of railway signal automatic control major. The usual performance and awareness in different modules are also evaluated. Assessment contents can be adjusted according to the practical situation.

（4）课程考核比例：过程性评价占 30%（期中考试 20%，平时作业 10%），总结性评价占 70%。

The proportion of course assessment: process evaluation accounts for 30% (including 20% of midterm evaluation and 10% of homework), summative assessment accounts for 70%.

四、实施要求 Implementation Requirements

1. 授课教师基本要求 Basic Requirements for Teachers

具有高等学校教师资格证，电工电子技术理论知识扎实，有较强的理论教学能力，熟悉电子仪器仪表操作，有较强的实践操作能力和实践教学管理经验。

With the teacher certificate higher education; solid theoretical knowledge of electrical and electronic technology; strong theory-teaching ability; familiar with electronic instrument operation; strong ability and experience in practical operations and teaching management.

2. 教学方法和策略 Teaching Methods and Strategies

（1）教学方法 Teaching methods。

本着“淡化理论、够用为度、培养技能、重在应用”的原则，课程注重培养学生分析和解决问题的能力以及对所学知识进行应用的能力。本课程主要推荐采用讲授教学法、讨论教学法、实验教学法、案例教学法、指导自学法等。

In line with the principle of "weaken theory teaching to be adequate for using, and emphasize application when cultivate skills", the course focuses on cultivating students' ability to analyze and solve problems and to apply the knowledge they have learned. This course mainly recommends the use of lecture teaching method, discussion teaching method, experimental teaching method, case teaching method, self-study teaching method, etc.

（2）教学策略 Teaching strategies。

教学过程中采用铁道信号自动控制专业教学资源库实现混合式教学，使学生了解基本电子元器件和集成电路的相关知识，熟悉电子电路结构和工作原理，具备进行简单电路设计与应用的能力。

Blended teaching is realized by the implement of the teaching resource database for railway signal automatic control major during the process. This course aims to help students to learn the relevant knowledge of basic electronic components and integrated circuits, to be familiar with the structure and working principle of electronic circuits, to have the ability to carry out simple circuit design and application.

在实践教学环节，采用企业实地考察，请企业专家、技术能手给学生授课，让学生清楚企业的工作流程、岗位职责要求和企业岗位工作的其他纪律规定。

As to the practical teaching aspect, field investigation is adopted. Enterpise experts and technical experts are invited to lecture in order to make students be clear about the workflows, requirements of job description and work disciplines and rules of posts.

第三节 "铁道概论"课程标准

Curriculum Standards for Introduction to the Railway

一、课程性质 Nature of the Course

1. 课程类型、课程功能 Types and Functions

"铁道概论"是铁道信号自动控制专业的专业基础课，也可以作为其他相关专业的专业拓展课程开设，课程共计 26 课时，1.5 学分。该课是各个专业了解、认识铁路行业相关基础知识的基本课程。

Introduction to the Railway is the specialized basic course for automatic control of railway signalling major and the extensive specialized course for other related majors as well, including 26 lessons and1.5 credits. It's the basic course to learn about the railway related fundamental knowledge for various professions.

其功能是对应铁路交通类专业人才培养目标，面向铁路交通企业中的信号、机车、供电、运营、车辆、工务等设备维护管理的相关岗位，为相关岗位奠定理论和技术基础。

In accordance with the objective of cultivating the railway transport talents, its function is to lay a theoretical and technical base for equipment maintenance management related positions, referring to railway signalling, locomotive, power supply, operation, vehicles, railway maintenance in railway transportation industry.

2. 课程功能定位 Orientation of the Function

表 1 课程功能定位分析

Table 1 Analysis of the Orientation of the Function

对接的工作岗位 Jobs	对接培养的职业岗位能力 Abilities
铁路行业信号、机车、供电、运营、车辆、工务等设备维护管理的相关岗位 Railway signalling, locomotives, power supply, operation, vehicle, railway maintenance and management positions in railway transportation industry	了解铁路交通线路、车站、车辆、供电、信号、通信、运营组织等各个系统的设备和基本构成 To understand each device and its construction in the railway transportation lines, stations, vehicles, power supply, signalling, communication and operation organization for certain system
	了解铁路交通各个系统设备的基本原理 To understand the fundamental principle of each device in railway transportation system

二、课程目标与内容 Teaching Objectives and Contents

1. 课程总目标 General Objectives

本课程从理论基础的角度出发，介绍铁路运输业当中各种设施设备的分类、构成以及作用和发展等内容。使学生了解铁路运输事业，对铁路相关设备有一个基本的认识，培养学生热爱铁路事业的基本思想观，树立工作的责任心，并为学习后续课程和电子技术在专业中的应用打好基础。

This course mainly introduces the classification, construction, function and development of different facilities and devices in railway transportation industry from the theoretical base. Its aims are to enable students to know about the railway transportation and acquire a general knowledge of railway-related facilities; to foster students'passion and responsibility for railway transportation and to lay a good foundation for the follow-up courses and application of electronic techniques in major.

2. 课程具体目标 Specific Objectives

全面、系统、扼要地介绍我国铁路运输业、铁路运输设备和生产过程，主要包括铁路运输组织、铁路线路、铁路车站、铁路车辆、铁路机车、铁路信号和通信、电气化铁路供电和高速铁路等知识。考虑到专业发展的需要，本专业侧重铁路信号和通信、运输组织、线路、车辆、电气化铁路等方面的内容。

To comprehensively and systematicly introduce railway transportation industry, devices and manufacturing of railway transportation in our country, mainly includes the knowledge of railway transportation organization, railway lines, railway stations, railway vehicles and locomotives, railway signalling and communication, power supply of electrified railway and high-speed rail. Considering the need of major development, special emphasis is to be put on the railway signalling and communication, railway transportation organization, railway stations, railway vehicles and electrified railway.

表 2　课程教学目标与内容 1

Table 2　Teaching Objectives and Contents 1

序号 No.	毕业要求指标点 Index point of graduation requirement	知识目标 Knowledge goals	技能目标 Ability goals	素质目标 Quality goals	教学内容 Teaching contents
1	铁路行业信号、机车、供电、运营、车辆、工务等设备维护管理的相关岗位 Related positions of equipment maintenance management, such as railway signalling, locomotives, power supply, operation, vehicle, railway maintenance	现代交通运输业 Modern transportation industry	初步具备制定交通发展规划的基本意识 To equip students with the basic awareness of drafting transportation development plan	树立轨道交通领域相关概念，具有进一步学习轨道交通相关专业的基本知识素质 To cultivate the relevant concepts in railway transportation field, to develop the basic knowledge to further study railway transportation related major	了解现代交通运输的作用、性质和种类，铁路运输业的地位及发展史 To know the function, nature, and types of modern transportation, as well as the position and history of railway transportation
2		铁路线路 Railway lines	初步具备轨道交通线路维护的基本能力 To develop the fundamental ability of maintaining rail transit line		了解线路的等级、分类，看懂线路标志和线路平、纵断面图，了解桥隧建筑物、轨道的组成及类型，理解限界的概念 To know the grades and classifications of railway line, to understand the road way signs, the section plan and track profile of railway line, to comprehend the bridge and tunnel structures, the constructions and types of rails and the notion of gauge
3		铁路车站 Railway stations	初步具备轨道交通车站规划和设计意识能力 Have the consciousness and ability of rail transit station planning and design		了解车站的作用和分类，中间站、区段站和编组站的任务、作业和设备特点。 To learn the functions and types of stations, the task, operation and equipment features of intermediate station, section station and marshalling station
4		铁路车辆 Railway vehicles	初步具备轨道交通车辆使用维护的基本能力 Have the basic ability to use and maintain rail transit vehicle		了解铁路车辆的分类、用途以及构造 To learn the classifications, functions and constructions of railway vehicles
5		铁路机车 Railway locomotives	初步具备轨道交通机车设备使用维护的基本能力 Have the basic ability to use and maintain rail transit locomotive equipment		了解铁路机车的类型、发展方向以及电气化铁路 To know the types, developing trend of railway locomotive and electrified railway

序号 No.	毕业要求指标点 Index point of graduation requirement	知识目标 Knowledge goals	技能目标 Ability goals	素质目标 Quality goals	教学内容 Teaching contents
6		铁路动车组 Railway train-set	动车组的检修运用 Maintenance of CRH train		了解基本结构、组成 To learn the fundamental constructions and structures of the Multiple Units
7	铁路行业信号、机车、供电、运营、车辆、工务等设备维护管理的相关岗位 Related positions of equipment maintenance management, such as railway signalling, locomotives, power supply, operation, vehicle, railway maintenance	铁路信号及通信 Railway signalling and communication	初步具备轨道交通信号及通信系统的使用及维护基本能力 Have the basic ability to use and maintain railway signalling and communication system		了解铁路信号的分类、设置，了解系统新设备、新技术和各种通信设备 To understand the classification and setting of railway signalling, to learn new equipment and technology and various kinds of communication equipment
8		铁路运输组织 Railway transportation organization	初步具备铁路运输组织的意识 Have the awareness of railway transportation organization		了解铁路旅客、货运组织业务和行车组织的方法、特点等 To know the operation and organization of railway passenger and freight transport

表 3　课程教学目标与内容 2

Table 3　Teaching Objectives and Contents 2

序号 No.	项目（模块） Items	任务（单元） Tasks	教学内容 Teaching contents	重点、难点 Key points and difficulties	学时 Hours
1	项目 1：绪论 Item 1: introduction	城轨交通发展概述 Introduction to the development of urban rail transit	了解现代交通运输的作用、性质和种类，铁路运输业的地位及发展史 To know the functions, nature and types of modern transportation, the position and history of railway transportation	重点：轨道交通的发展 Key point: the development of railway transportation 难点：铁路运输业的发展规 Difficulties: the rules of development of railway transportation	2
2	项目 2：铁路线路 Item 2: railway lines	线路等级，线路标志，线路平、纵断面图，轨道的组成，界限 Line grades, line markings, line plans and profile views, track composition, and boundaries	了解线路的等级、分类，看懂线路标志和线路平、纵断面图，了解桥隧建筑物、轨道的组成及类型，理解限界的概念 Understand the grade and classification of the lines, understand the line marks and profile views, understand the composition and types of bridges and tunnels, tracks, and understand the concept of delimitation	重点：线路分类、轨道组成 Key points: line classification and track composition; 难点：线路识别、平面纵断面、轨道结构 Difficulties: line identification, plane profile and track structure	4
3	项目 3：铁路车站 Item 3: railway stations	车站的作用和分类，中间站、区段站，编组站 Functions and classifications of stations, intermediate station, section station, marshalling station	了解车站的作用和分类，中间站、区段站和编组站的任务、作业和设备特点 To learn the functions and classifications of stations, the task, operation and features of intermediate station, section station and marshalling station	重点：车站分类、车站特点 Key points: classifications and features of stations 难点：车站类型、车站作业 Difficulties: types and operation of stations	4

续表

序号 No.	项目（模块） Items	任务（单元） Tasks	教学内容 Teaching contents	重点、难点 Key points and difficulties	学时 Hours
4	项目 4：铁路车辆 Item 4: railway vehicles	车辆的分类，车辆用途，车辆构造 Classifications, usage and constructions of railway vehicles	了解铁路车辆的分类、用途以及构造 To understand the classifications, usage and constructions of railway vehicles	重点：车辆构造 Key point: vehicles constructions 难点：车辆类型、车辆结构 Difficulties: the types and structures of vehicles	2
5	项目 5：铁路机车 Item 5: railway locomotives	机车的类型，机车发展方向，机车电气化一体 Types and developing tendency of locomotives, the integrated eletrified locomotives	了解铁路机车的类型、发展方向以及电气化铁路 To understand the types and developing tendency of locomotives and eletrified railway	重点：机车构造 Key point: constructions of locomotives 难点：机车类型、机车结构 Difficulties: types and structures of locomotives	2
6	项目 6：铁路动车组 Item 6: multiple Units	动车组的运用及特点 Operation and features of train-set	了解动车组的基本结构、组成及检修运用 To know the basic constructions, structures and maintenance of train-set	重点、难点：动车组的结构 Key points and difficulties: structures of train-set	2
7	项目 7：铁路信号与通信 item 7: railway signalling and communication	铁路信号的分类设置，信号系统新技术，通信设备类别 Classifications and setting-up of railway signalling, new technology of signalling system, categories of communication device	了解铁路信号的分类、设置，了解系统新设备、新技术和各种通信设备 To understand the classifications and setting-up of railway signalling, the new technology of signalling system, various communication device	重点：信号系统设置、通信设备 Key point: setting of signalling system and communication device 难点：信号基础设置、通信设备设置 Difficulties: fundamental settings of signalling and communication device	6
8	项目 8：铁路运输组织 Item 8: railway transportation organization	铁路旅客，货运组织，行车组织 Railway passenger, organization of freight transportand train operation	了解铁路旅客、货运组织业务和行车组织方法、特点等 To know the methods and features of railway passenger, organization of freight transportand train operation	重点：运输组织规律 Key point: rules of transportation organization 难点：客运、货运、行车 Difficulties: passenger transport, freight transport, operation	4

说明：本课程标准适用于 26～28 学时的“铁道概论”课程的教学，表 3 中的学时为建议和参考学时，实际教学内容和课时可结合课程标准，根据教学的专业和课时进行选择和调整。

Notes: This curriculum standard applies to the teaching of An Introduction to Railway, accounting for 2628teaching periods. The teaching hours in table 3 are arranged for reference, the actual teaching contents and periods can be adjusted according to the major and practical teaching hours.

三、课程考核 Course Assessment

（1）课程考核分为总结性评价和过程性评价，关注学生个体差异。

Course assessment consists of summative evaluation and process evaluation, fcusing on students' individual difference.

（2）总结性评价包括标准化试题的闭卷考试。

The summative evaluation includes standardized test.

过程性评价指使用铁道信号自动控制专业教学资源库开展线上线、下混合式教学，由线上成绩、线下成绩、线上作业和线上考试组成。对项目中的平时作业、认知参观进行考核。考核内容可以根据实践教学设备的变化进行相应的调整。

Process evaluation is composed of online and off-line performance, online assignment and online test by using the online and off-line blended teaching through teaching resources database of railway signalling automatic control major. The usual performance and awareness in different items are also evaluated. Assessment contents can be ajusted according to the practical situation.

（4）课程考核比例：过程性评价占 30%，总结性评价占 70%。

The proportion of course assessment: process evaluation accounts for 30%, while summative assessment accounts for 70%.

四、实施要求 Implementation Requirements

1. 授课教师基本要求 Basic Requirements for Teachers

（1）具备铁道信号专业或相关专业岗位工作经历，大学本科及以上学历，具有高等学校教师资格证书。

Work experiences related to railway signalling major or relevant major, bachelor degree and above, with the teacher certificate of higher education.

（2）具备相应技术职称或本专业三级及以上职业资格证书。

With relevant technical titles or professional vocational qualification certificate of level-3 and above.

（3）具有"双师型"教师证书。

With the certificate of dual qualified teacher.

（4）具备开发职业课程、组织与实施教学的能力。

Ability to develop vocational course and organize and implement teaching.

（5）专业教师每两年到现场实践锻炼应不少于两个月。

No less than two months' field practice every two years.

2. 教学方法和策略 Teaching Methods and Strategies

（1）教学方法 Teaching Methods。

主要采用项目化教学法、情景教学法、现场教学法和工作过程导向教学法。坚持"够用为度"的原则选择相关的知识，依据"即学即了解"的原则安排教学顺序。可以以项目教学形式，设计若干个具有代表性的项目，或采用项目讲解与实景知识相映衬的方式。

Project method, situational teaching method, field-based teaching method and work process-oriented teaching method are adopted. Related knowledge is chosen based on the principle that enough is enough, while teaching sequence is arranged according to the principle that learning isunderstanding. Project teaching form is used by designing several typical projects or project-explaining contrasting with realistic knowledge.

（2）教学策略 Teaching Strategies。

教学过程中采用铁道信号自动控制专业教学资源库实现混合式教学，如信号、车站、车辆、运营组织的认知部分内容，可在专业教学资源库预先给学生操作视频或微课学习，然后课堂上通过讲解和实操提醒注意事项，理论知识点也可通过专业教学资源库的课程组课、在线答疑、网络考试、作业布置和修改等功能实现混合式教学。

The blended teaching through teaching resources database of railway signalling automatic control major is adopted during teaching process. Perceivable knowledge in railway signalling, station, vehicle and operation organization can be studied in advance through operation videos or micro-lectures. In-class explanation and reminding on operation are followed afterwards. Theoretical knowledge explanation can be achieved through the functions of re-mixing the courses, FAQ, online testing, assigning and correcting homework in the resources database.

在实践教学环节，采用企业实地考察，请企业专家、技术能手来给学生授课，让学生清楚企业的工作流程、岗位职责要求和企业岗位工作的其他纪律规定。

As to the practical teaching aspect, field investigation is adopted. Enterprise experts and technical experts are invited to lecture in order to make students be clear about the workflows, requirements of job description and work disciplines and rules of posts.

第二章　专业核心课程 Core Courses

第一节　“铁路信号基础设备维护”课程标准

Curriculum Standard for Railway Signalling Infrastructure Maintenance

一、课程性质 Nature of Course

1. 课程类型、课程功能 Types and Functions

本课程是铁道信号自动控制专业的核心课，共计 84 课时，5 学分；是学生在学习了“铁道概论”“电子分析基础”课程、具备了对铁道信号系统初步和整体认知的能力基础上，开设的一门理论+实践课，其功能是对接铁道信号自动控制专业人才培养目标，面向铁路信号设备检修工作岗位，培养诊断、处理铁路信号基础设备故障、日常检修和施工作业的能力，并为后续“铁路车站自动控制系统维护”“铁路区间自动控制系统维护”“列车自动控制技术”等课程的学习奠定基础。

It's the core course of the railway signaling automatic control majors, including 84 lessons and 5 credits. It's an integration of theoretical and practical course that opens up on the basics of preliminary acknowledging of the general knowledge in railway signalling system after learning An Introduction to the Railway and The Basis of Circuit Analysis. In accordance with the objective of cultivating the talents, this course aims to foster the abilities of diagnosing and handling the faults of railway signalling devices as well as the daily maintenance and operation. Thus, it lays a foundation for the following-up courses like Automatic Control System Maintenance of Railway Stations, Automatic Control System Maintenance of Sections and Vehicle Automatic Control Technology.

2. 课程功能定位 Orientation of the Function

表 1　课程功能定位分析

Table 1 Analysis of the Orientation of the Function

对接的工作岗位 Jobs	对接培养的职业岗位能力 Abilities
车站、区间、驼峰信号设备维修信号工岗位 Signalman of stations, sections and humps signal devices maintenance	按照中国铁路总公司最新颁布的《铁路信号维护规则》对车站、区间、驼峰信号设备进行准确认知及测量的能力 Ability to understand and measure the signal devices of stations, sections and humps according to *The Maintenance Rules of Railway Signalling* newly issued by China Railway Corporation
机车信号设备维修信号工岗位 Signalman of locomotives signal devices	按照中国铁路总公司最新颁布的《铁路信号维护规则》对机车信号设备进行准确认知及测量的能力 Ability to understand and measure the locomotives signal devices according to *The Maintenance Rules of Railway Signalling* newly issued by China Railway Corporation
信号工程施工岗位 Construction worker of signalling engineering	按照铁路信号工程施工技术及工艺标准对相关信号设备进行施工、安装的能力 Ability to operate and install related signalling devices according to the construction technology and standards of railway signalling

二、课程目标与内容 Objective and Content

1. 课程总目标 General Objectives

让学生掌握铁路现场广泛使用的各种铁路信号基础设备的结构、工作原理、作用以及建立联锁、闭塞等基本概念。通过本课程的学习，使学生对铁路信号系统的结构、工作原理有进一步的认识。

To enable students to grasp the constructions, operating principles and functions of various kinds of railway signaling devices widely used in railway scenes, and to build up the concept of interlock and locking. Through the course learning, students will have a further understanding of the constructions and working principles of railway signaling system.

2. 课程具体目标 Specific Objectives

表 2　课程教学目标与内容 1

Table 2　Teaching Objective and Contents 1

<table>
<tr><th>序号
No.</th><th>毕业要求指标点
Index point of graduation requirement</th><th>知识目标
Knowledge goals</th><th>技能目标
Ability goals</th><th>素质目标
Quality goals</th><th>教学内容
Teaching contents</th></tr>
<tr><td>1</td><td rowspan="2">1. 明确铁路信号设备是铁路主要技术装备之一
Be clear that railway signal device is one of the main technical equipments in railway
2. 按照中国铁路总公司最新颁布的《铁路信号维护规则》对车站、区间、驼峰、车载信号设备进行准确认知及测量
Be able to accurately acknowledge and measure the stations, sections, humps and train signaling devices according to The Maintenance Rules of Railway Signaling newly issued by China Railway Corporation</td><td>信号继电器的分类、功能、作用、使用
Classifications, functions, usages and operation of signal relay</td><td>按照铁路信号设备需求识别相关继电器类型，按照相关继电器识别插座板与各种型号继电器内部接点和线圈的关系，识别各种继电器的部件、结构、原理、用途；掌握继电电路的识别及应用；理解继电电路的分析、继电电路的安全措施
To identify related relay types according to the requirements of railway signalling devices; To distinguish different relay plug boards and the relation between the internal junction point and coil, to identify the units, structures, principles and functions of various relays; To comprehend the recognition and applications of relay; To understand the analysis and safety principles of relay circuit</td><td rowspan="2">1. 规范的操作，细心和耐心地进行标准化工作的意识
To establish the awareness of operating with standard, carefulness and patience
2. 培养学生独立解决工作过程中出现的问题的能力
To foster students' ability of solving problems independently during the working process
3. 培养学生的团队协作精神
To cultivate students' teamwork spirit</td><td>信号继电器
Signal relay</td></tr>
<tr><td>2</td><td>信号机和信号表示器的分类、功能、作用、使用
Classifications, functions, usages and operation of signaling and signal indicators</td><td>识别色灯信号机；识别色灯信号机的机构；掌握色灯信号机的显示及设置原则；掌握色灯信号机的检修维护方法
To identify the color-light signal and its structures; To understand the indication, setting principles and maintenance methods of color-light signal</td><td>信号机和信号表示器
Signaling and signal indicators</td></tr>
</table>

续表

<table>
<tr><th>序号
No.</th><th>毕业要求指标点
Index point of graduation requirement</th><th>知识目标
Knowledge goals</th><th>技能目标
Ability goals</th><th>素质目标
Quality goals</th><th>教学内容
Teaching contents</th></tr>
<tr><td>3</td><td rowspan="3">1. 明确铁路信号设备是铁路主要技术装备之一
Be clear that railway signal device is one of the main technical equipments in railway
2. 按照中国铁路总公司最新颁布的《铁路信号维护规则》对车站、区间、驼峰、车载信号设备进行准确认知及测量
Be able to accurately acknowledge and measure the stations, sections, humps and train signaling devices according to The Maintenance Rules of Railway Signaling newly issued by China Railway Corporation</td><td>轨道电路的分类、功能、作用、使用
Classifications, functions and operations of track circuit</td><td>掌握工频、25Hz、移频轨道电路的基本组成；掌握道岔区段轨道电路和轨道电路极性交叉；判断轨道电路的基本工作状态和测试基本参数；掌握轨道电路的检修与维护
be knowledgeable about the fundamental structures of power frequency, 25Hz and frequency-shift track circuit; To understand the track circuit of switch section and polarity-crossing of track circuit; To judge the general working conditions and testing parameters of track circuit and know the inspection and maintenance of track circuit</td><td rowspan="3">1. 规范的操作，细心和耐心地进行标准化工作的意识
To establish the awareness of operating with standard, carefulness and patience
2. 培养学生独立解决工作过程中出现的问题的能力
To foster students' ability of solving problems independently during the working process
3. 培养学生的团队协作精神
To cultivate students' teamwork spirit</td><td>轨道电路
Track circuit</td></tr>
<tr><td>4</td><td>道岔转换与锁闭设备的分类、功能、作用、使用
Classifications, functions and operations of equipment in switch setting and locking</td><td>掌握ZD6、ZYJ7 S700K、ZD(J)9转辙机的结构，理解其动作过程、工作原理；
To know the structures, operating process and working principles of ZD6、ZYJ7 S700K、ZD(J)9 switch machine</td><td>道岔转换与锁闭设备
Switchs setting and locking equipments</td></tr>
<tr><td>5</td><td>防雷和接地装置的功能、作用、使用
Functions and operations of lighting protection and grounding devices</td><td>防雷的意义、元器件的使用，接地装置的设置及要求；掌握防雷和接地装置的检修与维护
To understand the significance of lighting protection and the usage of components, the setting and requirements of grounding devices; To master the inspection and maintenance of lighting protection and grounding devices</td><td>防雷和接地装置
Lighting protection and grounding devices</td></tr>
<tr><td>6</td><td>明确现代铁路信号系统的组成是铁路的主要技术装备，在保证行车安全、提高运输效率方面起着不可替代的作用
Be clear about the composition of modern railway signalling system is the main technical equipment of railway, which plays an irreplaceable role in assuring operation safety and improving the transportation efficiency</td><td>铁路信号系统概述
Introduction to railway signalling system</td><td>掌握铁路信号系统的组成、构成、作用
To understand the constructions and functions of railway signalling system</td><td>由小到大、由微观到宏观的认知新知识的能力，举一反三的能力
The ability of learning new knowledge gradually from micro to macro; The ability to draw inferences about other cases from one instance</td><td>铁路信号系统
Railway signalling system</td></tr>
</table>

表 3　课程教学安排 2

Table 3　teaching arrangement 2

序号 No.	项目（模块） Items	任务（单元） Tasks	教学内容 Teaching contents	重点、难点 Key points and difficulties	学时 Hours
1	项目 1：信号继电器 Item 1: signal relay	1.1 信号继电器概述 Introduction to signal relay	了解信号基础设备的组成及继电器工作原理、特点 To understand the composition of signalling fundamental devices and the operating principles and features of relay secure relay structure	重点：信号基础设备的组成 Key point: the composition of signalling fundamental devices 难点：继电器工作原理、特点 Difficulties: the operating principles and features of relay	2
2		1.2 安全型继电器 Safety relays	掌握安全型继结构及其工作原理、安全型继电器的特性，了解安全型继电器的接点特性 To know the constructions, features, operating principles and the contact features of safety relays	重点：安全型继电器的接点特性 Key point: the contact features of safety relays 难点：安全型继结构及其工作原理、安全型继电器的特性 Difficulties: operating principles and features of safety relays	4
3		1.3 时间、灯丝、交流二元型继电器 Timer, filaments and alternating binary relay	掌握时间、灯丝、交流二元型继电器的结构及工作原理 To grasp the structures and working principles of timer, filaments and alternating binary relay	重点：时间、灯丝、交流二元型继电器的结构 Key points: the structures of timer, filaments and alternating binary relay 难点：时间、灯丝、交流二元型继电器的工作原理 Difficulties: the working principles of timer, filaments and alternating binary relay	2
4		1.4 继电器的应用 The application of relays	继电电路的识别及应用，继电电路的分析，继电电路的安全措施 To distinguish the relay circuit and to know its application, analysis and safety measures	重点：继电电路的识别、应用和分析 Key points: identification, application and analysis of relay circuit 难点：继电电路的安全措施 Difficulties: safety measures of relay circuit	4
5		1.5 简单继电器电路的接线 The wiring of simple relay circuit	掌握简单继电器电路的接线方法及继电器的工作原理 To understand the wiring method of simple relay circuit and the working principles of relay	重点：简单继电器电路的接线方法 Key point: the wiring method of simple relay circuit 难点：继电器电路工作原理 Difficulties: working principles of relay	4
6	项目 2：信号机和信号表示器 Item 2: signaling and signal indicator	2.1 铁路信号基本知识 General knowledge of railway signalling	掌握色灯信号机的含义、分类、结构 To learn the notion, types and structures of color-light signal	重点：色灯信号机的含义、分类、结构 Key points: the notion, types and structures of color-light signal 难点：色灯信号机的含义、分类 Difficulties: the notion and types of color-light signal	2

续表

序号 No.	项目（模块） Items	任务（单元） Tasks	教学内容 Teaching contents	重点、难点 Key points and difficulties	学时 Hours
7	项目 2：信号机和信号表示器 Item 2: signaling and signal indicator	2.2 信号光源 Signal source	掌握色灯信号光源及透镜式色灯信号机灯丝转换原理 To master the color-light signal source and the filament conversion principles of lenticular color-light signal	重点：色灯信号点灯及灯丝转换原理 Key point: lighting and the filament conversion principles of color-light signal 难点：透镜式色灯信号机灯丝转换原理 Difficulties: the filament conversion principles of lenticular color-light signal	2
8		2.3 信号机的设置 The settings of signal machine	掌握信号机信号表示器的设置原则 To understand the setting rules of signal indicator	重点：信号机及信号表示器的设置原则 Key point: the setting rules of signal machine and signal indicator 难点：信号机及信号表示器的设置原则和命名 Difficulties: the setting rules and notion of signal machine and signal indicator	2
9		2.4 信号显示 Signal indication	掌握信号的基本显示系统、机构选用和灯光配列，掌握信号显示的意义及信号显示的距离要求 To understand the fundamental signaling display system, the determinate of constitutions and light series of signal, to understand the significance and the distance requirements of signal indication	重点：信号的基本显示系统及机构选用和灯光配列 Key points: the fundamental display system, the structure selection and light series of signalling 难点：信号的基本显示系统、灯光配列、显示制度和信号显示的意义 Difficulties: fundamental display system, light series, indication rules of signal and the meaning of signal indication	6
10		2.5 信号机的检修与维护 Inspection and maintenance of signal machine	掌握信号机的检修与维护 To grasp the inspection and maintenance of signal machine	重点：信号机的检修与维护 Difficulties: the inspection and maintenance of signal machine 难点：信号机的检修与维护 Difficulties: the inspection and maintenance of signal machine	2
11		2.6 信号机灯光调整与电气参数测试 Light adjustment of signal machine and electric parameter test	掌握信号机的灯光调整与电气参数测试 To understand light adjustment of signal machine and electric parameter test	重点：信号机的灯光调整与电气参数测试 Key points: light adjustment of signal machine and electric parameter test 难点：信号机的电气参数测试 Difficulties: the electric parameter test of signal machine	2
12	项目 3：轨道电路 Item 3: track circuit	3.1 轨道电路的组成及工作原理 The structures and working principles of track circuit	掌握轨道电路的组成、基本原理、作用、分类、划分和命名 To master the structures, working principles, functions, classification and naming of track circuit	重点：轨道电路的基本原理、作用、分类、划分和命名 Key points: basic principles, functions, classifications and notions of track circuit 难点：轨道电路的基本原理、划分和命名 Difficulties: basic principles, functions, classifications and notions of track circuit	2

续表

序号 No.	项目（模块） Items	任务（单元） Tasks	教学内容 Teaching contents	重点、难点 Key points and difficulties	学时 Hours
13	项目3：轨道电路 Item 3: track circuit	3.2 轨道电路区段划分及应用 The division and application of track circuit in sections	掌握轨道电路区段划分和命名 Be clear about the division and naming of section in track circuit	重点：轨道电路区段划分和命名 Key point: the division and naming of section in track circuit 难点：轨道电路区段划分 Difficulties: the section division of track circuit	2
14		3.3 道岔区段轨道电路 Track switch circuit	掌握道岔区段轨道电路和轨道电路极性交叉 To learn switch track circuit and the polar transposition of track circuit	重点：道岔区段轨道电路和轨道电路极性交叉 Key point: swited track circuit and the polar transposition of track circuit 难点：轨道电路极性交叉 Difficulties: the polar transposition of track circuit	2
15		3.4 工频交流连续式轨道电路 The continuous track circuit of industrial frequency alternate current (AC)	掌握工频交流轨道电路的组成及工作原理 To master the composition and working principles of industrial frequency AC track circuit	重点：工频交流轨道电路的组成及工作原理 Key points: the composition and working principles of industrial frequency AC track circuit 难点：工频交流轨道电路的工作原理 difficulties: the working principles of industrial frequency AC track circuit	2
16		3.5 轨道电路的基本工作状态与参数 The basic operation and parameters of track circuit	掌握轨道电路的基本状态及基本参数、调整方法、极性交叉测试 To understand the basic state and parameters, the adjustment method and polarity-crossing test of track circuit	重点：轨道电路的基本参数、调整方法、极性交叉测试 Key points: the basic parameters, the adjustment method and polarity-crossing test of track circuit 难点：轨道电路调整方法、极性交叉测试 Difficulties: the adjustment method and polarity-crossing test of track circuit	2
17		3.6 97型25Hz相敏轨道电路 97 mode 25Hz phase-sensitive track circuit	掌握97型25Hz相敏轨道电路的组成及工作原理 To grasp the structures and working principles of 97 mode 25Hz phase-sensitive track circuit	重点：97型25Hz相敏轨道电路的组成及工作原理 Key point: the structures and working principles of 97 mode 25Hz phase-sensitive track circuit 难点：97型25Hz相敏轨道电路的工作原理 Difficulties: working principles of 97 mode 25Hz phase-sensitive track circuit	2
18		3.7 JXW25型微电子相敏轨道电路 JXW25 micro-electronic phase-sensitive track circuit	掌握JXW25型微电子相敏轨道电路的组成及工作原理、电路测试 to understand the structures, working principles and circuit testing of JXW25 micro-electronic phase-sensitive track circuit	重点：JXW25型微电子相敏轨道电路的测试方法 Key point: testing methods of JXW25 micro-electronic phase-sensitive track circuit 难点：JXW25型微电子相敏轨道电路的测试方法 Difficulties: testing methods of JXW25 micro-electronic phase-sensitive track circuit	2

续表

序号 No.	项目（模块） Items	任务（单元） Tasks	教学内容 Teaching contents	重点、难点 Key points and difficulties	学时 Hours
19	项目3：轨道电路 Item 3: track circuit	3.8 25Hz 轨道电路的检修与维护 Inspection and maintenance of 25Hz track circuit	掌握25Hz轨道电路的检修与维护 To understand the inspection and maintenance of 25Hz track circuit	重点：25Hz 轨道电路的检修与维护 Key points: the inspection and maintenance of 25Hz track circuit 难点：25Hz 轨道电路的检修与维护 Difficulties: the inspection and maintenance of 25Hz track circuit	2
20		3.9 移频轨道电路 Frequency-shift track circuit	了解移频轨道电路的组成、原理 To understand the compositions and principles of frequency-shift track circuit	重点：移频轨道电路的组成 Key point: the compositions of frequency-shift track circuit 难点：移频轨道电路的原理 Difficulties: the principles of frequency-shift track circuit	2
21	项目4：道岔转换与锁闭设备 Item 4: switch the locking equipment	4.1 转辙机概述 Introduction to the switch machine	掌握转辙机的作用、分类、基本要求、设置 To grasp the functions, types, fundamental requirements and settings of switch machine	重点：转辙机的作用、分类、基本要求、设置 Key points: the functions, types, fundamental requirements and settings of switch machine 难点：转辙机作用、分类 Difficulties: the functions and types of switch machine	2
22		4.2 ZD6 型电动转辙机 ZD6 electric switcher	掌握转辙机各部件工作原理，掌握ZD6型电动转辙机的安装及电气参数测试 To understand the working principles of various components in switch machine and the installation and electrical parameter testing of ZD6 electric switcher	重点：转辙机各部件工作原理、安装及电气参数测试 Key points: the working principles of various components in switch machine and the installation and electrical parameter testing of switch machine 难点：转辙机各部件工作原理 Difficulties: the working principles of various components in switch machine	4
23		4.3 ZD6 型转辙机分解组装 The decomposition and assembly of ZD6 electric switcher	掌握 ZD6 电动转辙机分解组装方法 To know the decomposing and assembling methods of ZD6 electric switcher	重点：ZD6 电动转辙机分解组装方法 Key points: the decomposing and assembling methods of ZD6 electric switcher 难点：ZD6 电动转辙机分解组装方法 Difficulties: the decomposing and assembling methods of ZD6 electric switcher	4
24		4.4 外锁闭装置 External locking device	掌握外锁闭装置的结构、工作原理、检修与维护 To understand the structures, working principles, inspections and maintenance of external locking device	重点：外锁闭装置的结构、原理、检修与维护 Key points: the structures, principles, inspections and maintenance of external locking device 难点：外锁闭装置的结构 Difficulties: the structures of external locking device	4

序号 No.	项目（模块） Items	任务（单元） Tasks	教学内容 Teaching contents	重点、难点 Key points and difficulties	学时 Hours
25	项目 4：道岔转换与锁闭设备 Item 4: switch the locking equipment	4.5 S700K 电动转辙机 S700K electric switcher	掌握 S700K 型电动转辙机的特点、结构、工作原理 To understand the characteristics, structures and working principles of S700K electric switcher	重点：S700K 型电动转辙机的特点、结构、工作原理 Key points: the features, structures and working principles of S700K electric switcher 难点：S700K 型电动转辙机的原理 Difficulties: working principles of S700K electric switcher	2
26		4.6 ZD(J)9 电动转辙机 ZD(J)9 electric switcher	理解 ZD(J)9 电动转辙机的特点、结构、工作原理 To understand the characteristics, structures and working principles of ZD(J)9 electric switcher	重点：ZD(J)9 电动转辙机的特点、结构、工作原理 Key points: the characteristics, structures and working principles of ZD(J)9 electric switcher 难点：ZD(J)9 电动转辙机的工作原理 Difficulties: the working principles of ZD(J)9 electric switcher	2
27		4.7 ZYJ7 型电液转辙机 ZYJ7 electrohydraulic switch machine	理解 ZYJ7 型电液转辙机的结构、工作原理、检修与维护 To know the structures, working principles, inspection and maintenance of ZYJ7 electrohydraulic switch machine	重点：ZYJ7 型电液转辙机的类型、结构、工作原理、检修与维护 Key points: types, structures, working principles, inspection and maintenance of ZYJ7 electrohydraulic switch machine 难点：ZYJ7 型电液转辙机工作原理、检修与维护 Difficulties: working principles, inspection and maintenance of ZYJ7 electrohydraulic switch machine	4
28	项目 5：防雷和接地装置 Item 5: lightening protection and grounding devices	防雷和接地装置 Lightening protection and grounding devices	理解信号设备防雷元件的种类、接地装置的结构和工作原理及其检修与维护 To understand the types of lightening protection components of signalling devices, the structures and working principles of grounding devices and its inspection and maintenance	重点：信号设备防雷元件的种类、接地装置的结构 Key points: types of lightening protection components of signalling devices, the structure of grounding devices 难点：信号设备防雷元件、接地装置的工作原理 Difficulties: lightening protection components of signalling devices, working principles of grounding devices	4
29	项目 6：铁路信号系统 Item 6: railway signalling system	铁路信号系统概述 Introduction to the railway signalling system	理解铁路信号系统的组成 To understand the compositions of railway signalling system	重点：铁路信号系统的组成 Key point: the compositions of railway signalling system 难点：铁路信号系统的组成 Difficulties: the compositions of railway signalling system	2

说明：本课程标准适用于 8～88 学时的“铁路信号基础设备维护”课程的教学，表 3 中的学时为建议和参考学时，实际教学内容和课时可结合课程标准，根据教学的专业和课时进行选择和调整。

Notes: this curriculum standard applies to the teaching of Railway Signalling Infrastructure Maintenance, accounting for 80—88 teaching periods. The teaching hours in table 3 are arranged for reference, the actual teaching contents and periods can be adjusted according to the major and practical teaching hours.

三、课程考核 Course Assessment

（1）课程考核分为总结性评价和过程性评价，关注学生个体差异。

Course assessment consists of summative evaluation and process evaluation，fcusing on students' individual difference.

（2）总结性评价包括标准化试题的闭卷考试。

The summative evaluation includes standardized test.

（3）过程性评价指使用铁道信号自动控制专业教学资源库开展线上、线下混合式教学，由线上成绩、线下成绩、线上作业和线上考试组成。对项目中的平时作业、基本实践技能进行考核。考核内容可以根据实践教学设备的变化进行相应的调整。

Process evaluation is composed of online and off-line performance, online assignment and online test by using the online and off-line blended teaching through teaching resources database of railway signalling automatic control major. The usual performance and awareness in different items are also evaluated. Assessment contents can be adjusted according to the practical situation.

（4）课程考核比例：过程性评价占 50%，总结性评价占 50%。

The proportion of course assessment: process evaluation accounts for 50%, while summative assessment accounts for 50%.

四、实施要求 Implementation Requirements

1. 授课教师基本要求 Basic Requirements for Teachers

（1）具备铁道信号专业或相关专业岗位工作经历，大学本科及以上学历，具有高等学校教师资格证书。

Work experiences related to railway signalling major or relevant major, bachelor degree and above, with the teacher certificate of higher education.

（2）具备相应技术职称或本专业三级及以上职业资格证书。

With relevant technical titles or professional vocational qualification certificate of level-3and above.

（3）具有“双师型”教师证书。

With the certificate of dual qualified teacher.

（4）具备开发职业课程、组织与实施教学的能力；Ability to develop vocational course and organize and implement teaching.

（5）专业教师每两年到现场实践锻炼应不少于两个月。

No less than two months' field practice every two years.

2. 教学方法和策略 Teaching Methods and Strategies

（1）教学方法 Teaching Methods。

主要采用项目化教学、案例教学法、情景教学法、工作过程导向教学法。坚持“够用为度”的原则选择相关知识，依据“即学即用”的原则安排教学顺序。以项目教学为形式，选择若干个具有代表性的子系统作为项目，将知识点重新整理，作为实践与技能的背景知识安排在对应的项目中，让各种知识尽可能在“做中学”。

Project method, case teaching method, situational teaching method, and work process-oriented teaching method are adopted. Related knowledge is chosen based on the principle that enough is enough, while teaching sequence is arranged according to the principle that learning is understanding. Choose several typical subsystems as project to rearrange the knowledge points by using project teaching method. The practical and skillful background knowledge are arranged in the corresponding projects thus to realize learning knowledge by doing.

（2）教学策略 Teaching Strategies。

教学过程中采用铁道信号自动控制专业教学资源库实现混合式教学，例如继电器线圈图形符号、继电器基本电路、列车信号机的设置、站内调车信号机的设置、工频交流连续式轨道电路组成及原理、ZD6 转辙机机械故障调整等基本操作部分内容可在网络平台或采用其他手段预先给学生操作学习，然后通过实验课讲解和实作提醒考核点。还可在实验过程中结合学生需要采用视频循环播放的方式，以此提高学生掌握技能的能力。

The blended teaching through teaching resources database of railway signalling automatic control major is adopted during teaching process. Parts of the contents in basic operation like graphic symbols of relay coil, basic circuit of relay, settings of train signaller and station shunting signal, composition and working principles of industrial frequency AC track circuit and adjustments of mechanical fault in ZD6 electric switcher can be studied in advance through operation videos or online platforms. In-class explanation and reminding on operation are followed afterwards. Videos streaming during the experimental process is tailored to students' need thus to enhence students' ability to comprehend the skills.

在实践教学环节，采用企业实地考察，请企业专家、技术能手来给学生授课，让学生清楚企业的工作流程、岗位职责要求和企业岗位工作的其他纪律规定。

As to the practical teaching aspect, field investigation is adopted. Enterprise experts and technical experts are invited to lecture in order to make students be clear about the workflows, requirements of job description and work disciplines and rules of posts.

第二节 "铁路车站自动控制系统维护"课程标准

Curriculum Standard for Maintenance of Railway Station Automatic Control System

一、课程性质 Nature of the Course

1. 课程类型、课程功能 Types and Functions

本课程是铁道信号自动控制专业的核心课，共计 84 课时，5 学分；是学生在学习了"铁路信号基础设备维护"课程，具备信号继电器检修、信号机维护、轨道电路维护、转辙机维护、防雷及接地设置维护等能力的基础上，开设的一门理论+实践课。其功能是对接铁路信号专业人才培养目标，面向信号工工作岗位，培养学生电气集中联锁和计算机联锁设备的测试、检修和故障处理的能力，并为后续“列车运行自动控制系统维护”“铁路信号设计与施工”“铁路信号集中监测系统维护”“毕业设计”“信号工技能鉴定实训”课程的学习奠定基础。

It's the core course of railway signalling automatic control major, including 84 lessons and 5 credits. It's a theoretical and practical course based on the course study of the Railway Signalling Infrastructure Maintenance and on the condition that students have the ability to inspect and maintain the signal relay, signal, and track circuit, switch machine, lightening protection and grounding devices. In accordance with the objective of cultivating railway signalling talents, facing the signal workers, it fosters students' ability of testing, inspecting and maintaining and fault-handling in electric central interlocking and computer interlocking equipment, which lays a foundation for the study of the following-up course like Maintaincence of Train Operation Automatic Control System, Railway Signal Design and Constraltion, Graduation Project and Practical Training for Skill Appraisal of Signal Worker.

2. 课程功能定位 Orientation of the Function

表 1　课程功能定位分析

Table 1　Analysis of the Orientation of the Fumction

对接的工作岗位 Jobs	对接培养的职业岗位能力 Abilities
车站、驼峰信号设备维修信号工岗位 Signal worker of sations and humps signal device maintenance	按照中国铁路总公司最新颁布的《铁路信号维护规则》对车站、驼峰信号设备进行维护的能力 To maintain the stations and humps signal devices according to *The Maintenance Rules of Railway Signalling* newly issued by China Railway Corporation

二、课程目标与内容 Objective and Content

1. 课程总目标 General Objectives

掌握 6502 电气集中设备的基本组成、基本动作过程、基本电路原理及操作使用方法，具备 6502 电气集中设备的操作使用能力；掌握四线制道岔、五线制道岔控制电路结构、工作原理和故障处理方法，具备四线制道岔、五线制道岔控制电路的故障处理能力；掌握进站信号机、出站信号机和调车信号机点灯电路的组成、工作原理和故障处理方法，具备标准化作业及常见故障处理能力；掌握计算机联锁系统的基本知识，典型计算机联锁系统的组成、工作原理和日常维护程序及标准，具备标准化作业及常见故障处理能力。

To understand the compositions, operating process, circuit principles and operating methods of 6502 electric centralizing equipment, thus to equip students with the operating ability. To master the structures, working principles and fault handling approaches of four-wire and five-wire switchs control circuit thus to gain the ability of fault handling. To learn the structures, working principles and fault handling approaches of the home signal, starting signal and shunting signal lighting circuit thus to gain the ability of standardized operation and fault handling. To learn the fundamental knowledge of computer interlocking system, the compositions, working principles and routine maintenance procedures and standards, thus to have the ability of standardized operation and fault handling.

2. 课程具体目标 Specific Objectives

表 2　课程教学目标与内容 1

Table 2　Teaching Objectives and Contents 1

序号 No.	毕业要求指标点 Index point of graduation requirement	知识目标 Knowledge goals	技能目标 Ability goals	素质目标 Quality goals	教学内容 Teaching contents
1	掌握 6502 电气集中设备的基本组成、基本动作过程、基本电路原理及操作使用方法；具备 6502 电气集中设备的操作使用能力 To understand the basic components, fundamental operating process, basic circuit principles and operation methods of 6502 electric centralizing equipment; To attain the ability to operate 6502 electric centralizing equipment	熟练掌握车站联锁设备的组成，室内外设备的连接关系 To understand the compositions of the station interlocking equipments, the connecting relation between interior and outdoor equipments	能够描述出车站联锁设备的组成 Be able to describe the compositions of the station interlocking equipments	标准作业流程 Standardized operation	电气集中车站设备组成 The compositions of electric centralized station equipments
2		熟练掌握车站联锁设备的操作使用方法。To grasp the operation methods of station interlocking equipments	能够按照要求对车站联锁设备进行操作 To operate the station interlocking equipment according to the requirements	强化学生的岗位职业能力 To strengthen students' professional ability	电气集中车站设备功能；电气集中设备的操纵使用 The functions and operations of electric centralizing equipments
3		掌握联锁表的编制和各种联锁试验要求与方法 To learn the compiling of interlocking tables and the requirements and methods of various interlocking tests	能够进行联锁试验 Be able to test the interlocking	标准作业流程 Standardized operation	联锁表的基本概念；联锁表的编制 Basic concept of interlocking table and its compilation
4		掌握 6502 电气集中选择组电路和执行组电路的工作原理 To understand the working principles of selecting circuit and executive circuit in 6502 electric centralizing equipment	能处理 6502 电气集中电路的故障 Be able to handle the breakdown of 6502 electric centralizing equipment	安全工作意识 Safety awareness	6502 电气集中 1-15 线网络电路结构、各继电器的作用、设置与动作 The circuit structures of 1-15 wire in 6502 electric centralizing equipment, the functions, settings and operation of various relays
5	掌握四线制道岔控制电路的结构、工作原理和故障处理方法；具备四线制转辙机道岔控制电路故障处理能力 To understand the structures, working principles and fault-handling methods of four-wire switch control circuit; to gain the ability to deal with the breakdowns of control circuit in four-wire switch machine	熟练掌握四线制道岔控制电路的结构、工作原理和故障处理方法 To understand the structures, working principles and fault-handling methods of four-wire switch control circuit	能处理四线制转辙机道岔控制电路故障 Be able to deal with breakdowns of control circuit in four-wire switch machine	自主学习能力，团队协作意识 Self-learning ability and teamwork spirit	四线制道岔控制电路原理；四线制道岔控制电路故障分析方法 Principles and fault-handling methods of four-wire switch control circuit

续表

序号 No.	毕业要求指标点 Index point of graduation requirement	知识目标 Knowledge goals	技能目标 Ability goals	素质目标 Quality goals	教学内容 Teaching contents
6	掌握五线制道岔控制电路结构、工作原理和故障处理方法；具备五线制转辙机道岔控制电路故障处理能力 To understand the structures, working principles and fault-handling methods of five-wire switch control circuit; to gain the ability to deal with the breakdowns of control circuit in five-wire switch machine	熟练掌握五线制道岔控制电路结构、工作原理和故障处理方法 To understand the structures, working principles and fault-handling methods of five-wire switch control circuit	能处理五线制转辙机道岔控制电路故障 Be able to deal with breakdowns of control circuit in five-wire switch machine	自主学习能力，团队协作意识 Self-learning ability and teamwork spirit	五线制道岔控制电路原理；五线制道岔控制电路故障分析方法 Priciples and fault-handling methods of five-wire switch control circuit
7	掌握进站信号机点灯电路的组成、工作原理和故障处理方法，具备标准化作业及常见故障处理能力 To know the compositions, working principles and fault-handling methods of lighting circuit of home signal thus to gain the abilitiy of stardardized operation and fault-handling	熟练掌握进站信号机点灯电路的组成、工作原理和故障处理方法 To know the compositions, working principles and fault-handling methods of lighting circuit of home signal	能进行标准化作业；能处理进站信号机常见故障 Be able to operate standardizedly and deal with the common faults of home signal	规范操作意识，细心，耐心 Stardardized operation awareness, carefulness and patience	进站信号点灯电路；进站信号点灯电路测试和常见故障的分析处理方法 Lighting circuit of home signal; Lighting circuit testing and common fault-handling ways of home signal
8	掌握出站信号机点灯电路的组成、工作原理和故障处理方法，具备标准化作业及常见故障处理能力 To know the compositions, working principles and fault-handling methods of lighting circuit of starting signal thus to gain the abilitiy of stardardized operation and fault-handling	熟练掌握调车信号机点灯电路的组成、工作原理和故障处理方法 To know the compositions, working principles and fault-handling methods of lighting circuit of starting signal	能进行标准化作业；能处理出站信号机常见故障 Be able to operate standardizedly and deal with the common fault of starting signal	规范操作意识，细心，耐心 Stardardized operation awareness, carefulness and patience	出站信号点灯电路；出站信号点灯电路测试和常见故障的分析处理方法 Lighting circuit of starting signal; Lighting circuit testing and common fault-handling ways of starting signal
9	掌握调车信号机点灯电路的组成、工作原理和故障处理方法，具备标准化作业及常见故障处理能力 To know the compositions, working principles and fault-handling methods of lighting circuit of shunting signal thus to gain the abilitiy of stardardized operation and fault-handling	熟练掌握调车信号机点灯电路的组成、工作原理和故障处理方法 To know the compositions, working principles and fault-handling methods of lighting circuit of shunting signal	能进行标准化作业；能处理调车信号机常见故障 Be able to operate standardizedly and deal with the common fault of shunting signal	规范操作意识，细心，耐心 Stardardized operation awareness, carefulness and patience	调车信号点灯电路；调车信号点灯电路测试和常见故障的分析处理方法 Lighting circuit of starting signal; Lighting circuit testing and common fault-handling ways of shunting signal

续表

序号 No.	毕业要求指标点 Index point of graduation requirement	知识目标 Knowledge goals	技能目标 Ability goals	素质目标 Quality goals	教学内容 Teaching contents
10	掌握计算机联锁系统的基本知识，典型计算机联锁系统的组成、工作原理和日常维护程序及标准，具备标准化作业及常见故障处理能力 To learn the general knowledge of computer interlocking system, the constructions, working principles and daily maintenance procedure and standard of typical computer interlocking system, thus to gain the ability of standardized operation and fault-handling	熟悉TYJL-ADX型计算机联锁系统的硬件组成、各部分设备的功能；掌握TYJL-ADX型计算机联锁系统的设备维护常识与故障处理方法 Be familiar with the hardware structures of TYJL-ADX computer interlocking system and functions of each equipment; To learn the maintenance knowledge and fault-handling ways of TYJL-ADX computer interlocking system	能处理TYJL- ADX型计算机联锁系统的设备常见故障 Be able to handle the common breakdowns of TYJL-ADX computer interlocking system	培养计算机联锁系统安全操作意识 Awareness of safety operation of computer interlocking system	TYJL-ADX型计算机联锁系统的硬件组成、各部分设备的功能；TYJL-ADX型计算机联锁系统的设备维护常识与故障处理方法 The hardware structures of TYJL-ADX computer interlocking system and functions of each equipment; The maintenance knowledge and fault-handling ways of TYJL-ADX computer interlocking system
11		熟悉DS6-K5B型计算机联锁系统的硬件组成、各部分设备的功能；掌握DS6-K5B型计算机联锁系统的设备维护常识与故障处理方法 Be familiar with the hardware structures of DS6-K5B computer interlocking system and functions of each equipment; To learn the maintenance knowledge and fault-handling ways of DS6-K5B computer interlocking system	能处理DS6-K5B型计算机联锁系统的设备常见故障 Be able to handle the common breakdowns of DS6-K5B computer interlocking system	培养计算机联锁系统安全操作意识 Awareness of safety operation of computer interlocking system	DS6-K5B型计算机联锁系统的硬件组成、各部分设备的功能；DS6-K5B型计算机联锁系统的设备维护常识与故障处理方法 The hardware structures of DS6-K5B computer interlocking system and functions of each equipment; The maintenance knowledge and fault-handling ways of DS6-K5Bcomputer interlocking system

表3　课程教学目标与内容2

Table 3　Teaching Objectives and Contents 2

序号 No.	项目（模块） Items	任务（单元） Tasks	教学内容 Teaching contents	重点、难点 Key points and difficulties	学时 Hours
1	项目1：车站联锁知识 Item 1: knowledge of railway interlocking	1.1 车站联锁关系 Relation of stations interlocking	1. 进路与道岔之间的联锁关系 The interlocking relation between route and switch 2. 进路与进路之间的联锁关系 The interlocking relation between routes 3. 进路与信号机之间的联锁关系 The interlocking relation between route and signal machine 4. 进路与轨道区段之间的联锁关系 The interlocking relation between route and railway section	重点：进路与道岔之间的联锁关系；进路与进路之间的联锁关系；进路与信号机之间的联锁关系；进路与轨道区段之间的联锁关系 Key points: the interlocking relation between route and switch; the interlocking relation between routes; the interlocking relation between route and signal machine; the interlocking relation between route and railway section 难点：进路与道岔之间的联锁关系；进路与轨道区段之间的联锁关系 Difficulties: the interlocking relation between route and switch; the interlocking relation between route and railway section	2

续表

序号 No.	项目（模块） Items	任务（单元） Tasks	教学内容 Teaching contents	重点、难点 Key points and difficulties	学时 Hours
2	项目 1：车站联锁知识 Item 1: knowledge of railway interlocking	1.2 车站信号平面布置图 Layout plan of railway signal	1. 信号机的设置 The setting of signal machine 2. 轨道区段的划分 The division of railway sections	重点：信号机的设置，轨道区段的划分 Key points: the setting of signal machine, the division of railway sections 难点：轨道区段的划分 Difficulties: the division of railway sections	2
3		1.3 联锁表 The interlocking table	1. 联锁表的基本概念 Basic concept of interlocking table 2. 联锁表的编制 Compilation of the interlocking table	重点：联锁表的识读和编制 Key points: understanding and compilation of the interlocking table 难点：联锁表的编制 Difficulties: drawing of the interlocking table	2
4		1.4 电气集中车站设备组成与功能、操纵使用 Compositions, functions and operations of electric central station equipment	1. 电气集中车站设备组成 Compositions of electric central station equipment 2. 电气集中车站设备功能 Functions of electric central station equipment 3. 电气集中设备的操纵使用 Operations of electric central station equipment	重点：电气集中车站设备组成，电气集中车站设备功能 Key points: compositions of electric central station equipment, functions of electric central station equipment 难点：电气集中设备的操纵使用 Difficulties: operations of electric central station equipment	2
5		1.5 电气集中定型组合类型及选用 Compositions and selection of electric centralized stereotype	1. 电气集中定型组合类型 Composition of electric centralized stereotype 2.电气集中定型组合的选用 Selection of electric centralized stereotype	重点：电气集中定型组合类型 Key points: composition of electric centralized stereotype 难点：电气集中定型组合的选用 Difficulties: selection of electric centralized stereotype	2
6	项目 2：6502 电气集中设备维护 Item 2: maintenance of electric central equipment	2.1 记录电路 Circuit recording	1. 方向继电器电路的作用、设置与操作 Functions, settings and operations of directional relay circuit 2. 按钮继电器电路的作用、设置与操作 Indication significance of button indicator and route setting indicator 3. 按钮表示灯、进路排列表示灯的显示意义 Indication significance of button indicator and route setting indicator	重点：方向继电器电路作用、设置与动作；按钮表示灯、进路排列表示灯的显示意义 Key points: functions, settings and operations of directional relay circuit and indication significance of button indicator and route setting indicator 难点：按钮继电器电路的作用、设置与操作 Difficulties: functions,settings and operations of button relay circuit	2

续表

序号 No.	项目（模块） Items	任务（单元） Tasks	教学内容 Teaching contents	重点、难点 Key points and difficulties	学时 Hours
7	项目 2：6502 电气集中设备维护 Item 2: maintenance of electric central equipment	2.2 选岔电路 Selected switchs circuit	1～6 线网络选岔电路结构各继电器的作用、设置与动作 Functions,settings and operations of various relays in 1-6 network wiring selected switchs circuit structures	重点：1～6 线网络选岔电路结构各继电器的作用、设置与动作 Key points: functions, settings and operations of various relays in 1-6 wire selected switchs circuit structures 难点：1～6 线网络选岔电路结构各继电器的作用、设置与动作 Difficulties: functions,settings and operations of various relays in 1-6 network wiring selected switchs circuit structures	6
8		2.3 辅助开始继电器电路和终端继电器电路 FKJ circuit of auxiliary starting relay and exit relay	1. 辅助开始继电器电路作用、设置与动作 Functions, settings and operations of auxiliary starting relay circuit 2. 终端继电器电路作用、设置与动作 Functions, settings and operations of exit relay circuit	重点：辅助开始继电器电路作用、设置与动作；终端继电器电路作用、设置与动作 Key points: functions, settings and operations of auxiliary starting relay circuit and exit relay circuit 难点：辅助开始继电器电路作用、设置与动作 Difficulties: functions,settings and operations of auxiliary starting relay circuit	2
9		2.4 开始继电器电路 Starting relay circuit	1. 第 7 网络线的电路结构 Circuit structure of the seven network wiring 2. KJ 作用、设置、电路动作与表示 Functions, settings, circuit operation and indication of FKJ	重点：第 7 网络线的电路结构；KJ 作用、设置、电路动作与表示 Key points: circuit structure of the seven network wiring; Functions, settings, circuit operation and indication of FKJ 难点：第 7 网络线的电路结构 Difficulties: circuit structure of the seven network wiring	2
10		2.5 信号检查继电器电路 Signal-checking relay circuit	1. 第 8 网络线的电路结构 Circuit structure of the eight network wiring 2. XJJ 作用、设置与电路动作 Functions, settings and circuit operation of XJJ	重点：第 8 网络线的电路结构；XJJ 作用、设置、电路动作与表示 Key points: circuit structure of the eight network wiring; Functions, settings and circuit operation of XJJ 难点：第 8 网络线的电路结构；XJJ 作用、设置、电路动作与表示 Difficulties: circuit structure of the eight network wiring; Functions, settings and circuit operation of XJJ	6
11		2.6 区段检查及股道检查继电器电路 Relay circuit of section and track checking	1. 第 9、10 网络线的电路结构 Circuit structure of the nine and ten network wiring 2. QJJ 作用、设置与电路动作 Functions, settings and circuit operation of QJJ 3. GJJ 作用、设置与电路动作 Functions, settings and circuit operation of GJJ	重点：第 9、10 网络线的电路结构；QJJ、GJJ 作用、设置与电路动作 Key points: circuit structure of the nine and ten network wiring; functions, settings and circuit operation of QJJ and GJJ 难点：第 9、10 网络线的电路结构 Difficulties: circuit structure of the nine and ten network wiring	2

续表

序号 No.	项目（模块） Items	任务（单元） Tasks	教学内容 Teaching contents	重点、难点 Key points and difficulties	学时 Hours
12		2.7 信号继电器电路 signal relay circuit	1. 第 11 网络线的电路结构 Circuit structure of 11 network wiring 2. LXJ、DXJ、YXJ 作用、设置与电路动作 Functions, settings and circuit operation of LXJ、DXJ、YXJ 3. 进站、出站信号控制的辅助继电器电路 Auxiliary relay circuit controlled by home and starting signal	重点：第 11 网络线的电路结构；LXJ、DXJ、YXJ 作用、设置与电路动作；进站、出站信号控制的辅助继电器电路 Key points: circuit structure of 11 network wiring；functions, settings and circuit operation of LXJ、DXJ、YXJ 难点：第 11 网络线的电路结构；LXJ、DXJ、YXJ 作用、设置与电路动作 Difficulties: circuit structure of 11 network wiring; functions, settings and circuit operation of LXJ、DXJ、YXJ	2
13	项目 2：6502 电气集中设备维护 Item 2: maintenance of electric central equipment	2.8 电气集中锁闭、解锁方式及解锁条件、时机 The ways, conditions and timing of electric centralized locking and delocking	1. 电气集中锁闭、解锁方式 Ways of electric centralized locking and delocking 2. 电气集中解锁条件、时机 Conditions and timing of electric centralized delocking	重点：电气集中解锁条件、时机 Conditions and timing of electric centralized delocking 难点：电气集中锁闭、解锁方式 Ways of electric centralized locking and delocking	2
14		2.9 解锁电路 Release circuit	1. 第 12、13 网络线的电路结构 Circuit structure of the twelve and thirteen network wiring 2. 解锁网络有关继电器的作用、设置与动作规律 Functions, settings and operation rules of delocking network related relays	重点：第 12、13 网络线的电路结构 Key points: circuit structure of the twelve and thirteen network wiring 难点：解锁网络有关继电器的作用、设置与动作规律 Difficulties: Functions, settings and operation rules of delocking network related relays	8
15	项目 3：道岔控制电路设备维护与故障处理 Item 3: the equipments maintenance and fault-handling of switch control circuit	3.1 四线制道岔控制电路原理及故障分析方法 Principles and fault analysis methods of four-wire switch control circuit	1 四线制道岔控制电路原理 Priciples of four-wire switch control circuit 2. 四线制道岔控制电路故障分析方法 Fault analysis methods of four-wire switch control circuit	重点：四线制道岔控制电路原理 Key points: principles of four-wire switch control circuit 难点：四线制道岔控制电路故障分析方法 Difficulties: fault analysis methods of four-wire switch control circuit	4
16		3.2 六线制道岔控制电路原理及故障分析方法 Principles and fault analysis methods of six-wire switch control circuit	1. 六线制道岔控制电路原理 Principles of six-wire switch control circuit 2. 六线制道岔控制电路故障分析方法 Fault analysis methods of six-wire switch control circuit	重点：六线制道岔控制电路原理 Key points: principles of six-wire switch control circuit 难点：六线制道岔控制电路故障分析方法 Difficulties: fault analysis methods of six-wire switch control circuit	4

续表

序号 No.	项目（模块） Items	任务（单元） Tasks	教学内容 Teaching contents	重点、难点 Key points and difficulties	学时 Hours
17	项目 3：道岔控制电路设备维护与故障处理 Item 3: the equipments maintenance and fault-handling of switch control circuit	3.3 五线制道岔控制电路原理及故障分析方法 Principles and fault analysis methods of five-wire switch control circuit	1. 五线制道岔控制电路原理 Principles of five-wire switch control circuit 2. 五线制道岔控制电路故障分析方法 Fault analysis methods of five-wire switch control circuit	重点：五线制道岔控制电路原理 Key points: principals of five-wire switch control circuit 难点：五线制道岔控制电路故障分析方法 Difficulties: fault analysis methods of five-wire switch control circuit	4
18		3.4 多动道岔控制电路原理及故障分析方法 Principles and fault-handling methods of multiple switchs control circuit	1. 多动道岔控制电路原理 Principles of multiple switchs control circuit 2. 多动道岔控制电路故障分析方法 Fault-handling methods of multiple switchs control circuit	重点：多动道岔控制电路原理 key points: principles of multiple switchs control circuit 难点：多动道岔控制电路故障分析方法 Difficulties: fault-handling methods of multiple switchs control circuit	4
19	项目 4：信号机点灯电路故障处理 Item 4: fault-handling of lighting circuit in signal machine	4.1 信号机点灯电路的工作原理 working principles of lighting circuit in signal controller	1. 进站信号点灯电路 Lighting circuit of home signal 2. 出站兼调车信号点灯电路 Lighting circuit of starting signal and shunting signal 3. 调车信号点灯电路 Lighting circuit of shunting signal	重点：进站信号点灯电路；出站兼调车信号点灯电路 Key points: lighting circuit of home signal, starting signal and shunting signal 难点：进站信号点灯电路；出站兼调车信号点灯电路 Difficulties: lighting circuit of home signal, starting signal and shunting signal	4
20		4.2 信号机点灯电路常见故障分析处理方法 The fault analysis and handling approaches of lighting circuit in signal machine	1. 主灯丝断丝报警电路 Alarm circuit of broken main filament 2. 信号点灯电路测试和常见故障的分析处理方法 Testing and common fault-handling ways of signal lighting circuit	重点：信号点灯电路测试和常见故障的分析处理方法 Key points: testing and common fault-handling ways of signal lighting circuit 难点：信号点灯电路测试和常见故障的分析处理方法 Difficulties: testing and common fault-handling ways of signal lighting circuit	4
21	项目 5：计算机联锁设备维护 Item 5: maintenance of computer interlocking equipment	5.1 JD1-A 型计算机联锁系统 JD1-A computer interlocking system	1. JD1-A 型计算机联锁系统的硬件组成、各单元模块的功能与表示 The hardware structures, functions and representations of each item in JD1-A computer interlocking system 2. JD1-A 型计算机联锁系统各部设备之间的连接关系与信息传输路径；接口电路的组成与控制原理 The connection between each device and information transmission route in JD1-A computer interlocking system; the compositions and working principles of interface circuit 3. JD1-A 型计算机联锁系统的设备维护常识与故障处理方法 The general knowledge of equipment maintenance and fault handling methods in JD1-A computer interlocking system	重点：JD1-A 型计算机联锁系统各部设备之间的连接关系与信息传输路径；接口电路的组成与控制原理 Key points: the connection between each device and information transmission route in JD1-A computer interlocking system; the compositions and working principles of interface circuit 难点：JD1-A 型计算机联锁系统的设备维护常识与故障处理方法 Difficulties: the general knowledge of equipment maintenance and fault handling methods in JD1-A computer interlocking system	6

续表

序号 No.	项目（模块） Items	任务（单元） Tasks	教学内容 Teaching contents	重点、难点 Key points and difficulties	学时 Hours
22	项目5：计算机联锁设备维护 Item 5: maintenance of computer interlocking equipment	5.2 TYJL-ADX计算机联锁系统 TYJL-ADX computer interlocking system	1. TYJL-ADX型计算机联锁系统的硬件组成、各部分设备的功能 The hardware structures, functions and representations of each item in TYJL-ADX computer interlocking system 2. TYJL-ADX型计算机联锁系统各部设备之间的连接关系与信息传输路径；接口电路的组成与控制原理 The connection between each device and information transmission route in TYJL-ADX computer interlocking system; the compositions and working principles of interface circuit 3. TYJL-ADX型计算机联锁系统的设备维护常识与故障处理方法 The general knowledge of equipment maintenance and fault handling methods in TYJL- ADX computer interlocking system	重点：TYJL-ADX型计算机联锁系统各部设备之间的连接关系与信息传输路径；接口电路的组成与控制原理； Key points: the connection between each device and information transmission route in TYJL-ADX computer interlocking system; the compositions and working principles of interface circuit 难点：TYJL-ADX型计算机联锁系统的设备维护常识与故障处理方法 Difficulties: the general knowledge of equipment maintenance and fault handling methods in TYJL-ADX computer interlocking system	6
23		5.3 DS6-K5B 计算机联锁系统 DS6-K5B computer interlocking system	1. DS6-K5B型计算机联锁系统的硬件组成、各部分设备的功能 The hardware structures, functions and representations of each item in DS6-K5B computer interlocking system 2. DS6-K5B型计算机联锁系统各部设备之间的连接关系与信息传输路径；接口电路的组成与控制原理 The connection between each device and information transmission route in DS6-K5B computer interlocking system; the compositions and working principles of interface circuit 3. DS6-K5B型计算机联锁系统的设备维护常识与故障处理方法 The general knowledge of equipment maintenance and fault handling methods in DS6-K5B computer interlocking system	重点：DS6-K5B型计算机联锁系统各部设备之间的连接关系与信息传输路径；接口电路的组成与控制原理 Key points: the connection between each device and information transmission route in DS6-K5B computer interlocking system; the compositions and working principles of interface circuit 难点：DS6-K5B型计算机联锁系统的设备维护常识与故障处理方法 Difficulties: the general knowledge of equipment maintenance and fault handling methods in DS6-K5B computer interlocking system	6

说明：本课程标准适用于80～88学时的“铁路车站自动控制系统维护”课程的教学，表3中的学时为建议和参考学时，实际教学内容和课时可结合课程标准，根据教学的专业和课时进行选择和调整。

Notes: this curriculum standard applies to the teaching of Maintenance of Railway Station Automatic Control System, accounting for 80—88 teaching periods. The teaching hours in table 3 are arranged for reference, the actual teaching contents and periods can be adjusted according to the major and practical teaching hours.

三、课程考核 Course Assessment

（1）课程考核分为总结性评价和过程性评价，关注学生个体差异。

Course assessment consists of summative evaluation and process evaluation，fcusing on students' individual difference.

（2）总结性评价包括标准化试题的闭卷考试。

The summative evaluation includes standardized test.

（3）过程性评价指使用铁道信号自动控制专业教学资源库开展线上、线下混合式教学，由线上成绩、线下成绩、线上作业和线上考试组成。对项目中的平时作业、基本实践技能进行考核。考核内容可以根据实践教学设备的变化进行相应的调整。

Process evaluation is composed of online and off-line performance, online assignment and online test by using the online and off-line blended teaching through teaching resources database of railway signalling automatic control major. The usual performance and awareness in different items are also evaluated. Assessment contents can be ajusted according to the practical situation.

（4）课程考核比例：过程性评价占 50%，总结性评价占 50%。

The proportion of course assessment: process evaluation accounts for 50%, while summative assessment accounts for 50%.

四、实施要求 Implementation Requirements

1. 授课教师基本要求 Basic Requirements for Teachers

（1）具备铁道信号专业或相关专业岗位工作经历，大学本科及以上学历，具有高等学校教师资格证书。

Work experiences related to railway signalling major or relevant major, bachelor degree and above, with the teacher certificate of higher education.

（2）具备相应技术职称或本专业三级及以上职业资格证书。

With relevant technical titles or professional vocational qualification certificate of level-3and above.

（3）具有“双师型”教师证书。

With the certificate of dual qualified teacher.

（4）具备开发职业课程、组织与实施教学的能力。

Ability to develop vocational course and organize and implement teaching.

（5）专业教师每两年到现场实践锻炼应不少于两个月。

No less than two months' field practice every two years.

2. 教学方法和策略 Teaching methods and strategies

（1）教学方法 Teaching methods。

主要采用项目化教学、案例教学法、情景教学法、工作过程导向教学法。坚持“够用为度”的原则选择相关知识，依据“即学即用”的原则安排教学顺序，以项目教学为形式，选择若干个具有代表性的子系统作为项目，将知识点重新整理，作为实践与技能的背景知识安排在对应的项目中，让各种知识尽可能在“做中学”。

Project method, case teaching method, situational teaching method and work process-oriented teaching method are adopted. Related knowledge is chosen based on the principle that enough is enough, while teaching sequence is arranged according to the principle that learning is understanding. Choose several typical subsystems as project to rearrange the knowledge points by using project teaching method. The practical and skillful background knowledge are arranged in the corresponding projects thus to realize learning knowledge by doing.

（2）教学策略 Teaching strategies。

教学过程中结合铁道信号自动控制专业教学资源库和现场教学，例如选择组电路开路故障查找、执行组开路故障查找、四线制道岔控制电路故障查找、五线制道岔控制电路故障查找、控制台操作办理等基本操作部分内容学习，可在网络平台或采用其他手段预先给学生操作学习，然后通过实验课讲解和实作提醒考核点。还可在实验过程中结合学生需要采用视频循环播放的方式，以此提高学生掌握技能的能力。

The blended teaching through teaching resources database of railway signaling automatic control major is adopted during teaching process. Parts of the contents in basic operation like open circuit fault examination in selecting circuit, executive circuit, four-wire and five-wire switch control circuit and control panel operation can be studied in advance through operation videos or online platforms. In-class explanation and reminding on operation are followed afterwards. Videos streaming during the experimental process is tailored to students' need thus to enhance students' ability to comprehend the skills.

在实践教学环节，采用企业实地考察，请企业专家、技术能手来给学生授课，让学生清楚企业的工作流程、岗位职责要求和企业岗位工作的其他纪律规定。

As to the practical teaching aspect, field investigation is adopted. Enterprise experts and technical experts are invited to lecture in order to make Students be clear about the workflows, requirements of job description and work disciplines and rules of posts.

第三节 "铁路区间自动控制系统维护"课程标准

Curriculum Standard for Maintenance of Railway Section Automatic Control System

一、课程性质 Nature of the Course

1. 课程类型、课程功能 Types and Functions

本课程是铁道信号自动控制专业的核心课，共计 60 课时，3.5 学分；是学生在学习了"铁路信号基础设备维护"课程，具备信号继电器检修、信号机维护、轨道电路维护、转辙机维护、防雷及接地设置维护等能力的基础上，开设的一门理论+实践课；其功能是对接铁路信号专业人才培养目标，面向信号工工作岗位，培养学生区间自动闭塞、站间闭塞、半自动闭塞控制系统的测试、检修和故障处理能力，并为后续“列车运行自动控制系统维护”“铁路信号设计与施工”“铁路信号集中监测系统维护”“毕业设计”“信号工技能鉴定实训”课程的学习奠定基础。

This course is the core course of railway signalling automatic control major, including to lessons and 3.5 credits. It's a theoretical and practical course for students who has learned the Maintenance of Basic Railway Signal Devices and are able to maintain the signal relay, signal machine, track circuit, switch machine, lightening-protection and grounding devices. In accordance with the objective of cultivating railway signalling talents, it fosters Students' ability of testing, inspecting and maintaining the control system of railway section automatic block, the interval of blocks and semi-automatic block and lays a foundation for the study of the following-up courses like Maintaincence of Train Operation Automatic Control System, Railway Signal Design and Construction, Maintenance of Railway Signal Centralized Supervision System, Graduation Project and Practical Training for Skill Appraisal of Signal Worker.

2. 课程功能定位 Orientation of the Function

表 1　课程功能定位分析

Table 1　Analysis of the Orientation of the Function

对接的工作岗位 Jobs	对接培养的职业岗位能力 Abilities
车站与区间信号设备维修信号工、电子与电气设备检修信号工、机车信号设备维修信号工 Maintenance signal worker of stations and sections signal equipment, electronic and electric equipment and locomotives signal equipment	按照中国铁路总公司最新颁布的《铁路信号维护规则》对区间信号设备进行维护的能力 To maintain section signalling devices according to *The Maintenance Rules of Railway Signalling* newly issued by China Railway Corporation

二、课程目标与内容 Objective and content

1. 课程总目标 General Objectives

能按照信号检修作业标准进行铁路区间信号设备测试、检修、故障处理及施工。包括测试、分析管内闭塞系统电气特性；熟练维修半自动闭塞系统；熟练维修自动站间闭塞系统；熟练维修自动闭塞系统；熟练处理各种闭塞系统的常见故障。培养遵纪守法、团结协作、认真负责、艰苦奋斗、精检细修、爱护公物、文明生产、安全生产等良好的职业素质。

Be able to test, inspect, maintain and operate the railway sections signal equipments according to the standardized operation of signal inspection and maintenance, which includes testing and analyzing the electrical characteristics of blocking systems, maintaining the semi-automatic block system, automatic inter-station block system and the automatic block system, and handling the common fault of various blocking systems. To cultivate the professional quality of discipline, teamwork spirit, responsibility, hardworking, precision, public property protecting and safe and civilized production.

2. 课程具体目标 Specific Objectives

表 2 课程教学目标与内容 1

Table 2 Teaching Objectives and Contents 1

<table>
<tr><th>序号
No.</th><th>毕业要求指标点
Index point of graduation requirement</th><th>知识目标
Knowledge goals</th><th>技能目标
Ability goals</th><th>素质目标
Quality goals</th><th>教学内容
Teaching contents</th></tr>
<tr><td>1</td><td>区间闭塞和闭塞系统的认知
To learn the section block and blocking system</td><td>1. 了解区间、闭塞、闭塞制度和行车闭塞制式的发展
To understand the section, blocking, blocking system and the development of driving block system
2. 了解半自动闭塞的技术特征、设备组成、基本原理和技术经济效益
To know the technical features, equipment composition, working principles and technical and economic benefits of the semi-automatic block system
3. 了解站间闭塞的基本概念、基本原理、技术特征、基本原理和技术经济效益
To know the basic concepts, principles, technical features and technical and economic benefits of inter-section blocking
4. 了解移频自动闭塞技术特征、设备组成、基本原理、技术条件和技术经济效益
To understand the technical features,equipment composition, principles, technical conditions, technical and economic benefits of the frequency-shift automatic blocking</td><td>认识自动闭塞、半自动闭塞、自动站间闭塞的结构、设备及特点
To learn the structures and equipment, features of the automatic block system, the semi-automatic block system and the automatic inter-station block</td><td>培养新知识的学习热情
To foster the passion of leaning new knowledge</td><td>1.区间闭塞和闭塞系统的基本概念
Basic concepts of inter-section blocking and blocking system
2. 半自动闭塞的技术特征、设备组成、基本原理和技术经济效益
The technical features, equipment composition, working principles and technical and economic benefits of the semi- automatic block system
3. 自动闭塞技术特征、设备组成、基本原理、技术条件和技术经济效益
The technical features, equipment composition, working principles and technical and economic benefits of the automatic block system</td></tr>
<tr><td rowspan="2">2</td><td>了解半自动闭塞系统
To know the semi-automatic block system</td><td>了解半自动闭塞的作用；理解半自动闭塞的主要技术特点和技术要求
To understand the functions, main technical features and technical requirements of the semi-automatic block system</td><td>认识半自动闭塞设备
To know the equipment of semi- automatic block system</td><td>培养学生设备认知能力
To foster students' ability of identifying equioment</td><td rowspan="2">1. 系统构成及主要技术条件
System structures and main technical conditions
2. 设备组成
Equipments compositions
3. 电路原理
Circuit principles
4. 办理方法
Operating methods
5. 与车站结合电路
Circuit connected with station
6. 微电子半自动闭塞设备构成及原理
The structures and principles of micro semi-automatic blocking system equipment
7. 半自动闭塞设备的维护内容，检修作业标准，作业工具和仪表的应用
The maintenance, standardization and application of working tools and instruments of semi-automatic blocking system equipment</td></tr>
<tr><td>掌握 64D 型半自动闭塞系统的工作原理
To understand the working principles of 64D semi-automatic blocking system</td><td>掌握 64D 型半自动闭塞的构成、设备组成、办理手续、电路工作原理以及继电半自动闭塞与车站联锁的结合电路
To know the structures, equipments compositions, handling procedures, circuit principles and the combined circuit between relay semi-automatic block and station interlocking</td><td>1. 了解 64 继电半自动闭塞设备的结构、原理
To understand the structures and principles of 64D relay semi-automatic blocking equipments
2. 掌握 64 继电半自动闭塞的办理方法
To grasp the handling procedures of 64D relay semi-automatic blocking
3. 了解 64 继电半自动闭塞设备的电路动作原理
To understand the circuit working principles of 64D relay semi-automatic blocking equipments</td><td>培养学生设备维护能力和独立解决问题的能力
To cultivate Students' ability of maintaining the equipments and handling problems independently</td></tr>
</table>

续表

序号 No.	毕业要求指标点 Index point of graduation requirement	知识目标 Knowledge goals	技能目标 Ability goals	素质目标 Quality goals	教学内容 Teaching contents
2	了解微电子半自动闭塞 To know the micro-electronic semi-automatic blocking	了解微电子半自动闭塞传输设备组成和基本原理、采集电路、驱动电路和传输设备 To understand the transmission equipment structures, basic principles, acquisition circuit,driving circuit and transmission equipments of the micro-electronic semi-automatic blocking	认识微电子半自动闭塞设备 To know the equipments of micro-electronic semi-automatic blocking	培养学习能力和独立解决问题的能力 To cultivate students' ability of learning and handling problems independently	
	了解半自动闭塞的维护方法 To know the maintenance methods of the semi-automatic blocking	了解 64D 型半自动闭塞设备的维护内容、检修作业标准，熟悉电路图，熟练运用检维修工具和仪表 To know the maintenance and inspection standardized operation of 64D semi-automatic blocking equipment; be familiar with the circuit diagram and the application of maintenance tools and instruments	1. 了解配线施工、导通实验及故障处理的方法 To know the wiring construction, guide circuit testing and fault-handling methods 2. 分析系统存在的不足，提出改进的措施和建议 Analyze the system deficiency and put forward improvement measures and suggestions	培养学生独立分析和解决问题能力；培养学生设备、维护认知的能力 To cultivate Students' ability of learning and handling problems independently, and the ability of identifying and maintaining the equipments	
3	了解计轴设备作用、结构和工作原理 To understand the functions, structures and working principle of axle-counters	了解计轴设备作用及结构。理解计轴设备主要技术条件及工作原理 To understand the functions, structures, main technical conditions and working principles of axle-counters	了解计轴设备作用及结构 To understand the functions and structures of axle-counters	培养学生独立分析和解决问题能力；培养学生设备、维护认知的能力 To cultivate students' ability of learning and handling problems independently, and the ability of identifying and maintaining the equipments	1. 系统构成及主要技术条件 System structures and main technical conditions 2. 设备组成 Composition of equipments 3. 电路原理 cIrcuit principles 4. 办理方法 Operating methods 5. 与车站结合电路 Circuit connected with stations 6. 计轴自动闭塞的设备的维护内容，检修作业标准，作业工具和仪表的应用 The maintenance, standardized inspection and application of working tools and instruments of axle-counting auto-block
	掌握计轴自动站间闭塞主要技术条件、系统构成、电路和工作原理 To grasp the main technical conditions, system compositions, circuit and working principles of axle-counting station auto-block	掌握计轴自动站间闭塞系统构成、电路和工作原理，理解主要技术条件 To understand the structures, circuit, working principles and main technical conditions of axle-counting station auto-block system	掌握电路的动作程序，操作办理的方法 To grasp the operating procedures and operation approaches of circuit	培养学生独立分析和解决问题能力；培养学生设备、维护认知的能力 To cultivate Students' ability of learning and handling problems independently, and the ability of identifying and maintaining the equipments	

续表

序号 No.	毕业要求指标点 Index point of graduation requirement	知识目标 Knowledge goals	技能目标 Ability goals	素质目标 Quality goals	教学内容 Teaching contents
3	掌握计轴自动站间闭塞的维护方法 To know the maintenance methods of axle-counting station auto-block	掌握计轴自动站间闭塞设备的维护内容及质量标准，熟悉电路图，能查找电路断路故障，熟练运用维修作业工具和仪表，进行简单检修作业 To grasp the maintenance contents and quality standard of axle-counting station auto-block equipments; be familiar with the circuit diagram and be able to find out the open circuit fault; to skillfully apply the working tools and instruments of inspection and maintenance to carry out the simple inspection	1. 掌握配线施工、导通实验及故障处理的方法 To know the wiring construction, guide circuit testing and fault-handling methods 2. 分析系统存在的不足，提出改进的措施和建议 Analyze the system deficiency and put forward improvement measures and suggestions	培养学生独立分析和解决问题能力；培养学生设备、维护认知的能力 To cultivate students' ability of learning and handling problems independently, and the ability of identifying and maintaining the equipments	
4	了解ZPW-2000系列自动闭塞的技术条件和特点 To understand the technical conditions and features of ZPW-2000 series automatic blocking 掌握ZPW-2000A自动闭塞的构成及工作原理 To grasp the structures and working principles of ZPW-2000A series automatic blocking 了解ZPW-2000R自动闭塞的构成及工作原理 To grasp the structures and working principles of ZPW-2000R series automatic blocking 掌握ZPW-2000系列构成的双向四显示自动闭塞的电路工作原理 To understand the working principle of bi-directional four-aspects automatic blocking circuit constituted by the ZPW-2000 series 看懂自动闭塞的电路图	了解ZPW-2000系列自动闭塞的技术条件和特点 To understand the technical conditions and features of ZPW-2000 series automatic blocking	了解ZPW-2000系列自动闭塞的技术条件 To understand the technical conditions of ZPW-2000 series automatic blocking	培养学生独立分析问题能力 To cultivate students' ability of handling problems independently	1. ZPW-2000系列自动闭塞的特点 Features of ZPW-2000 series automatic blocking 2. ZPW-2000系列自动闭塞的技术条件 The technical conditions of ZPW-2000 series automatic blocking
		掌握ZPW-2000系列自动闭塞的结构原理；理解ZPW-2000系统各部分设备的功能；掌握ZPW-2000轨道电路的应用 To understand the structure principles and functions of different equipments of ZPW-2000 series automatic blocking system; To grasp the application of ZPW-2000 track circuit	分析和处理ZPW-2000轨道电路的故障 Be able to analyze and handle the fault of ZPW-2000 track circuit	培养学生设备维护能力和独立解决问题的能力 To cultivate students' ability of maintaining equipments and handling problems independently	1. 系统组成 2. 系统结构 3. 轨道电路的应用原理 1. System compositions 2. System structures 3. Application principles of track circuit
		理解ZPW-2000系列构成的双向四显示自动闭塞系统、掌握移频发送原理、接收原理、四显示信号点灯电路原理，掌握三接近闭塞分区电路原理，掌握二接近闭塞分区电路原理，掌握一接近闭塞分区电路原理，掌握一般闭塞分区电路原理与车站结合电路原理	分析和处理闭塞分区电路故障 Be able to analyze and handle the circuit fault of blocking sections	培养学生设备维护能力 To cultivate students' ability of maintaining equipments	1. 四显示双线双向自动闭塞各工程设计 Construction design of bi-directional four-aspects automatic blocking 2. 三接近闭塞分区电路 three-close blocking section circuit 3. 二接近闭塞分区电路 Two-close blocking section circuit

续表

序号 No.	毕业要求指标点 Index point of graduation requirement	知识目标 Knowledge goals	技能目标 Ability goals	素质目标 Quality goals	教学内容 Teaching contents
4	To know the circuit diagram of automatic blocking 了解自动闭塞的维护 To know the maintenance of automatic blocking	To learn the bi-directional four-aspects automatic blocking system constructed by ZPW-2000 series; To understand the principles of frequency-shifting sending and receiving, four-aspects signal lighting circuit principles; To know the circuit principles of three-close blocking section; To understand the general blocking section circuit principles andprinciples of integrated circuit between stations 看懂闭塞分区电路图 To understand the circuit diagram of blocking section 了解自动闭塞维护内容、标准 To know the maintenance contents and standard of auto-blocking			4. 一接近闭塞分区电路 One-close blocking section circuit 5. 一般闭塞分区电路 General block section circuit 6. 与车站结合电路 Circuit Integrated with stations 7. 报警电路原理 The principle of alarm circuit 8. 站间联系电路原理 The circuit principles of between stations
5	了解自动闭塞改变运行方向电路的作用和运用 To understand the functions and applications of auto-blocking circuit in changing the driving direction	了解改变运行方向概念、作用、电路结构和设备 To know the concept, functions, circuit structures and equipment of changing driving direction	掌握改变运行方向的应用 To know the application of changing driving direction	培养学生独立分析问题能力 To cultivate students' ability of handling problems independantly	1. 改变运行方向概念 The concept of changing driving direction 2. 改变运行方向作用 The function of changing driving direction 3. 改变运行方向的操作设备 The operating equipment of changing driving direction
	掌握改变运行方向的办理 To understand the operation of changing driving direction	理解改变运行方向操作含义；掌握操作办理方法 To know the operation meanings and approaches of changing driving direction	掌握改变运行方向的办理 To learn The operation of changing driving direction	培养学生计算能力、设备的认知能力 To cultivate the ability of calculation and equipments identification	1. 改变运行方向操作步骤手续 Operating procedures of changing driving direction 2. 正常办理步骤和操作 Normal operating steps and operation 3. 辅助办理步骤和操作 Auxiliary operating steps and operation
	掌握改变运行方向的动作原理 To understand the operating principle of changing driving direction	掌握改变运行方向的动作程序、电路图的含义 To understand the operating procedures and circuit meaning of changing driving direction	分析四线制改变运行方向的动作程序 To understand the operating procedure of four-wire changing driving direction	培养学生设备维护能力和独立解决问题的能力 To cultivate students' ability of maintaining equipments and handling problems independantly	1. 正常办理电路动作顺序 Operating procedures of normal operating circuit 2. 辅助办理电路动作顺序 Operating procedures of auxiliary operating circuit 3. 局部电路工作原理 The working principle of local circuit 4. 方向继电器电路原理 The circuit of directional relay

续表

序号 No.	毕业要求指标点 Index point of graduation requirement	知识目标 Knowledge goals	技能目标 Ability goals	素质目标 Quality goals	教学内容 Teaching contents
5	了解改变运行方向电路的维护 To know the circuit maintenance of changing driving direction	了解改变运行方向电路图、动作程序、故障处理程序和方法 To understand the circuit diagram, operating procedures, fault-handling procedures and meanthods of changing driving direction			看懂改变运行方向电路图 To understand the circuit diagram of changing driving direction
6	了解高速铁路自动闭塞的特点及原理 To understand the characteristics and principle of high-speed rail auto-blocking	了解高速铁路自动闭塞的特点及原理 To understand the characteristics and principle of high-speed rail auto-blocking	了解高速铁路自动闭塞的特点及原理 To understand the characteristics and principle of high-speed rail auto- blocking	培养学生独立分析问题能力 To cultivate students' ability of handling problems independantly	1. 高速铁路自动闭塞的特点 The characteristics of high-speed rail auto-blocking 2. 高速铁路自动闭塞的原理 The principle of high-speed rail auto-blocking
	掌握客运专线ZPW-2000A轨道电路的特点、结构和工作原理 To understand the characteristics, structures and working principles of ZPW-2000A track circuit in passenger dedicated line	掌握客运专线ZPW-2000A轨道电路的特点、结构和工作原理 To understand the characteristics, structures and working principles of ZPW-2000A track circuit in passenger dedicated line	能正确画出客运专线ZPW-2000A轨道电路的结构框图，描述其特点，叙述各部分设备的作用 Be able to accurately draw the structure diagram of ZPW-2000A track circuit in passenger dedicated line and describe its characteristics and functions of each equipment	接受新知识、举一反三的能力 Be able to learn new knowledge and drawing inferences about other cases from one instance	1. 临时限速服务器系统 Temporary speed-limited service system 2. 列控中心 Train control center; 3. 地面电子单元(LEU) Land electronic unit 4. 应答器 Transponder
	掌握高速铁路自动闭塞电路原理 To understand the principles of high-speed rail auto-blocking circuit	掌握200～250km/h高速铁路自动闭塞电路原理；掌握300～350km/h高速铁路自动闭塞电路原理 To comprehend the principle of 200～250km/h and 300～2350km/h high-speed rail auto-blocking circuit 掌握高速轨道电路与列控中心的通信 To grasp the communication between high-speed track circuit and train operation control center	分析高速铁路自动闭塞电路 Be able to analyze the high-speed rail auto-blocking circuit	培养学生设备维护能力 To cultivate students' ability of maintaining equipments	1. 200～250km/h高速铁路自动闭塞电路原理 The principle of 200～250km/h high-speed rail auto-blocking circuit 2. 300～350km/h高速铁路自动闭塞电路原理 The principle of 300～2350km/h high-speed rail auto-blocking circuit
	了解高速铁路自动闭塞系统维护 To know the maintenance of high-speed rail auto-blocking system	了解高速铁路自动闭塞系统维护 To know the maintenance of high-speed rail auto-blocking system	高速铁路自动闭塞系统维护方法 The maintenance methods of high-speed rail auto-blocking system	培养学生设备维护能力 To cultivate students' ability of maintaining equipments	高速铁路自动闭塞系统设备 Equipments of high-speed rail auto-blocking system

表 3 课程教学安排 2

Table 3 Teaching objectives and contents 2

序号 NO.	项目（模块） Items	任务（单元） Tasks	教学内容 Teaching contents	重点、难点 Key points and difficulties	学时 Hours
1	项目 1：闭塞和闭塞系统的认知 Item 1：the recognition of blocking and blocking system	1.1 闭塞和闭塞系统的认知 The recognition of blocking and blocking system	1. 区间闭塞和闭塞系统的基本概括、闭塞系统分类 2. 半自动闭塞、自动站间闭塞、自动闭塞的系统构成、技术特征和发展概括及适用范围 1. The general introduction and classifications of sections blocking and blocking systems 2. The system compositions, technical features, development and application of semi-auto-blocking, auto section blocking and auto-blocking	重点：闭塞系统的构成和应用范围 Key points: the structure and application range of blocking system 难点：三种闭塞系统的区别 Difficulties: differences of the three blocking systems	2
2		1.2 半自动闭塞认知 The recognition of semi-auto-blocking			
3		1.3 自动站间闭塞认知 The recognition of inter-station auto-blocking			
4		1.4 自动闭塞认知 The recognition of auto-blocking			
5	项目 2：半自动闭塞维护 Item 2：maintenance of semi-automatic blocking	2.1 半自动闭塞系统认知 The recognition of semi-automatic blocking system	1. 半自动闭塞系统的作用 Functions of semi-automatic blocking system 2. 主要技术特点 Main technical features 3. 技术要求 Technical requirements	重点：半自动闭塞系统的作用及特点 Key points: functions and features of semi-automatic blocking system 难点：技术要求 Difficulties: technical requirements	2
6		2.2 64D 型继电半自动闭塞系统认知 The recognition of 64D relay semi-automatic blocking system	1. 64D 型继电半自动闭塞系统的构成原理 Constitution principles of 64D relay semi-automatic blocking system; 2. 设备组成 Equipment composition 3. 操作办理手续 Operating procedures 4. 电路动作程序及电路原理 Circuit operation procedure and circuit principles 5. 与车站联锁的结合电路 Combined circuit with inter-station locking	重点：64D 型继电半自动闭塞系统的构成原理、设备组成、办理手续、工作原理、电路原理 Key points: Constitution principles, operating procedures and circuit principles of 64D relay semi-automatic blocking system 难点：电路原理 Difficulties: circuit principles	12
7		2.3 微电子半自动闭塞 Microelectronic semi-automatic blocking	1. 微电子半自动闭塞传输设备 Transmission equipment of microelectronic semi-automatic blocking 2. 采集电路 Acquisition circuit 3. 驱动电路 Driving circuit 4. 传输设备切换结合电路原理 Circuit principle of integrating transmission switches' equipment	重点：微电子半自动闭塞传输设备、采集电路、驱动电路、传输设备切换结合电路原理 Key points: transmission equipment, acquisition circuit, driving circuit and circuit principle of switching transmission equipment of microelectronic semi-automatic blocking 难点：传输设备切换结合电路原理 Difficulties: circuit principle of switching transmission equipment	2

序号 NO.	项目（模块） Items	任务（单元） Tasks	教学内容 Teaching contents	重点、难点 Key points and difficulties	学时 Hours
8	项目 3：自动站间闭塞维护 Item 3: maintenance of automatic section blocking	3.1 计轴设备认知 The recognition of axle-counting equipments	1. 计轴设备的作用 The functions of axle-counting equipments 2. 主要部件的结构和工作原理 Structures and working principles of the main components	重点：计轴设备的主要部件结构和工作原理 Key points: structures and working principles of the main components in axle-counting equipments 难点：计轴设备的工作原理 Difficulties: working principles of axle-counting equipments	2
9		3.2 计轴设备的工作原理 The working principles of axle-counting equipment	1. 计轴自动站间闭塞技术条件 The technical conditions of axle-counting station auto-block 2.系统构成 The system structure 3. 计轴自动站间闭塞电路及原理 The circuit and principle of axle-counting station auto-block 4. 计轴自动站间闭塞办理手续 The handling procedures of axle-counting station auto-block	重点：计轴自动站间闭塞电路及原理、办理手续 Key points: the circuit and principle and handling procedures of axle-counting station auto-block 难点：电路及原理 Difficulties: circuit and principles	4
10	项目 4：ZPW-2000 系列自动闭塞维护 Item 4: ZPW-2000 automatic block	4.1 ZPW-2000 系列自动闭塞认知 The recognition of ZPW-2000 automatic block	1. ZPW-2000 系列自动闭塞的技术条件和特点 The technical conditions and features of ZPW-2000 automatic block	重点：电码化的作用、范围 Key points: the function and range of coding 难点：站内轨道电路电码化设计原则 Difficulties: the design principle of station track circuit coding	2
11		4.2 ZPW-2000A 型自动闭塞认知 The recognition of ZPW-2000A automatic block	1. ZPW-2000A 型自动闭塞的构成 The structures of ZPW-2000A automatic block 2. 谐振无绝缘轨道电路工作原理 The working principles of resonant jointless track circuit 3. 室外设备和室内设备各部件的作用结构和工作原理 The structures, functions and working principles of various components of outdoor and indoor equipments 4. ZPW-2000A 型自动闭塞的传输安全性和传输长度 The transmission safety and length of ZPW-2000A automatic block	重点：ZPW-2000A 型自动闭塞的构成；室外设备和室内设备各部件的作用结构和工作原理 Key points: the structures of ZPW-2000A automatic block; the structures, functions and working principles of various components of outdoor and indoor equipments 难点：ZPW-2000A 型自动闭塞的传输安全性和传输长度 Difficulties: the transmission safety and length of ZPW-2000A automatic block	4

续表

序号 NO.	项目（模块） Items	任务（单元） Tasks	教学内容 Teaching contents	重点、难点 Key points and difficulties	学时 Hours
12	项目 4：ZPW-2000 系列自动闭塞维护 Item 4: ZPW-2000 automatic block	4.3 ZPW-2000R 型自动闭塞认知 The recognition of ZPW-2000R automatic block	ZPW-2000R 型自动闭塞的构成 The structures of ZPW-2000R automatic block 2. 谐振无绝缘轨道电路工作原理 The working principles of resonant jointless track circuit 3. 室外设备和室内设备各部件的作用结构和工作原理 The structures, functions and working principles of various components of outdoor and indoor equipments 4. ZPW-2000R 型自动闭塞的传输安全性和故障—安全措施 The transmission safety and fault-safe measures of ZPW-2000R automatic block	重点：ZPW-2000R 型自动闭塞的构成；室外设备和室内设备各部件的作用结构和工作原理 Key points: the structures of ZPW-2000R automatic block; the structures, functions and working principles of various components of outdoor and indoor equipments 难点：ZPW-2000R 型自动闭塞的传输安全性和传输长度 Difficulties: the transmission safety and fault-safe measures of ZPW-2000R automatic block	2
13		4.4 ZPW-2000 系列自动闭塞电路认知 The recognition of ZPW-2000 automatic block circuit	1. ZPW-2000 系列构成的双线双向的四显示自动闭塞工程设计 The engineering design of double track bidirectional four-aspect automatic block constructed by ZPW-2000 2. 闭塞分区电路 Circuit of block section 3. 站间联系电路 Circuit between stations 4. 区间设备报警电路 Alarm circuit of interval equipments 5. 与车站联锁的结合电路 Integrated circuit between stations interlocking	重点：ZPW-2000 系列构成的双线双向的四显示自动闭塞电路 Key points: circuit of double track bidirectional four-aspect automatic block constructed by ZPW-2000 难点：与车站联锁的结合电路 Difficulties: integrated circuit between stations interlocking	6
14		4.5 自动闭塞设备维护 Equipment maintenance of automatic block	1. ZPW-2000 系列自动闭塞的维护内容 Maintenance contents of ZPW-2000 automatic block 2. ZPW-2000 系列自动闭塞的故障处理方法 Fault-handling methods of ZPW-2000 automatic block	重点：ZPW-2000 系列自动闭塞的维护内容 Key points: maintenance contents of ZPW-2000 automatic block 难点：ZPW-2000 系列自动闭塞的故障处理方法 Difficulties: fault-handling methods of ZPW-2000 automatic block	2
15	项目 5：改变运行方向电路维护 Item 5: circuit maintenance of changing operating direction	5.1 自动闭塞改变运行方向电路认知 The circuit recognition of automatic block changing operating direction	1. 自动闭塞改变运行方向电路的作用和应用 The function and application of circuit in automatic block changing operating direction 2. 改变运行方向电路的办理方法 The operation of changing driving direction	重点：改变运行方向电路的办理方法 Key points: the operation of changing driving direction 难点：改变运行方向电路的应用 Difficulties: The application of circuit in changing operating direction	2

续表

序号 NO.	项目（模块） Items	任务（单元） Tasks	教学内容 Teaching contents	重点、难点 Key points and difficulties	学时 Hours
16	项目 5：改变运行方向电路维护 Item 5：circuit maintenance of changing operating direction	5.2 自动闭塞改变运行方向电路原理认知 The circuit principle recognition of automatic block changing operating direction	1. 改变运行方向电路组成 The circuit structure of changing operating direction 2. 改变运行方向电路原理 The circuit principle recognition of changing operating direction 3. 改变运行方向电路动作程序 The circuit operating procedures of changing operating direction	重点：改变运行方向电路组成；改变运行方向电路原理；改变运行方向电路动作程序 Key points: the circuit structure, principles and operating procedures of changing operating direction 难点：改变运行方向电路原理 Difficulties: the circuit principle of changing operating direction	8
17		5.3 改变运行方向电路维护 The circuit maintenance of automatic block changing operating direction	1. 改变运行方向电路维护内容 The circuit maintenance contents of changing operating direction 2. 改变运行方向电路常见故障处理方法 The common fault-handling ways of circuit in changing operating direction	重点：改变运行方向电路维护内容； Key points: the circuit maintenance contents of changing operating direction 难点：改变运行方向电路常见故障处理方法 Difficulties: the common fault-handling ways of circuit in changing operating direction	2
18	项目 6：高速铁路自动闭塞系统 Item 6：high-speed rail automatic blocking system	6.1 高速铁路自动闭塞系统认知 The recognition of high-speed rail automatic blocking system	1. 主要技术原则 The main technical principles 2. 主要工作模式 The main working mode 3. 闭塞分区的划分 Division of block sections 4. 列车安全防护距离 Train-protection distance 5. CTCS-3 级列控系统与 CTCS-2 级列控系统的异同 The similarities and differences between the train control systems CTCS-3 and CTCS-2	重点：CTCS-3 级列控系统结构 Key points: structure of CTCS-3 train control system 难点：CTCS-3 级列控系统地面与车载设备 Difficulties: ground and on-board equipments of CTCS-3 train control system	2
19		6.2 客运专线 ZPW-2000A 型轨道电路认知 The recognition of track circuit in ZPW-2000A passenger dedicated line	客运专线 ZPW-2000A 型轨道电路的特点、结构和工作原理 Features, structures and working principles of track circuit in ZPW-2000A passenger dedicated line	重点：客运专线 ZPW-2000A 型轨道电路的特点、结构和工作原理 Key points: features, structures and working principles of track circuit in ZPW-2000A passenger dedicated line 难点：客运专线 ZPW-2000A 型轨道电路的工作原理 Difficulties：working principles of track circuit in ZPW-2000A passenger dedicated line	2

续表

序号 NO.	项目（模块） Items	任务（单元） Tasks	教学内容 Teaching contents	重点、难点 Key points and difficulties	学时 Hours
20	项目 6：高速铁路自动闭塞系统 Item 6：high-speed rail automatic blocking system	6.3 高速铁路自动闭塞电路认知 The recognition of high-speed rail automatic blocking circuit	1. 200-250km/h 高速铁路自动闭塞电路原理 The principle of 200-250km/h high-speed rail automatic blocking circuit 2. 300-350km/h 高速铁路自动闭塞电路原理 The principle of 200-250km/h high-speed rail automatic blocking circuit 3. 列控中心与轨道电路的通信 The communication between train control center and track circuit	重点：200～250km/h 高速铁路自动闭塞电路原理 Key points: the principle of 200-250km/h high-speed rail automatic blocking circuit 难点：列控中心与轨道电路的通信 Difficulties: the communication between train control center and track circuit	2
21		6.4 高速铁路自动闭塞系统维护 The maintenance of high-speed rail automatic blocking system	1. 高速铁路自动闭塞的维修事项 The maintenance of high- speed rail automatic block 2. 高速铁路自动闭塞的常见故障处理方法 The common fault-handling methods of high-speed rail automatic block	重点：高速铁路自动闭塞的维修事项 Key points: the maintenance of high-speed rail automatic block 难点：高速铁路自动闭塞的常见故障处理方法 Difficulties: the common fault-handling methods of high-speed rail automatic block	4

说明：本课程标准适用于 60～68 学时的“铁路区间自动控制系统维护”课程的教学，表 3 中的学时为建议和参考学时，实际教学内容和课时可结合课程标准，根据教学的专业和课时进行选择和调整。

Notes: this curriculum standard applies to the teaching of Maintenance of Railway Section Automatic Control System, accounting for 60—68 teaching periods. The teaching hours in table 3 are arranged for reference, the actual teaching contents and periods can be adjusted according to the major and practical teaching hours.

三、课程考核 Course assessment

（1）课程考核分为总结性评价和过程性评价，关注学生个体差异。

Course assessment consists of summative evaluation and process evaluation，focusing on students' individual difference.

（2）总结性评价包括标准化试题的闭卷考试。

The summative evaluation includes standardized test.

（3）过程性评价指使用铁道信号自动控制专业教学资源库开展线上、线下混合式教学，由线上成绩、线下成绩、线上作业和线上考试组成。对项目中的平时作业、基本实践技能进行考核。考核内容可以根据实践教学设备的变化进行相应的调整。

Process evaluation is composed of online and off-line performance, online assignment and online test by using the online and off-line blended teaching through teaching resources database of railway signalling automatic control major. The usual performance and awareness in different items are also evaluated. Assessment contents can be adjusted according to the practical situation.

（4）课程考核比例：过程性评价占 40%，总结性评价占 60%。

The proportion of course assessment: process evaluation 40%, while summative assessment accounts for 60%.

四、实施要求 Implementation Requirements

1. 授课教师基本要求 Basic Requirements for Teachers

（1）具备铁道信号专业或相关专业岗位工作经历，大学本科及以上学历，具有高等学校教师资格证书.

Work experiences related to railway signalling major or relevant major, bachelor degree and above, with the teacher certificate in an institution of higher education.

（2）具备相应技术职称或本专业三级及以上职业资格证书。

With relevant technical titles or professional vocational qualification certificate of level-3 and above.

（3）具有“双师型”教师证书。

With the certificate of dual qualified teacher.

（4）具备开发职业课程、组织与实施教学的能力。

Ability to develop vocational course and organize and implement teaching.

（5）专业教师每两年到现场实践锻炼应不少于两个月。

No less than two months' field practice every two years.

2. 教学方法和策略 Teaching Methods and Strategies

（1）教学方法 Teaching methods。

主要采用项目化教学法、情景教学法和工作过程导向教学法。根据现场 ZPW-2000A 设备检修和故障处理的任务作为代表性的项目，理论知识的教学紧密围绕技能训练开展，应用大量的视频和图片，通过对比、举例、通俗的比喻等方法使学生更好地理解和掌握相关知识，运用多媒体教学手段化解教学难点。

Project method, situational teaching method and work process-oriented teaching method are adopted. With the equipment inspection and maintenance and fault-handling assignments of ZPW-2000A as the representative project, teaching of theoretical knowledge revolves around skill training. Through the methods of comparison, illustrations and common metaphor, plenty of videos and pictures are applied to make Students better understand and master related knowledge. Multimedia teaching approaches are adopted to resolve difficulties in teaching.

（2）教学策略 Teaching strategies。

教学过程中采用铁道信号自动控制专业教学资源库实现混合式教学，如 CD96 移频在线测试仪、ZPW-2000A 室内设备和室外设备参数测试、改变运行方向电路操作办理、故障处理程序和处理方法、客运专线 ZPW-2000A 设备检修等操作内容，可在专业教学资源库预先给学生操作视频或微课来学习，然后通过实验课讲解和实作提醒考核点。还可在实验过程中结合学生需要采用视频循环播放的方式，以此提高学生掌握技能的能力。

The blended teaching through teaching resources database of railway signaling automatic control major is adopted during teaching process. Some of the operating contents like CD96 frequency-shift on-line tester, parameter testing of ZPW-2000A indoor and outdoor equipments, operation of changing driving direction circuit, fault-handling procedures and methods, ZPW-2000A equipments inspection and maintenance of passenger dedicated line can be studied in advance through operation videos or micro-lectures. In-class explanation and reminding on operation are followed afterwards in experimental lesson.Videos streaming during the experimental process tailors to Students' need thus to enhance Students' ability to comprehend the skills.

在实践教学环节，采用企业实地考察，请企业专家、技术能手来给学生授课，让学生清楚企业的工作流程、岗位职责要求和企业岗位工作的其他纪律规定。

As to the practical teaching aspect, field investigation is adopted. Enterprise experts and technical experts are invited to lecture in order to make students be clear about the workflows, requirements of job description and work disciplines and rules of posts.

第四节 “列车运行自动控制系统维护”课程标准

Curriculum Standard for Maintenance of Train Operation Automatic Control System

一、课程性质 Nature of the Course

1. 课程类型、课程功能 Types and Functions

本课程是铁道信号自动控制专业的核心课，共计 60 课时，3.5 学分；是学生在学习了“铁路信号基础设备维护”“铁路车站自动控制系统维护”“铁路区间自动控制系统维护”课程，具备自动闭塞、移频轨道电路等知识的基础上，开设的一门理论+实践课。其功能是对接铁道信号自动控制专业人才培养目标，面向车站与区间信号设备维修信号工、电子与电气设备检修信号工、机车信号设备维修信号工等工作岗位，培养学生按照信号检修作业标准进行列车运行控制系统相关设备的日常维护、设备检修和故障分析处理的能力，并为后续“铁路信号设计与施工”“铁路信号集中监测系统维护”课程的学习奠定基础。

This course is the core course of railway signalling automatic control major, including 60 lssons and 3.5 credits. It's a theoretical and practical course for students who has learned the Maintenance of Railway Signal Devices, Maintenance of Railway Station Automatic Control System and Maintenance of Railway Sections Automatic Control System and has mastered the auto-block and frequency-shift track circuit. In accordance with the objective of cultivating railway signalling automatic control talents, it fosters Students' ability of daily maintenance of train operation control system, the inspecting and maintaining ability and fault-handling ability, which lays a foundation for the study of the following-up courses like Railway Signalling Design and Construction and Maintenance of Railway Signal Centralized Supervision System.

2. 课程功能定位 Orientation of the Function

表 1 课程功能定位分析

Table 1 Analysis of the Orientation of the Function

对接的工作岗位 Jobs	对接培养的职业岗位能力 Abilities
车站与区间信号设备维修信号工、电子与电气设备检修信号工、机车信号设备维修信号工 Maintenance signalman of stations and sections signal equipments, electronic and electric equipments and locomotives signal equipments	按照中国铁路总公司最新颁布的《铁路信号维护规则》对列车运行自动控制系统进行维护的能力 To maintain the train operation automatic control system according to *The Maintenance Rules of Railway Signalling* newly issued by China Railway Corporation

二、课程目标与内容 Objective and Content

1. 课程总目标 General Objectives

学生通过本课程的学习，能够熟悉机车信号车载设备的功能与原理，熟悉 LKJ2000 监控装置的原理，掌握站内轨道电路电码化技术，掌握 CTCS-2、CTCS-3 级列控系统的结构与功能，熟悉 RBC 技术原理，以及完成相应职业岗位工作任务所需的方法和社会能力。

Students are able to understand the functions and principles of locomotive signal on-board equipments, the principles of LKJ2000 supervision device, the coding technique of instation track circuit, the structures and functions of CTCS-2，CTCS-3 train control system, the technical principles of RBC and master the methods of completing the task of corresponding positions after learning this course.

2. 课程具体目标 Specific Objectives

表 2 课程教学目标与内容 1

Table 2 Teaching Objectives and Content 1

序号 NO.	毕业要求指标点 Index point of graduation requirement	知识目标 Knowledge goals	技能目标 Ability goals	素质目标 Quality goals	教学内容 Teaching contents
1	了解列车运行系统概述 Understand the introduction of train operation system	了解列车运行控制系统的概念；了解机车信号、列车运行监控记录装置、列车超速防护、中国列车运行控制系统（CTCS）和站内轨道电码化等的发展历程；理解 CTCS 的应用、系统结构 To understand the concept of train operation control system; To learn the development of locomotive signal, train operation supervision and recording device, automatic train protection, Chinese train control system (CTCS) and instation track coding; To know the application and structures of CTCS	能认识列车运行控制系统的结构、设备 To know the structure and devices of train operation control system	培养学习新知识的热情 To foster the passion of learning new knowledge	1. 列车运行控制系统的发展 The development of train operation control system 2. CTCS 应用等级的特点 Features of CTCS's application degree
	理解 ATP 的概念、功能、工作原理 To understand the concept, function and principle of automatic train protection（ATP）	了解列车超速防护（ATP）的概念；理解 ATP 的功能；掌握列车制动控制模式的工作原理；理解列车运行测速、测距和列车定位的方法及其原理；了解紧急制动和常用制动的区别；理解人控优先和机控优先的区别 To understand the concept and function of automatic train protection（ATP）; To grasp the working principle of train braking control mode; To know the measurement of range and speed in train operation, the approaches and principles of train positioning; To understand the differences between emergency brake and common brake, the differences between manual control and mechanical control	能分析列车制动控制模式的工作原理，能应用测速测距和列车定位方法分析列控系统 Be able to analyze the working principle of train braking control mode and the train control system by using the way of measuring speed and range and train positioning	培养系统分析能力 To cultivate the ability of systematic analysis	1. ATP 基本概念 Basic concept of ATP 2. ATP 功能及分类 Functions and classifications of ATP 3. 列车制动控制模式 Train braking control mode

续表

序号 NO.	毕业要求指标点 Index point of graduation requirement	知识目标 Knowledge goals	技能目标 Ability goals	素质目标 Quality goals	教学内容 Teaching contents
2	掌握 JT1-CZ2000 型机车信号设备 To understand the JT1-CZ2000 locomotive signal device	理解 JT1-CZ2000 型机车信号系统构成；了解 JT1-CZ2000 型机车信号系统的主要技术条件 To understand the structures and main technical conditions of JT1-CZ2000 locomotive signal system	能分析 JT1-CZ2000 型机车信号系统 Be able to analyze the JT1-CZ2000 locomotive signal system	培养学生设备认知能力 The ability to identify the equipments	1. 系统构成及主要技术条件 System structure and main technical conditions 2. 机车信号主机 Locomotive signal host 3. 双路接收线圈 Dual-path receiving coil 4. 机车信号机 Locomotive signal controller 5. 系统连接 System connection
	掌握机车信号低频信息定义、分配及使用 To understand the definition, distribution and application of locomotive signal low-frequency information	掌握机车信号主机的结构、功能、基本原理和接口连接；掌握双路接收线圈的结构、基本工作原理和连接；理解机车信号机的结构和连接；理解系统连接方式和连接接口 To understand the structures, functions, basic principles and interface connection of locomotive signal host; To know the structure, basic principles and connection of dual-path receiving coil; To understand the connecting ways and interface	能分析和处理机车信号主机的板卡、双路接收线圈、机车信号机、机车信号接口故障 Be able to analyze and handle the PCB of locomotive signal host, dual-path receiving coil, locomotive signal controller and the connection fault signal controller	培养学生设备维护能力和独立解决问题的能力 To cultivate students' ability of maintaining equipments and handling problems independantly	
		掌握机车信号自动闭塞区段、特殊区段、CTCS-2 和 CTCS-3 区段信息定义、低频信息分配 To understand the information definition and low-frequency information distribution of locomotive signal automatic blocking section, special section, CTCS-2 and CTCS-3 section 掌握机车信号自动闭塞区段、特殊区段、CTCS-2 和 CTCS-3 区段机车信号信息使用 To understand the information application of locomotive signal automatic blocking section, special section, CTCS-2 and CTCS-3 section	能分析机车信号的低频信息分配、机车信号信息使用 Be able to analyze the low-frequency information distribution and the information application of locomotive signal	培养学生独立分析和解决问题能力；培养学生设备、维护认知的能力 To cultivate students' ability of maintaining equipments and handling problems independantly	1. 机车信号信息定义 Definition of locomotive signal information 2. 低频信息分配 The low-frequency information distribution 3. 机车信号信息使用 The information application of locomotive signal
3	了解 LKJ2000 型监控装置 To know the LKJ2000 supervision device	了解 LKJ2000 型监控装置的特点、功能；理解监控装置速度监控的依据、基本原理、速度控制模式等 To learn the characteristics and functions of LKJ2000 supervision devices; To understand the speed supervision's basis, principles and speed supervision mode of supervision device	能分析监控装置速度监控的工作原理、速度控制曲线 Be able to analyze speed supervision's working principle and speed control curve of supervision devices	培养学生独立分析问题能力 To foster students' ability of analyzing problems independently	1. LKJ2000 型监控装置的特点 The characteristics of LKJ2000 supervisor device 2. LKJ2000 型监控装置的功能 The functions of LKJ2000 swpervisor device 3. 监控装置速度控制模式 Speed supervision mode of supervision device

续表

序号 NO.	毕业要求指标点 Index point of graduation requirement	知识目标 Knowledge goals	技能目标 Ability goals	素质目标 Quality goals	教学内容 Teaching contents
3	掌握LKJ2000型监控装置系统的组成及工作原理 To understand the system composition and working principles of LKJ-2000 supervision device	掌握LKJ2000型列车运行监控记录装置的组成及各部分的功能；理解系统通信结构；理解信号输入/输出电路；掌握监控主机箱的结构和功能；了解监控显示器、事故状态记录器的结构和功能 To know the compositions and functions of various parts in LKJ2000 train operation supervision device; To understand the system communication structure and the signal input/output circuit; To grasp the structure and functions of central supervision; To know the structure and function of the supervision display and accident data recorder	能分析和处理LKJ2000型列车运行监控记录装置的设备故障 Be able to analyze and handle the equipment fault of LKJ2000 train operation supervision device	培养学生设备维护能力和独立解决问题的能力 To cultivate students' ability of maintaining equipments and handling problems independantly	1. 系统组成 System composition 2. 系统通信结构 Structure of communication system 3. 信号输入/输出电路 Signal input/output circuit 4. 监控主机箱 Central supervision 5. 监控显示器 Supervision display 6. 事故状态记录器 Accident data recorder
	理解列车运行监控装置的相关设备 To know the related equipment of train operation supervision device	理解列车运行监控装置的转储器、机车安全信息综合监测装置、铁路车号自动识别系统（ATIS）车载设备、列车运行状态信息系统、双指针速度表、数模转换盒的结构和功能 To know the transferring unit of train operation supervision device, integrated supervision device of locomotive safety information, on-board equipment of ATIS, LAIS (train running information system), dual pointer speedometer and digital-analog conversion box	能分析和处理列车运行监控装置的相关设备故障 Be able to analyze and handle the related equipment faults of train operation supervision device	培养学生设备维护能力 To cultivate students' ability of maintaining equipments	1. 转储器 The transferring unit 2. 机车安全信息综合监测装置 Integrated supervision device of locomotive safety information 3. 铁路车号自动识别系统车载设备 On-board equipment of ATIS 4. 列车运行状态信息系统 LAIS (train running information system) 5. 双针速度表 Dual pointer speedometer 6. 数模转换盒 Dual pointer speedometer and data switch box
4	理解站内轨道电路电码化概述 To understand the general introduction to the instation track circuit coding	掌握站内轨道电路电码化的概念和范围；了解站内轨道电路电码化发送信息；理解站内轨道电路电码化方式，二线制电码化电路和四线制电码化电路的区别 To know the concept and range of instation track circuit coding; To understand the information-sending and receiving of instation circuit code, the coding way and the differences between two-wire and four-wire code circuit	能分析站内轨道电路电码化范围和方式 Be able to analyze the coding range and way of instation track circuit	培养学生独立分析问题能力 To cultivate students' ability of analyzing problems independantly	1. 站内轨道电路电码化 The instation track circuit coding 2. 站内轨道电路电码化范围 Range of the instation track circuit coding 3. 站内轨道电路电码化发送的信息 The information-sending and receiving of the instation track circuit coding 4. 站内轨道电路电码化方式 Ways of the instation track circuit coding 5. 二线制电码化电路和四线制电码化电路 Two-wire and four-wire code circuit

续表

序号 NO.	毕业要求指标点 Index point of graduation requirement	知识目标 Knowledge goals	技能目标 Ability goals	素质目标 Quality goals	教学内容 Teaching contents
4	理解电码化器材 To understand coding equipments	理解电码化机柜的结构和功能；理解电码化发码设备、隔离设备、防雷匹配设备的结构和功能；掌握补偿电容的计算 To know the structure and function of coding cab, the code-sending device, isolation device and lightning- protection matching device; To grasp the calculation of compensating capacitance	能分析电码化器材的结构和补偿电容的计算 Be able to analyze the structure of coding equipments and the calculation of compensating capacitance	培养学生计算能力、设备的认知能力 To foster students' ability of calculating and equipments recognition	1. 电码化机柜 Coding cab 2. 电码化发码设备 The code-sending device 3. 隔离设备 Isolation device 4. 防雷匹配设备 Lightning-protection matching device 5. 补偿电容 Compensating capacitance
	掌握叠加方式轨道电路电码化 To understand the overlay track circuit coding	了解叠加方式轨道电路电码化设计原则和 ZPW-2000 系列叠加电码化类型；掌握站内电码化载频频率的排列；了解叠加方式站内轨道电路电码化组合及其运用；掌握正线预叠加电码化电路；掌握到发线股道电码化电路；掌握机车信号载频的锁频和载频自动切换电路和原理；理解 25.7Hz 转频码的发送原理 To know the design principle of the overlay track circuit coding, types of ZPW-2000 overlay coding, arrangement of carrier frequency, combination and application of overlay instation track circuit coding, main line pre-overlay coding circuit and the departure line circuit coding; To understand the frequency locking, auto-switching circuit and principle of locomotive signal carrier frequency; To understand the sending principles of 25.7Hz transferring frequency coding	能看懂和分析二线制叠加方式站内轨道电路电码化电路 Be able to understand and analyze the two-wire overlay instation track circuit coding	培养学生设备维护能力和独立解决问题的能力 To cultivate students' ability of identifying and maintaining equipments and handling problems independantly	1. 叠加方式轨道电路电码化设计原则 The design principle of the overlay track circuit coding 2. 叠加方式站内轨道电路电码化简述 Introduction to the overlay track circuit coding between stations 3. 二线制叠加方式站内轨道电路电码化电路 The two-wire overlay instation track circuit coding 4. 四线制叠加方式站内轨道电路电码化电路 The four-wire overlay instation track circuit coding 5. 机车信号载频自动切换 Locomotive signal carrier frequency auto-switching
5	理解 CTCS-2 级列控系统总体结构 To understand the general structure of CTCS-2 train operation control system	理解 CTCS-2 级列控系统的地面设备、车载设备；掌握 CTCS-2 级列控系统基本工作原理 To know the ground equipments and on-board equipments and the fundamental working principles of CTCS-2 train operation control system	能分析 CTCS-2 级列控系统结构和工作原理 Be able to analyze the structure and working principles of CTCS-2 train operation control system	培养学生独立分析问题的能力 To cultivate Students' ability of analyzing problems independantly	1. 系统总体结构 General structure of system 2. 列控地面设备 Train operation control ground equipments 3. 列控车载设备 Train operation controlon-board equipments system 4. CUCS-2 级列控系统基本工作原理 The fundamental working principles of CTCS-2 train operation control system

续表

序号 NO.	毕业要求指标点 Index point of graduation requirement	知识目标 Knowledge goals	技能目标 Ability goals	素质目标 Quality goals	教学内容 Teaching contents
5	掌握 CTCS-2 级列控系统地面设备 To grasp the ground equipments of CTCS-2 train operation control system	理解临时限速服务器系统的功能和结构；了解列控中心的由来；掌握列控中心的功能；掌握列控中心各单元结构及功能；掌握列控中心各单元板卡面板显示及接口；理解列控中心与外部系统的通信；掌握列控中心的基本原理；理解地面电子单元（LEU）的设置、功能、结构、工作原理、接口连接和室外系统；掌握应答器的设备、功能、工作原理、编号和名称；了解应答器的分类、结构、应答器组和设置 To comprehend the function and structure of TSRS (Temporary Speed Restrict System), the origin, functions, structures and functions of various units of train control center; To grasp the PCB display and interface of various units in train control system; To understand the basic principle of train control center; To comprehend the setting, function, structure, working principle, interface connection and outdoor system of LEU; To understand the equipments, functions, working principles, numbering and names of transponder; To know the classifications, structures of transponder and transponder units and settings	能分析和处理临时限速服务器系统设备、列控中心各单元板卡和应答器的故障；能分析列控中心、应答器的结构和工作原理；能分析 LEU、应答器的接口 Be able to analyze and handle the fault of TSRS, the PCB and transponder of train control center; Be able to analyze the structures and working principles of train control center and transponder, the LEU and the interface of transponder	认识新知识的能力、举一反三的能力 Ability to learn new knowledge and draw inferences about other cases from one instance	1. 临时限速服务器系统 TSRS (temporary speed restrict system) 2. 列控中心 Train control center 3. 地面电子单元 LEU 4. 应答器 Train control center
	掌握 CTCS-2 级列控系统车载设备 To understand on-board equipments of CTCS-2 train operation control system	理解列控车载设备的功能；了解列车车载设备的特点；掌握车载设备系统构成；掌握车载列控系统工作模式；理解车载信号人机界面 To comprehend the functions and features of on-board equipments of train operation control system; To grasp the system structures and working mode of on-board equipments; To understand the man-computer interface of on-board signal	能分析和处理列控车载设备的故障 Be able to analyze and deal with the faults of on-board equipments of train control system	培养学生设备维护能力 To foster students' ability to maintain equipments	1. 列控车载设备的功能 Functions of on-board equipments of train control system 2. 列控车载设备的特点 Features of on-board equipments of train control system 3. 列车车载设备系统构成 Structures of on-board equipments of train control system 4. CTCS2-200H 型车载列控系统工作模式 Working mode of on-board train control system 5. 车载信号 On-board signal

续表

序号 NO.	毕业要求指标点 Index point of graduation requirement	知识目标 Knowledge goals	技能目标 Ability goals	素质目标 Quality goals	教学内容 Teaching contents
6	了解 CTCS-3 级列控系统运营需求 To know the operating requirement of CTCS-3 train operation control system	了解主要技术原则；理解主要工作模式；了解闭塞分区划分、列车安全防护距离；掌握 CTCS-3 级列控系统和 CTCS-2 级列控系统的异同 To comprehend the main technical principles and working modes; To understand the divisions of section blocking and the train safety protection distance; To know the differences and similarities between CTCS-3 and CTCS-2 train operation control system	能分析 CTCS-3 级列控系统与 CTCS-2 级列控系统的异同 Be able to analyze the differences and similiarities between CTCS-3 and CTCS-2 train operation control system	培养学生独立分析问题 To cultivate students' ability of analyzing problems independantly	1. 主要技术原则 Main technical rules 2.主要工作模式 Main working modes 3. 闭塞分区的划分 Division of sections 4. 列车安全防护距离 Protection distance of train safety 5. CTCS-3 级列控系统与 CTCS-2 级列控系统的异同 The differences and similarities between CTCS-3 and CTCS-2 train operation control system
	掌握 CTCS-3 级列控系统总体结构 To understand the general structure of CTCS-3 train operation control system	掌握 CTCS-3 级列控系统结构 To comprehend the general structure of CTCS-3 train operation control system	能分析 CTCS-3 级列控系统结构 Be able to analyze the general structure of CTCS-3 train operation control system	认识新知识的能力、举一反三的能力 Ability to learn new knowledge and draw inferences about other cases from one instance	1. 系统总体结构 General structure of the system 2. 系统地面设备结构 Ground equipment structure of the system
	掌握 CTCS-3 级列控地面设备 To grasp the ground equipments of CTCS-3 train operation control system	了解无线闭塞中心 RBC 的配置原则；掌握 RBC 的功能；了解 RBC 的主要技术指标；掌握 RBC 的设备配置；理解 RBC 系统外部接口和客专配置 To learn the setting principles, functions, main technical points and the equipments allocation of RBC (radio blocking center); To understand the external interface and the setting of passenger line in RBC system	能分析 RBC 的设备配置和故障 Be able to analyze the equipment setting and faults of RBC	培养学生设备维护能力和独立解决问题的能力 To cultivate Students' ability of maintaining equipments and handling problems independently	1. 无线闭塞中心 RBC Radio blocking center 2. GSM-R 通信网络 GSM-R communication network 3. RBC 系统外部接口 External Interfaceof RBC system 4. 临时限速服务器、列控中心、信号系统安全数据网、LEU 和应答器 TSRS (temporary speed restrict system), train control center, safety data network of signal system, LEU and transponder

表 3　课程教学安排 2

Table 3　Teaching Objectives and Contents 2

序号 NO.	项目（模块）Items	任务（单元）Tasks	教学内容 Teaching contents	重点、难点 Key points and difficulties	学时 Hours
1	项目 1:列车运行控制系统概述 Item 1: general introduction to the train control system	1.1 列车运行系统概述 General introduction to the train operation system	1. 列车运行控制系统的发展 The development of train operation control system 2. CTCS 应用等级的特点 Characteristics of CTCS application degree	重点:CTCS 应用等级的划分及特点 Key points: division and characteristics of CTCS application degree 难点：站内轨道电路电码化介绍 Difficulties: introduction to the instation track circuit coding	2

续表

序号 NO.	项目（模块） Items	任务（单元） Tasks	教学内容 Teaching contents	重点、难点 Key points and difficulties	学时 Hours
2	项目1：列车运行控制系统概述 Item 1: general introduction to the train control system	1.2 ATP 概述 General introduction of ATP	1. ATP 基本概念 Basic concept of ATP 2. ATP 功能及分类 Functions and classifications of ATP 3. 列车制动控制模式 Train braking control mode	重点：ATP 的功能及分类 Key points: functions and classifications of ATP 难点：列车制动控制模式 Difficulties: train braking control mode	2
3		2.1JT1-CZ2000 型机车信号组成和原理 The composition and principles of JT1-CZ2000 locomotive signal	1. 系统构成及主要技术条件 Structure composition and main technical conditions 2. 机车信号主机 Locomotive signal host 3. 双路接收线圈 Dual-path receiving coil 4. 机车信号机 Locomotive signal controller 5. 系统连接 System connection	重点：机车信号系统设备结构、JT1-CZ 2000 机车信号工作原理； Key points: the equipment structure of locomotive signal system and the working principle of JT1-CZ2000 locomotive signal 难点：机车信号系统设备结构、JT1-CZ 2000 机车信号工作原理 Difficulties: the equipment structure of locomotive signal system and the working principle of JT1-CZ2000 locomotive signal	4
4	项目2：机车信号车载设备 Item 2: locomotive signal on-board equipments	2.2 机车信号低频信息定义、分配及应用 The low-frequency information definition, distribution and application of locomotive signalling	1. 机车信号信息定义 The definition of locomotive signalling 2. 低频信息分配 Distribution of low frequency information 3. 机车信号信息使用 The application of locomotive signalling	重点：机车信号信息的使用 Key points: the application of locomotive signalling 难点：机车信号信息的使用 Difficulties: the application of locomotive signalling	2
5		2.3 机车信号点灯控制实验 The lighting control experiment of locomotive signalling	1. 机车信号设备认知 The recognition of locomotive signalling equipments 2. 国产移频信号载频与低频使用情况 The use of carrier frequency and low frequency in domestic frequency shift signalling 3. 机车信号点灯控制 Locomotive signalling lighting control 4. 低频信息的测试与应用 Testing and application of low frequency information	重点：机车信号点灯控制，低频信息的测试与应用； Key points: locomotive signalling lighting control, testing and application of low frequency information 难点：低频信息的测试与应用 Difficulties: testing and application of low frequency information	2
6	项目3：列车运行监控记录装置 Item 3: train running supervision and record device	3.1 LKJ2000 型监控装置概述 Introduction of LKJ2000 supervision equipments	1. LKJ2000 型监控装置的特点； Features of LKJ2000 supervision equipments 2. LKJ2000 型监控装置的功能； Functions of LKJ2000 supervision equipments 3. 监控装置速度控制模式 Speed control mode of supervision and record equipments	重点：LKJ2000 监控记录装置的特点、功能 Key points: features and functions of LKJ2000 supervision equipments 难点：监控记录装置速度控制模式 Difficulties: speed control mode of supervision and record equipments	2

序号 NO.	项目（模块） Items	任务（单元） Tasks	教学内容 Teaching contents	重点、难点 Key points and difficulties	学时 Hours
7	项目 3：列车运行监控记录装置 Item 3: train running supervision and record device	3.2 LKJ2000 型监控装置系统组成及工作原理 System structure and working principles of supervision and record equipments	1. 系统组成 System structure 2. 系统通信结构 Structure of system communication 3. 信号输入/输出电路 Signal input/output circuit 4. 监控主机箱 Central supervision 5. 监控显示器 Supervision display 6. 事故状态记录器 Accident data recorder	重点：LKJ2000 监控记录装置系统组成 Key points: system structure of supervision and record equipments 难点：LKJ2000 监控记录装置工作原理 Difficulties: working principles of supervision and record equipments	2
8		3.3 列车运行监控装置的相关设备 The related equipment of train operation supervision device	1. 转储器 The transferring unit 2. 机车安全信息综合监测装置 Integrated supervision device of locomotive safety information 3. 铁路车号自动识别系统车载设备 On-board equipments of automatic train identification system 4. 列车运行状态信息系统 LAIS (Train Running Status Information System) 5. 双针速度表 Dual pointer speed indicator 6. 数模转换盒 Data switch box	重点：TAX2 系统组成及功能 Key points: structure and function of TAX2 system 难点：TAX2 的工作原理 Difficulties: working principle of TAX2 system	2
9		3.4 LKJ2000 监控记录装置的操作实验 The operating experiment of LKJ2000 supervision equipments	1. 了解监控记录装置操作步骤 To know operating procedures of supervision equipments 2. 掌握监控记录装置操作方法 To grasp the operation approaches of supervision equipments	重点：监控记录装置操作步骤 Key points: operating procedures of supervision equipments 难点：监控记录装置操作方法 Difficulties: operation approaches of supervision equipments	2
10	项目 4：站内轨道电路电码化 Item 4: instation track circuit coding	4.1 站内轨道电路电码化概述 Introduction to the instation track circuit coding	1. 站内轨道电路电码化 Instation track circuit coding 2. 站内轨道电路电码化范围 Range of instation track circuit coding 3. 站内轨道电路电码化发送的信息 Sending and receiving information of instation track circuit coding 4. 站内轨道电路电码化方式 Ways of instation track circuit coding 5. 二线制电码化电路和四线制电码化电路 Two-wire and four-wire coding circuit	重点：电码化的作用、范围 Key points: functions and range of coding 难点：站内轨道电路电码化设计原则 Difficulties: the design principles of instation track circuit coding	2

续表

序号 NO.	项目（模块）Items	任务（单元）Tasks	教学内容 Teaching contents	重点、难点 Key points and difficulties	学时 Hours
11	项目 4：站内轨道电路电码化 Item 4: instation track circuit coding	4.2 电码化器材 Coding equipments	1. 电码化机柜 Coding cab 2. 电码化发码设备 The code-sending device 3. 隔离设备 Isolation device 4. 防雷匹配设备 Lightning-protection matching device 5. 补偿电容 The calculation of compensating capacitance	重点：电码化发码设备 Key point: the code-sending device 难点：补偿电容距离的计算 difficulties: the calculation of compensating capacitance	2
12		4.3 叠加方式轨道电路电码化 The overlay track circuit coding	1. 叠加方式轨道电路电码化设计原则 The design principle of the overlay track circuit coding 2. 叠加方式站内轨道电路电码化简述 Introduction to the overlay instation track circuit coding 3. 二线制叠加方式站内轨道电路电码化电路 Two-wire overlay instation track circuit coding 4. 四线制叠加方式站内轨道电路电码化电路 Four-wire overlay instation track circuit coding 5. 机车信号载频自动切换 Automatic switch of locomotive signalling carrier frequency	重点：二线制叠加方式站内轨道电路电码化电路 Key point: two-wire overlay instation track coding circuit 难点：机车信号载频自动切换 difficulties: automatic switch of locomotive signalling carrier frequency	10
13		4.4 站内电码化参数测试和故障处理实验 Parameter test and fault-handling experiment of instation coding	1. 电码化系统设备构成 The equipment structure of coding system 2. 电码化电路 Code circuit 3. 电码化参数测量 Parameter test of instation coding 4. 简单故障处理 Simple fault handling	重点：电码化参数测量 Key point: parameter test of instation coding 难点：简单故障处理 Difficulties: simple fault handling	2
14	项目 5：CTCS-2 级列控系统 Item 5: CTCS-3 train control system	5.1 CTCS-2 级列控系统总体结构 General structure of CTCS-2 train control system	1. 系统总体结构 General structure of the system 2. 列控地面设备 Train control grounding device 3. 列控车载设备 Train control on-board equipments 4. CTCS-2 级列控系统基本工作原理 Fundamental working principles of CTCS-2 train control system	重点：CTCS-2 级列控系统结构 Key point: structure of CTCS-2 train control system 难点：CTCS-2 级列控系统原理 Difficulties: principle of CTCS-2 train control system	2

续表

序号 NO.	项目（模块） Items	任务（单元） Tasks	教学内容 Teaching contents	重点、难点 Key points and difficulties	学时 Hours
15	项目 5：CTCS-2 级列控系统 Item 5: CTCS-3 train control system	5.2 CUCS-2 级列控系统地面设备 Ground equipments of CTCS-2 train control system	1. 临时限速服务器系统 TSRS (Temporary Speed Restrict System) 2. 列控中心 Train control center 3. 地面电子单元 LEU 4. 应答器 Transponder 5. 列控中心设备的功能与通信接口 Functions and communication interface of train control center equipments	重点：CTCS-2 级列控中心结构及作用、CTCS-2 级列控中心设备与其他系统间的通信接口、LEU、应答器机构及作用 Key points: structure and function of CTCS-2 train control system, equipments of CTCS-2 train control system and the communication interface with other systems, LEU, structure and function of transponder 难点：列控中心基本原理，列控中心的功能、LEU 原理；列控中心区间占用逻辑检查功能 Difficulties: the basic principles and functions of train control center, principle of LEU; Logical checking function of train control center section	10
16		5.2 CTCS-2 级列控系统地面设备认知实验 The recognition experiment of CTCS-2 train control system ground equipment	掌握地面设备的组成及应用 To understand the composition and application of grounding device	重点、难点：列控中心地面设备认知 Key points and difficulties: the recognition of train control system ground equipment	2
17		5.3 CTCS-2 级列控设备 CTCS-2 train control equipments	1. 列控车载设备的功能 The functions of train control on-board equipments 2. 列控车载设备的特点 Characteristics of train control on-board equipments 3. 列车车载设备系统构成 System structure of train control on-board equipments 4. CTCS2-200H 型车载列控系统工作模式 Working mode of CTCS2-200H train control system 5. 车载信号 Cab signal	重点：CTCS-2 级列控车载设备组成 Key point: composition of CTCS-2 train control on-board equipments 难点：CTCS-2 级车载原理 Difficulties: principles of CTCS-2 train control on-board equipments	4
18		5.3 CTCS-2 级列控车载设备认知实验 The recognition experiment of CTCS-2 train control system on-board equipment	掌握车载设备结构组成及应用 To understand structure and application of on-board equipments	重点、难点：CTCS-2 级列控车载设备组成 Key points and difficulties: Composition of CTCS-2 train control system on-board equipment	2

序号 NO.	项目（模块） Items	任务（单元） Tasks	教学内容 Teaching contents	重点、难点 Key points and difficulties	学时 Hours
19	项目 6：CTCS-3 级列控系统 Item 6: CTCS-3 train control system	6.1 CTCS-3 级列控系统运营需求 The operating requirements of CTCS-3 train control system	1. 主要技术原则 Main technical principles 2. 主要工作模式 Main working mode 3. 闭塞分区的划分 Division of sections 4. 列车安全防护距离 Train safety protection distance 5. CTCS-3 级列控系统与 CTCS-2 级列控系统的异同 Similarities and differences between CTCS-3 and CTCS-2 train control system	重点：CTCS-3 级列控系统结构 Key point: structures of CTCS-3 train control system 难点：CTCS-3 级列控系统地面与车载设备 Difficulties: ground and on-board equipments of CTCS-3 train control system	2
20		6.2 CTCS-3 级列控系统总体结构 The general structure of CTCS-3 train control system	1. 系统总体结构 General structure of the system 2. 系统地面设备结构 Structure of system grounding devices	重点：系统总体结构 Key point: general structure of the system 难点：系统地面设备结构 Difficulties: structure of system grounding devices	2
21		6.3 CTCS-3 级列控系统地面设备 The ground equipments of CTCS-3 train control system	1. 无线闭塞中心 RBC (Radio Blocking Center) 2. GSM-R 通信网络 GSM-R communication network	重点：无线闭塞中心设备结构及功能 Key points: equipment structure and functions of RBC 难点：无线闭塞中心设备原理 Difficulties: principles of RBC	2
22		6.4 RBC 外部接口与客专配置 The external interface and the setting of passenger line in RBC system	1. RBC 系统外部接口 External interface of RBC system 2. 临时限速服务器、列控中心、信号系统安全数据网、LEU 和应答器 Temporary speed-limited service system, train control center, signalling system safety data network, LEU (Land Electronic Unit) and transponder	重点：无线闭塞中心在客专上的配置 Key point: the setting of passenger line in RBC system 难点：无线闭塞中心在客专上的配置 Difficulties: the setting of passenger line in RBC system	2

说明：本课程标准适用于 60～68 学时的“列车运行自动控制系统维护”课程的教学，表 3 中的学时为建议和参考学时，实际教学内容和课时可结合课程标准，根据教学的专业和课时进行选择和调整。

Notes: this curriculum standard applies to the teaching of the Maintenance of Train Operation Automatic Control System, accounting for 60—68 teaching periods. The teaching hours in table 3 are arranged for reference, the actual teaching contents and periods can be adjusted according to the major and practical teaching hours.

三、课程考核 Course Assessment

（1）课程考核分为总结性评价和过程性评价，关注学生个体差异。

Course assessment consists of summative evaluation and process evaluation, focusing on students' individual difference.

（2）总结性评价包括标准化试题的闭卷考试。

The summative evaluation includes standardized test.

（3）过程性评价指使用铁道信号自动控制专业教学资源库开展线上、线下混合式教学，由线上成绩、线下成绩、线上作业和线上考试组成。对项目中的平时作业、基本实践技能进行考核。考核内容可以根据实践教学设备的变化进行相应的调整。

Process evaluation is composed of online and off-line performance, online assignment and online test by using the online and off-line blended teaching through teaching resources database of railway signalling automatic control major. The usual performance and awareness in different items are also evaluated. Assessment contents can be ajusted according to the practical situation.

（4）课程考核比例：过程性评价占 50%，总结性评价占 50%。

The proportion of course assessment: process evaluation 50%, while summative assessment accounts for 50%.

四、实施要求 Implementation Requirements

1. 授课教师基本要求 Basic Requirements for Teachers

（1）具备铁道信号专业或相关专业岗位工作经历，大学本科及以上学历，具有高等学校教师资格证书。

Work experiences related to railway signalling major or relevant major, bachelor degree and above, with the teacher certificate of higher education.

（2）具备相应技术职称或本专业三级及以上职业资格证书。

With relevant technical titles or professional vocational qualification certificate of level-3and above.

（3）具有“双师型”教师证书。

With the certificate of dual qualified teacher.

（4）具备开发职业课程、组织与实施教学的能力。

Ability to develop vocational course and organize and implement teaching.

（5）专业教师每两年到现场实践锻炼应不少于两个月。

No less than two months' field practice every two years.

2. 教学方法和策略 Teaching Methods and Strategies

（1）教学方法 Teaching methods。

主要采用项目化教学法、情景教学法和工作过程导向教学法。铁路运营企业列车运行控制系统设备检修和故障处理的任务作为代表性的项目，理论知识的教学紧密围绕技能训练开展，应用大量的视频和图片，通过对比、举例、通俗的比喻等方法使学生更好地理解和掌握相关知识，运用多媒体教学手段化解教学难点。

Project method, situational teaching method and work process-oriented teaching method are adopted. With the equipments inspection and maintenance and fault-handling assignments of train operating control system in railway transportation as the representative project, teaching of theoretical knowledge revolves around the skill training. Through the methods of comparison, illustrations and common metaphor, plenty of videos and pictures are applied to make students better understand and master related knowledge. Multi-media teaching approaches are adopted to resolve difficulties in teaching.

（2）教学策略 Teaching strategies。

教学过程中采用铁道信号自动控制专业教学资源库实现混合式教学，如机车信号点灯、低频信息的测试与应用、站内电码化参数测试和故障处理、CTCS-2 级列控系统设备检修等操作内容，可在专业教学资源库预先给学生操作视频或微课来学习，然后课堂上通过讲解和实操提醒注意事项。理论知识点也可以通过专业教学资源库的课程组课、在线答疑、网络考试、作业布置和修改等功能实现混合式教学。

The blended teaching through teaching resources database of railway signaling automatic control major is adopted during teaching process. Parts of the operating contents like locomotive signal lighting, testing and application of low-frequency information, parameter testing and fault-handling of instation coding, inspection and maintenance of CTCS-2 train control system equipments can be studied in advance through operation videos or micro-lectures. In-class explanation and reminding operation are followed afterwards. Theoretical knowledge explanation can be achieved through the functions of re-mixing the courses, FAQ, online testing, assigning and correcting homework in the resources database.

在实践教学环节，可采用企业实地考察，请企业专家、技术能手来给学生授课，让学生清楚企业的工作流程、岗位职责要求和企业岗位工作的其他纪律规定。

As to the practical teaching aspect, field investigation is adopted. Enterprise experts and technical experts are invited to lecture in order to make Students be clear about the workflows, requirements of job description and work disciplines and rules of posts.

第五节 “铁路信号设计与施工”课程标准

Curriculum Standard for Railway Signal Design and Construction

一、课程的性质 Nature of the Course

1. 课程类型、课程功能 Types and Functions

“铁路信号设计与施工”是铁道信号自动控制专业的核心课，共计 60 课时，3.5 学分；是学生在学习了“铁路信号基础设备维护”“铁路车站自动控制系统维护”“铁路区间自动控制系统维护”课程，具备一定的铁路信号系统知识的基础上，开设的一门理论+实践课。其功能是对接铁道信号自动控制专业人才培养目标，面向铁路信号工、信号工程施工、铁路信号设计研究员岗位，培养学生按照铁路信号施工设计标准进行相关设备的安装、调试的能力，为其将来胜任铁路信号工工作岗位打下坚实的基础。

Railway Signal Design and Construction is the core course of railway signalling automatic control major, including 60 lessons and 3.5 credits in total. It’s a theoretical and practical course for students who have learnt the Maintenance of Railway Signal Devices, Maintenance of Railway Station Automatic Control system and Maintenance of Railway Sections Automatic Control System and has gained a basic understanding of the railway signalling system. In accordance with the objective of cultivating railway signalling automatic control talents, students who have learnt this course will be quatified for positions like railway signal worker, signal engineer and researcher of railway signal design. It fosters students’ ability of installing and adjusting related equipments according to the railway signalling construction standard, thus laying a foundation for the job of railway signalling worker.

2. 课程功能定位 Orientation of the Function

表 1　课程功能定位分析

Table 1　Analysis of the Orientation of the Function

对接的工作岗位 Jobs	对接培养的职业岗位能力 Abilities
铁路信号工、信号工程施工、铁路信号设计研究员岗位 Railway signal worker, signal engineer and researcher of railway signal design	能按照铁路信号工程施工技术及工艺标准对相关信号设备进行施工、安装的能力 Be able to construct and install related signalling equipments according to the railway signalling construction technology and standards

二、课程目标与内容 Objective and Content

1. 课程总目标 General Objectives

综合运用铁路信号的专业知识，解决铁路信号设备、产品等在工程设计、施工安装等方面的实际问题。培养学生掌握铁路信号工程设计的基本规范、规程，掌握铁路信号工程设备施工安装的基本工艺、基本流程等。

To solve the practical problems of engineering design, construction and installation in railway signalling equipments and products by applying the railway signalling professional knowledge. Enable the students to grasp the basic norms and rules of railway signalling engineering design and the basic technology and procedures of railway signalling construction and installation.

2. 课程具体目标 Specific Objectives

对铁路信号设备工程设计与施工全过程有一个比较系统的了解；能看懂实际站例的信号设备工程图纸；能进行信号设备施工的一般图纸设计；能进行坐标和电缆长度、芯线数计算；能处理施工中遇到一般故障和问题。

To systematically comprehend the engineering design and construction process in railway signalling equipments and understand the engineering drawings of railway signalling in practice; Be able to design the general drawings of railway signalling equipment construction; To calculate the coordinate, the cable length and the number of core wire; To handle the general fault and problem during the construction.

表 2　课程教学目标与内容 1

Table 2　Teaching objectives and contents 1

序号 NO.	毕业要求指标点 Index point of graduation requirement	知识目标 Knowledge goals	技能目标 Ability goals	素质目标 Quality goals	教学内容 Teaching contents
1	了解勘测调查的依据、内容和要求 To know the basis, contents and requirements of survey	掌握初步设计的任务及工作内容 To understand the task and main contents of preliminary design	依据任务书，能进行现场勘测，掌握现场设计所需资料的收集方法 Be able to carry out the field survey and collect the relevant data for field design according to the assignment	培养业务学习热情、积累现场维护知识 To foster the learning passion and accumulate the field maintenance knowledge	勘测调查 Field survey

续表

序号 NO.	毕业要求指标点 Index point of graduation requirement	知识目标 Knowledge goals	技能目标 Ability goals	素质目标 Quality goals	教学内容 Teaching contents
2	掌握车站信号平面布置图的设计内容 To understand the design contents of layout of station signal	掌握车站信号设备平面布置图设计的原则、步骤和方法 To grasp the principles, steps and ways of designing the layout of station signal	了解集中区的划分原则，信号机、轨道电路、道岔等信号设备位置的确定，理解信号机的布置方法、轨道区段的划分原则和方法 To know the division principles of concentrated area, the position confirmation of signal equipments of signal controller, track circuit and switchs; To understand the setting ways of signal controller, the division principles and ways of track sections	能根据车站信号设备平面布置图，准确确定各种信号设备设计的准确位置 Be able to confirm the accurate position of various signal equipments according to the layout of station signal	车站信号设备平面布置图设计 The design of layout of station signal
3	掌握电缆径路图的设计内容 To understand the design contents of cable pathway	掌握轨道区段设置、电缆芯数的计算、电缆箱盒选用 To know the settings of track sections, the calculation of cable cores and the choose of cable box	掌握坐标计算方法、电缆径路选择，电缆长度及芯线的确定方法 To grasp the calculating methods of coordinates, the selection of cable pathway, the length of cable and the confirmation of core wire	能独自完成车站电缆径路图设计 Be able to complete the design of cable pathway independently	车站电缆径路图设计 The design of station cable pathway
4	掌握车站信号平面图、双轨图及电缆径路图设计的内容 To learn the design contents of station signal layout, double-track diagram and the content of cable pathway desigr	掌握车站信号平面图、双轨图及电缆径路图的设计方法 To learn the design methods of station signal layout, double-track diagram and cable pathway	掌握车站信号平面图、双轨图及电缆径路图设计的内容及标准 To learn the contents and standards of station signal layout, double-track diagram and cable pathway design	能根据电缆径路图，完成电缆的敷设和设备的安装及导通 Be able to complete the cable laying, the installation and conduction of the equipments according to the cable pathway	平面图、双轨图及电缆径路图认知 The recognition of layout, double-track diagram and cable pathway
5	掌握室内设备布置图、组合排列表设计的内容 To understand the design contents of indoor equipment layout and combined arrangement list	掌握室内设备布置图、组合排列表设计的方法 To understand the design methods of indoor equipment layout and combined arrangement list	掌握室内设备布置的方法及组合的选用 To comprehend the setting ways of indoor equioments and selection of combination	根据设计图，完成室内设备的安装 Be able to finish the installation of indoor equipments according to the design	室内信号设备布置图及组合排列表 The indoor equipment layout and combined arrangement list
6	掌握接口电路图设计的内容 To understand the design contents of interface diagram	掌握信号机、道岔及轨道电路接口电路的设计方法 To learn the design method of interface circuit in signal controller, switchs and track circuit	掌握接口电路图设计的内容及方法 To learn the design contents and methods of interface diagram	能看懂接口电路图的内容及一般的故障处理方法 Be able to understand the contents of interface diagram and common fault-handling methods	接口电路图的设计 The design of interface diagram

续表

序号 NO.	毕业要求指标点 Index point of graduation requirement	知识目标 Knowledge goals	技能目标 Ability goals	素质目标 Quality goals	教学内容 Teaching contents
7	掌握信号机点灯电路图的设计内容 To know the design contents of lighting circuit diagram in signal controller	掌握信号机点灯电路图的设计步骤和方法 To undertand the design steps and methods of lighting circuit diagram in signal controller	掌握进站、出站及调车等信号机点灯电路相对固定的定型图 To comprehend the stereotype diagram of lighting circuit in home signal, starting signal and shunting signal	掌握信号机点灯电路的工作原理及故障处理方法 To understand the working principles and fault-handling methods of signal lighting circuit	信号机点灯电路图设计 Design of signal lighting circuit diagram
8	掌握道岔控制电路图的设计内容 To understand the design content of switch control circuit	掌握道岔控制电路图的设计步骤和方法 To grasp the design steps and ways of switch control circuit	掌握单动、双动道岔控制电路相对固定的定型图 To comprehend the stereotype diagram of single and dual switchs control circuit	掌握道岔控制电路的工作原理及故障处理方法 To know the working principles and fault-handling methods of switch control circuit	道岔控制电路图设计 The design of switch control circuit
9	掌握轨道电路的设计原则、步骤和方法 To learn the design principle, procedures and methods of track circuit	掌握扼流变压器、25Hz 轨道电路的设计原则及轨道电路组合类型的选用 To understand the design rules of impedance transformer and 25Hz track circuit, the selection of track circuit combination	掌握轨道电路的工作原理 To understand the working principles of track circuit	掌握轨道电路的故障处理方法 To comprehend the fault-handling methods of track circuit	轨道电路图设计 Design of track circuit diagram
10	掌握站内电码化电路设计内容 To know the design contents of instation coding circuit	掌握站内电码化电路正线接车、正线发车、正线股道、侧线股道的设计方法 The design methods of main line receiving, departuring, track and side track of instation coding circuit	掌握站内电码化电路的工作原理 To understand the working principles of instation coding circuit	掌握站内电码化电路的故障处理方法 To comprehend the fault-handling methods of instation coding circuit	站内电码化电路图设计 Design of instation coding circuit
11	掌握室内设备配线图表设计的内容 To understand the design contents of wiring diagram of indoor equipments	掌握室内各种机柜配线图表设计的构成及方法 To know the design structure and methods of wiring diagram of various indoor cabs	掌握室内设备配线图表的设备端子及电源端子配线意义 To comprehend the wiring significance of device terminals and power supply terminals in wiring diagram of indoor equipments	能根据室内设备配线图表完成设备端子间配线 Be able to complete the wiring of device terminals according to the wiring diagram of indoor equipments	室内设备配线图表设计 Design of wiring diagram of indoor equipments
12	掌握室外设备配线图表设计的内容 To understand the design contents of wiring diagram of outdoor equipments	掌握室外设备配线图表设计的方法 To understand the design methods of wiring diagram of outdoor equipments	掌握室外设备配线图表的设备端子配线意义 To comprehend the wiring significance of device terminals in wiring diagram of outdoor equipments	能根据室外设备配线图表完成设备端子间配线 Be able to complete the wiring of device terminals according to the wiring diagram of outdoor equipments	室外设备配线图表设计 Design of wiring diagram of outdoor equipments

续表

序号 NO.	毕业要求指标点 Index point of graduation requirement	知识目标 Knowledge goals	技能目标 Ability goals	素质目标 Quality goals	教学内容 Teaching contents
13	掌握区间信号设备平面布置图设计的内容 To understand the design contents of section signal equipments layout	掌握区间信号设备平面布置图设计的原则、步骤和方法 To comprehend the design principles, procedures and methods of section signal equipments layout	掌握解区间信号设备的定位方法 To grasp the location methods of section signal equipments	能根据区间信号设备平面布置图完成设备安装 Be able to install the facilities according to the section signal equipments layout	区间信号平面布置图 Layout of section signal
14	掌握区间电缆径路图的设计内容 To know the design contents of section cable pathway	掌握区间电缆使用原则、长度计算、芯数确定、方向和型号的确定方法 To understand the application principles, length calculating, core confirmation, methods of determinating the direction and types of section cable	掌握区间电缆的使用类型及设计标准 To comprehend the application types and design standard of section cable	能根据电缆径路图完成区间电缆敷设及设备安装 Be able to complete the cable laying and the installation of the equipments according to the cable pathway	区间电缆径路图 Section cable pathway
15	掌握自动闭塞电路图的设计的内容 To know the design contents of automatic block circuit diagram	掌握自动闭塞电路图的设计步骤和方法 To understand the design procedures and ways of automatic block circuit diagram	了解自动闭塞分区电路、N+1电路、站间联系电路、报警电路及区间信号采集电路的工作原理 To understand the working principles of automatic block circuit diagram, N+1 circuit, communication circuit between stations, alarm circuit and acquisition circuit of section signal	能根据电路图完成自动闭塞电路设备的维修 Be able to maintain the equipments of automatic block circuit according to the circuit diagram	自动闭塞电路图 Automatic block circuit diagram
16	掌握自动闭塞室内设备配线图表设计的内容 To know the design contents of wiring chart of automatic block indoor equipments	掌握自动闭塞室内配线图表设计步骤和方法 To understand the design procedures and ways of wiring chart of automatic block indoor equipments	掌握室内设备配线图表的设备端子及电源端子配线意义 To comprehend the wiring significance of device terminals and power supply terminals in the indoor equipments wiring chart	根据室内配线图表完成设备配线 Be able to wire the equipments according to the indoor equipments wiring chart	自动闭塞室内配线图表设计 Design of wiring chart of automatic block indoor equipments
17	掌握室外设备配线图表设计的内容 To know the design contents of wiring chart of automatic block outdoor equipments	掌握室外设备配线图表设计的步骤和方法 To understand the design procedures and ways of wiring chart of automatic block outdoor equipments	掌握室外设备配线图表的设备端子配线意义 To comprehend the wiring significance of device terminals in the outdoor equipments wiring chart	能根据室外设备配线图表完成设备端子间配线 Be able to wire the device terminals according to the outdoor equipments wiring chart	自动闭塞室外配线图表设计 Design of wiring chart of automatic block outdoor equipments

续表

序号 NO.	毕业要求指标点 Index point of graduation requirement	知识目标 Knowledge goals	技能目标 Ability goals	素质目标 Quality goals	教学内容 Teaching contents
18	掌握6502电气集中工程图纸的全部内容 To know the contents of 6502 electric interlocking engineering drawings	掌握工程图纸与实物的对应关系 To comprehend the corresponding relation between engineering drawings and object	掌握工程图纸设计内容及设备配线方法 To understand the design contents of engineering drawings and methods of wiring equipments	能根据工程图进行设备安装及维修 Be able to install and maitain the equipments according to the engineering drawings	6502电气集中工程图纸识图 Be able to read 6502 electric interlocking engineering drawings
19	掌握图纸设计内容及设备配线 To know the layout design contents and equipments wiring	掌握工程图纸与实物的对应关系 To comprehend the corresponding relation between engineering drawings and object	进一步掌握室内设备配线图表的设备端子及电源端子配线意义 To further comprehend the wiring significance of device terminals and power supply terminals in the indoor equipments wiring chart	进一步提高设备配线速度和质量 To further improve the speed and quality of equipment wiring	室内设备配线图识读 Be able to read the indoor equipments wiring chart

表3　课程教学目标与内容2

Table 3　Teaching Objectives and Content 2

序号 NO.	项目（模块） Items	任务（单元） Tasks	教学内容 Teaching contents	重点、难点 Key points and difficulties	学时 Hours
1	项目1：计算机联锁工程设计 Item 1: engineering design of computer interlocking	1.1 勘测调查 Survey	勘测调查的内容 Contents of survey	重点、难点：地形、地貌的确认 Key points and difficulties: Confirmation of terrain and landform	2
2		1.2 车站信号设备平面布置图设计 Design of railway station signal equipment layout	车站信号设备平面布置图设计的原则、步骤和方法 The design principles, procedures and methods of railway station signal equipment layout	重点、难点：车站信号设备平面布置图设计的方法 Key points and difficulties: design methods of railway station signal equipment layout	4
3		1.3 车站电缆径路图 Station cable pathway	车站电缆径路图设计内容、步骤和方法 Design contents, procedures and methods of station cable pathway	重点、难点：坐标计算，电缆长度和芯线计算 Key points and difficulties: calculation of coordinate, cable length and core wires	8
4		1.4 现场教学：平面图、双轨图及电缆径路图 On-the-spot teaching: layout plan, dual-track diagram and cable pathway	平面图、双轨图及电缆径路图认知 The recognition of layout plan, dual-track diagram and cable pathway	重点、难点：电缆径路图的认知 Key points and difficulties: the recognition of cable pathway	2
5		1.5 室内信号设备布置图及组合排列表 The indoor signal equipment layout and combination arrangement table	室内信号设备布置图及组合排列表的设计方法 Design method of the indoor signal equipment layout and combination arrangement table	重点、难点：组合排列表的设计方法 Key points and difficulties: design method of combination arrangement table	2

续表

序号 NO.	项目（模块） Items	任务（单元） Tasks	教学内容 Teaching contents	重点、难点 Key points and difficulties	学时 Hours
6	项目 1：计算机联锁工程设计 Item 1: engineering design of computer interlocking	1.6 联锁表设计 Design of interlock table	联锁表设计步骤和方法 Design steps and methods of interlock table	重点、难点：信号机显示、朝中道岔位置 Key points and difficulties: signal display and middle-oriented switch position	2
7		1.7 接口电路图 Interface circuit diagram	接口电路图的设计内容和方法 Design contents and methods of interface circuit diagram	重点、难点：接口电路图的设计方法 Key points and difficulties: design methods of interface circuit diagram	2
8		1.8 信号机点灯电路图 Lighting circuit diagram of signal controller	信号机点灯电路图的设计内容和方法 Design contents and ways of signal controller lighting circuit diagram	重点、难点：信号机点灯电路图的设计内容和方法 Key points and difficulties: design contents and ways of signal controller lighting circuit diagram	2
9		1.9 道岔控制电路图 Switch control circuit diagram	道岔控制电路图的设计内容和方法 Design contents and ways of switch control circuit diagram	重点、难点：道岔控制电路图的设计方法 Key points and difficulties: design ways of switch control circuit diagram	2
10		1.10 轨道电路图 Track circuit diagram	轨道电路图的设计内容和方法 Design contents and ways of track circuit diagram	重点、难点：轨道电路图的设计方法 Key points and difficulties: design methods of track circuit diagram	2
11		1.11 站内电码化电路图 Instation coding circuit diagram	站内电码化电路图的设计内容和方法 Design contents and ways of instation coding circuit diagram	重点、难点：站内电码化电路图的设计方法 Key points and difficulties: design methods of instation coding circuit diagram	2
12		1.12 室内配线图表设计 Design of indoor equipment wiring chart	室内配线图表的设计内容和方法 Design contents and methods of indoor equipment wiring chart	重点、难点：室内配线图表的设计方法 Key points and difficulties: design methods of indoor equipment wiring chart	4
13		1.13 室外配线图表设计 Design of outdoor equipment wiring chart	室外配线图表的设计内容和方法 Design contents and methods of outdoor equipment wiring chart	重点、难点：室外配线图表的设计方法 Key points and difficulties: design methods of outdoor equipment wiring chart	4
14	项目 2：自动闭塞工程设计 Item 2: design of automatic blocking engineer	2.1 区间信号平面布置图 Layout of section signal	区间信号平面布置图的设计内容和方法 Design contents and methods of layout of section signal	重点、难点：区间信号平面布置图的设计方法 Key points and difficulties: design methods of layout of section signal	2
15		2.2 区间电路径路图 Layout of section circuit pathway	区间电路径路图的设计内容和方法 Design contents and methods of section circuit pathway	重点、难点：区间电路径路图的设计方法 Key points and difficulties: design methods of section circuit pathway	2

续表

序号 NO.	项目（模块） Items	任务（单元） Tasks	教学内容 Teaching contents	重点、难点 Key points and difficulties	学时 Hours
16	项目 2: 自动闭塞工程设计 Item 2: design of automatic blocking engineer	2.3 自动闭塞电路图 Automatic blocking circuit diagram	自动闭塞电路图的设计内容和方法 Design contents and methods of automatic blocking circuit diagram	重点、难点：自动闭塞电路图的设计方法 Key points and difficulties: design methods of automatic blocking circuit diagram	4
17		2.4 自动闭塞室内配线图表设计 Design of wiring chart of automatic block indoor equipments	自动闭塞室内配线图表的设计内容和方法 Design contents and methods of wiring chart of automatic block indoor equipments	重点、难点：自动闭塞室内配线图表的设计方法 Key points and difficulties: design methods of wiring chart of automatic block indoor equipments	4
18		2.5 自动闭塞室外配线图表设计 Design of wiring chart of automatic block outdoor equipments	自动闭塞室外配线图表的设计内容和方法 Design contents and methods of wiring chart of automatic block outdoor equipments	重点、难点：自动闭塞室外配线图表的设计方 Key points and difficulties: design contents and methods of wiring chart of automatic block indoor equipments	4
19	项目 3: 工程施工 Item 3: engineering construction	3.1 6502 电气集中工程图纸识图 Recognition of 6502 electric interlocking engineering drawings	6502 电气集中工程图纸识图 Recognition of 6502 electric interlocking engineering drawings	重点、难点：工程图与现场实物核对 Key points and difficulties: verification of engineering drawings and material object	6
20		3.2 室内设备配线图识读 Recognition of wiring chart of indoor equipments	室内设备配线图识读 Recognition of wiring chart of indoor equipments	重点、难点：现场配线实行核对 Key points and difficulties: verification of on-site wiring	6
21		3.3 室外设备：箱盒类型、配线图识读 Outdoor equipments: types of caple box and Recognition of wiring chart	室外设备配线图识读 Recognition of wiring chart of outdoor equipments	重点、难点：现场配线实行核对 Key points and difficulties: verification of on-site wiring	6

说明：本课程标准适用于 60～68 学时的“铁路信号设计与施工”课程的教学，表 3 中的学时为建议和参考学时，实际教学内容和课时可结合课程标准，根据教学的专业和课时进行选择和调整。

Notes: this curriculum standard applies to the teaching of Railway Signalling Design and Construction, accounting for 60—68 teaching periods. The teaching hours in table 3 are arranged for reference, the actual teaching contents and periods can be adjusted according to the major and practical teaching hours.

三、课程考核 Course Assessment

（1）课程考核分为总结性评价和过程性评价，关注学生个体差异。

Course assessment consists of summative evaluation and process evaluation，focusing on Students' individual difference.

（2）总结性评价包括标准化试题的闭卷考试。

The summative evaluation includes standardized test.

（3）过程性评价指使用铁道信号自动控制专业教学资源库开展线上线、下混合式教学，由线上成绩、线下成绩、线上作业和线上考试组成。对项目中的平时作业、基本实践技能进行考核。考核内容可以根据实践教学设备的变化进行相应的调整。

Process evaluation is composed of online and off-line performance, online assignment and online test by using the online and off-line blended teaching through teaching resources database of railway signalling automatic control major. The usual performance and awareness in different items are also evaluated. Assessment contents can be ajusted according to the practical situation.

（4）课程考核比例：过程性评价占 50%，总结性评价占 50%。

The proportion of course assessment: process evaluation 50%, while summative assessment accounts for 50%.

四、实施要求 Implementation Requirements

1. 授课教师基本要求 Basic Requirements for Teachers

（1）具备铁道信号专业或相关专业岗位工作经历，大学本科及以上学历，具有高等学校教师资格证书。

Work experiences related to railway signalling major or relevant major, bachelor degree and above, with the teacher certificate of higher education.

（2）具备相应技术职称或本专业三级及以上职业资格证书。

With relevant technical titles or professional vocational qualification certificate of level3 and above.

（3）具有“双师型”教师证书。

With the certificate of dual qualified teacher.

（4）具备开发职业课程、组织与实施教学的能力。

Ability to develop vocational course and organize and implement teaching.

（5）专业教师每两年到现场实践锻炼应不少于两个月。

No less than two months' field practice every two years.

2. 教学方法和策略 Teaching meThods and Strategies

（1）教学方法 Teaching methods。

主要采用项目化教学法、情景教学法和工作过程导向教学法。将铁路运营企业铁路信号系统设备设计、安装与调试的任务作为代表性的项目，理论知识的教学紧密围绕技能训练开展，应用大量的视频和图片，通过对比、举例、通俗的比喻等方法使学生更好地理解和掌握相关知识，运用多媒体教学手段化解教学难点。

Project method, situational teaching method and work process-oriented teaching method are adopted. With the assignments of equipments design, installation and debugging of railway signal system in train operation as the representative project, teaching of theoretical knowledge revolves around the skill training. Through the methods of comparison, illustration and common metaphor, plenty of videos and pictures are applied to make Students better understand and master related knowledge. Multi-media teaching approaches are adopted to resolve difficulties in teaching.

（2）教学策略 Teaching strategies。

教学过程中采用铁道信号自动控制专业教学资源库实现混合式教学，如平面图、双轨图及电缆径路图设计、道岔控制电路图设计等操作内容，可在专业教学资源库预先给学生操作视频或微课来学习，然后课堂上通过讲解和实操提醒注意事项。理论知识点也可通过专业教学资源库的课程组课、在线答疑、网络考试、作业布置和修改等功能实现混合式教学。

The blended teaching through teaching resources database of railway signalling automatic control major is adopted during teaching process. Parts of the operating contents like design of layout, double-track layout, cable pathway and switch-control circuit diagram can be studied in advance through operation videos or micro-lectures in the database. In-class explanation and reminding on operation are followed afterwards. Blending learning can be achieved through the use of re-mixing the courses, FAQ, online testing, assigning and correcting homework in the resources database.

在实践教学环节，采用企业实地考察，请企业专家、技术能手来给学生授课，让学生清楚企业的工作流程、岗位职责要求和企业岗位工作的其他纪律规定。

As to the practical teaching aspect, field investigation is adopted. Enterprise experts and technical experts are invited to lecture in order to make Students be clear about the workflows, requirements of job description and work disciplines and rules of posts.

第六节　“铁路信号集中监测系统运用与维护”课程标准

Curriculum Standard for Operation and Maintenance of Railway Signal Central Supervision System

一、课程性质 Nature of the Course

1. 课程类型、课程功能 Types and Functions

本课程是铁道信号自动控制专业的核心课，共计 40 课时，2.5 学分；是学生在学习了“铁路信号基础设备维护”“铁路车站自动控制系统维护”“铁路区间自动控制系统维护”课程，具备一定的铁路信号系统知识的基础上，开设的一门理论+实践课，其功能是对接铁道信号自动控制专业人才培养目标，面向车站与区间信号设备维修信号工、电子与电气设备检修信号工等工作岗位，培养学生按照信号检修作业标准进行列车运行控制系统相关设备的日常维护、设备检修和故障分析处理的能力，为其将来胜任铁路信号工工作岗位打下坚实的基础。

Operation and Maintenance of Railway Signal Central Supervision System is the core course of railway signalling automatic control major, including 40 lessons and 2.5 credits in total. It’s a theoretical and practical course for students who have learnt Maintenance of Railway Signal Devices, Maintenance of Railway Station Automatic Control System and Maintenance of Railway Sections Automatic Control System and who have gained a basic understanding of the railway signalling system. In accordance with the objective of cultivating railway signalling automatic control talents, students who have learnt this course will be qualified for jobs like signal worker of railway section equipments maintenance and electrical and electronic equipment maintenance. It fosters students’ ability of daily maintenance, devices inspection and fault-handling of related equipments in train operation control system according to the railway signalling inspection and maintenance standard, thus lays a solid foundation for the job of railway signalling worker.

2. 课程功能定位 Orientation of the Function

表 1 课程功能定位分析

Table 1 Analysis of Orientation of the Funition

对接的工作岗位 Jobs	对接培养的职业岗位能力 Abilities
车站与区间信号设备维修信号工、电子与电气设备检修信号工、机车信号设备维修信号工 Signal worker of railway section equipments maintenance, electrical and electronic equipment maintenance and locomotive signal equipment maintenance	按照中国铁路总公司最新颁布的《铁路信号维护规则》对铁路信号集中监测系统进行运用与维护的能力 Ability of operating and maintaining the railway signal central supervision and control system according to *Maintenance Rules of Railway Signalling* newly issued by China Railway Corporation

二、课程目标与内容 Objective and Content

1. 课程总目标 General Objectives

监督信号设备运行情况、发现信号设备隐患、加强信号设备结合部管理、分析信号设备故障原因、辅助信号维修人员处理故障、指导现场维修、反映设备运用质量、提高维修人员设备维护水平和维护效率，保障行车安全和服务运输生产，以保证信号设备安全、可靠、稳定地运行。

To supervision the operation of signal equipments, discover its hidden trouble and strengthen its joint parts management and analyze the signal equipments breakdown reason; To assist signal maintenance worker with the fault-handling and guide the field maintenance and make a feedback of the operation quality of equipments; To improve the maintenance level and efficiency of maintenance worker and to ensure the train operation safety and to serve the transportation production in order to assure safe, sound and stable operation of signal equipments.

2. 课程具体目标 Specific Objectives

表 2 课程教学目标与内容 1

Table 2 Teaching Objectives and Contents 1

序号 No.	毕业要求指标点 Index point of graduation requirement	知识目标 Knowledge goals	技能目标 Ability goals	素质目标 Quality goals	教学内容 Teaching content
1	了解信号监测系统的结构和用途；运用系统维护信号设备，快速处理信号设备故障 To know the structure and purpose of signal supervision system; To use the system to maintain signal equipments and deal with signal equipment fault rapidly	熟悉信号监测系统的结构和用途 Be familiar with the structure and purpose of signal supervision system	掌握电压、电流、开关量信息采集处理的原理 To comprehend the principle of voltage, current and switch signal acquisition	培养合格的铁路信号维修工 To cultivate qualified railway signal worker	信号集中监测设备认知 The recognition of signal central supervision equipment
2	了解信号集中监测系统的信号处理方法；掌握数据采集原理，通过监测系统，了解设备的运行情况及安全隐患 To understand signal processing method of signal central supervision system and principle of data acquisition ; To know the operation and hidden danger of equipments through supervision system	掌握信号集中监测系统数据采集和处理的方法 To comprehend data acquisition and processing method of signal central supervision system	通过收集数据，能判断设备工作性能及运行情况 Be able to judge the working performance and operation of equipments through data acquisition	通过数据对比，快速分析和处理设备故障 To analyze and deal with the equipment fault rapidly by data comparison	信号集中监测数据采集和处理系统认知 The recognition of data acquisition and processing in signal central supervision system

序号 No.	毕业要求指标点 Index point of graduation requirement	知识目标 Knowledge goals	技能目标 Ability goals	素质目标 Quality goals	教学内容 Teaching content
3	掌握电源屏、列车信号机点灯回路电流监测的功能、电路的设备和故障处理 To learn the power supply screen, supervision functions of lighting return current in train signal controller, circuit facilities and fault-handling	掌握电源屏、列车信号机点灯回路电流监测采集原理 To understand the acquisition principle of the power supply screen and lighting return current supervision of train signal controller	掌握电源屏、列车信号机点灯回路电流监测的设备和故障处理 To know the equipments and fault-handling of the power supply screen and lighting return current supervision of train signal controller	通过监测系统监督检查电源屏和信号机的工作状态，并进行维护 Be able to supervise the operation state of power supply screen and signal controller and carry out the maintenance	电源屏、列车信号机点灯回路电流监测设备维护 The equipments maintenance of the power supply screen and lighting return current supervision of train signal controller
4	掌握轨道电路、转辙机等设备的监测和故障处理 To understand the supervison and fault-handling of relevant equipments in track circuit and switch machine	掌握轨道电路监测采集的工作原理 To know the working principle of supervison and acquisition of track circuit	根据采集数据判断设备的工作情况 Be able to judge the working condition of equipments according to the collected data	能熟练进行日常检修和故障处理 Be able to conduct daily inspection and maintenance and deal with breakdowns	轨道电路监测设备维护 Maintenance of track circuit monitoring faeility
5		掌握转辙机监测采集的工作原理 To know the working principle of supervison and acquisition of switch machine	根据采集数据判断设备的工作情况 Be able to judge the working condition of equipments according to the collected data	能熟练进行日常检修和故障处理 Be able to conduct daily inspection and maintenance and deal with breakdowns	转辙机监测设备维护 Maintenance of switch machine monitoring faeility
6	掌握外电网综合质量、电缆绝缘和电源漏流的监测和故障处理 To learn the supervision and fault-handling of comprehensive quality of external power network, cable insulation and leakage flow of power supply	掌握外电网、电缆绝缘、电源漏流监测的工作原理 To understand the working principle of the supervision of external power network, cable insulation and leakage flow of power supply	掌握外电网综合质量、电缆绝缘和电源漏流监测的设备和故障处理 To learn the equipments and fault-handling of comprehensive quality of external power network, cable insulation and leakage flow of power supply	能熟练进行日常检修和故障处理 Be able to condcut daily inspection and maintenance and deal with breakdowns	外电网综合质量、电缆绝缘和电源漏流监测设备维护 Maintenance of supervision equipment of comprehensive quality of external power network, cable insulation and leakage flow of power supply
7	掌握道岔表示电压监测的功能 To understand the functions of voltage supervision in switch indication	掌握道岔表示电压监测的工作原理 To understand the working principle of voltage supervision in switch indication	掌握道岔表示电压监测的设备和故障处理 To learn the equipments and fault-handling of voltage supervision in switch indication	能熟练掌握道岔表示电压监测及设备维护 To skillfully grasp the supervision and equipment maintenance of voltage supervision in switch indication	道岔表示电压监测设备维护 The equipment maintenance of voltage supervision in switch indication
8	掌握列车主灯丝断丝、熔丝断丝监测的功能 To know the functions of monitoring broken wires of train main filament and fuse and broken wires	掌握列车主灯丝断丝、熔丝断丝监测的工作原理 To understand the working principle of monitoring broken wires of train main filament and fuse and broken wires	掌握列车主灯丝断丝、熔丝断丝监测的设备和故障处理 To understand the equipments and fault-handling of monitoring broken wires of train main filament and fuse and broken wires	熟练掌握列车主灯丝断丝、熔丝断丝的故障判断和处理 To skillfully grasp the judging and handling fault of broken wires of train main filament and fuse and broken wires	列车主灯丝断丝、熔丝断丝监测设备维护 Equipments maintenance of broken wires of train main filament and fuse and broken wires

续表

序号 No.	毕业要求指标点 Index point of graduation requirement	知识目标 Knowledge goals	技能目标 Ability goals	素质目标 Quality goals	教学内容 Teaching content
9	掌握站机报警信息调看及信息统计；熟悉再现回放操作 To know the gathering and counting of alarm information in jointed station and locomotive; to know the operation of replay	熟悉信号集中监测系统操作主界面及其他功能操作 Be familiar with the main operating interface of signal centralized supervision system	掌握信号设备的工作状态及故障处理 To grasp the working conditions and fault-handling of signal equipments	熟练掌握站机的操作和数据分析 To understand the operation and data analysis of jointed station and locomotive	站机的日常操作 The daily operation of jointed station and locomotive
10	掌握转辙机、轨道电路的分析 To understand the analysis of switch machine and track circuit	掌握道岔、轨道电路典型故障案例分析 To know the typical fault case analysis of switch and track circuit	掌握转辙机和轨道电路的监测曲线分析、故障处理方法 To understand the analysis of supervision curves and fault-handling methods in switch machine and track circuit	熟练掌握信号设备的故障分析和处理方法 Be familiar with the fault analysis and handling method of signal equipments	信号集中监测设备案例分析 Case study of signal centralized supervision equipments
11	掌握道岔控制电路的监测，确保道岔使用安全 To know the supervision of switch-controlled circuit in order to ensure the operating safety of switch	掌握道岔控制电路监测的工作原理 To understand the working principles of switch-controlled circuit supervision	掌握道岔控制电路的安全工作状态 To understand the safety working state of switch-controlled circuit	及时判断道岔控制电路的工作状态 Be able to judge the working condition of switch-controlled circuit	实验一：道岔控制电路监测项目测量实验 Experiment 1: the measuring experiment of switch-controlled circuit supervision
12	掌握 TJWX-2010 信号集中监测车站子系统软件的使用方法 To understand the using method of subsystem software of TJWX-2010 signal centralized supervision station	掌握 TJWX-2010 信号集中监测调阅信号设备信息数据的方法 To comprehend the methods of browsing and adjusting the information data of signal equipments in TJWX-2010 signal centralized supervision	掌握 TJWX-2010 信号集中监测分析和处理信号设备故障的方法 To understand the analysis and signal equipments fault-handling ways of TJWX-2010 signal centralized supervision	熟练掌握 TJWX-2010 信号微机监测的操作方法 To comprehend the operation methods of TJWX-2010 signal microcomputer supervision system	实验二：TJWX-2010 信号微机监测的操作使用 Experiment 2 : operation of TJWX-2010 signal microcomputer supervision system

表 3　课程教学目标与内容 2

Table 3　Teaching Objectives and Contents 2

序号 No.	项目（模块） Items	任务（单元） Tasks	教学内容 Teaching contents	重点、难点、考核点 Key points, difficulties and evaluation points	学时 Hours
1	项目 1：信号集中监测系统概述 Item1: general introduction to signal centralized supervision system	1.1 信号集中监测设备认知 Recognition of signal centralized supervision devices	信号集中监测设备的结构及功能 Structure and function of signal centralized supervision devices	重点、难点：车站监测系统设备的结构、功能；电压、电流、开关量信息采集处理的原理 Key points and difficulties: structure and function of station supervision system equipments; the acquisition principles of voltage, current and switch signal	2

续表

序号 No.	项目（模块） Items	任务（单元） Tasks	教学内容 Teaching contents	重点、难点、考核点 Key points, difficulties and evaluation points	学时 Hours
2	项目1：信号集中监测系统概述 Item1: general introduction to signal centralized supervision system	1.2 信号集中监测数据采集处理系统认知 Recognition of data acquisition system in signal centralized supervision	信号设备监测数据的采集 Data acquisition of signal supervision	重点、难点：信号设备数据采集原理 Key points and difficulties: Data acquisition principles of signal equipments	2
3	项目2：信号集中监测系统维护 Item 2: maintenance of signal centralized supervsion system	2.1 电源屏、列车信号机点灯回路电流监测采集原理 The acquisition principle of the power supply screen and lighting loop current supervision of train signal controller	电源屏、列车信号机点灯回路电流的监测内容和原理 The supervision contents and principles of the power supply screen and lighting loop current supervision of train signal controller	重点、难点：电源屏、列车信号机点灯回路电流监测的工作原理 Key points and difficulties: the working principles of the power supply screen and lighting loop current supervision of train signal controller	2
4		2.2 轨道电路监测设备维护 Maintenance of track circuit supervision devices	轨道电路监测的内容和原理 Supervision contents and principles of track circuit	重点、难点：轨道电路监测采集原理 Key points and difficulties: the working principle of track circuit supervision and acquisition	4
5		2.3 转辙机监测设备维护 Maintenance of switch machine supervision devices	直流、交流转辙机监测的内容和原理 The supervision contents and principles of DC/AC switch machine	重点、难点：直流、交流转辙机监测采集原理 Key points and difficulties: the supervision and acquisition principle of DC/AC switch machine	4
6		2.4 外电网综合质量、电缆绝缘和电源漏流监测设备维护 Maintenance of comprehensive quality of external power network, cable insulation and leakage flow of power supply	外电网综合质量、电缆绝缘和电源漏流监测的内容和原理 Contents and principles of the supervision of external power network, cable insulation and leakage flow of power supply	重点、难点：外电网综合质量、电缆绝缘和电源漏流监测采集原理 Key points and difficulties: the supervision and acquisition principle of of external power network, cable insulation and leakage flow of power supply	2
7		2.5 道岔表示电压监测设备维护 The equipment maintenance of voltage supervision in switch indication	道岔表示电压监测采集原理 The acquisition principle of voltage supervision in switch indication	重点、难点：道岔表示电压监测采集原理 Key points and difficulties: the and acquisition principle of voltage supervision in switch indication	4
8		2.6 列车主灯丝断丝、熔丝断丝监测设备维护 Supervision equipments maintenance of broken wires of train main filament and fuse and broken wires	列车主灯丝断丝、熔丝断丝监测采集原理 The acquisition principle of broken wires of train main filament and fuse and broken wires supervision	重点、难点：列车主灯丝断丝、熔丝断丝监测采集原理 Key points and difficulties: the acquisition principle of broken wires of train main filament and fuse and broken wires supervision	2

续表

序号 No.	项目（模块） Items	任务（单元） Tasks	教学内容 Teaching contents	重点、难点、考核点 Key points, difficulties and evaluation points	学时 Hours
9	项目3：信号集中监测系统应用 Item 3 application of signal centralized supervision system	3.1 站机的日常操作 Daily operation of jointed station and locomotive	信号集中监测系统操作主界面，调阅数据和测试数据方法；电缆绝缘、电源屏对地漏流的测试；站机报警信息调看及信息统计；再现回放操作；站机其他功能操作 The main operating interface of signal centralized supervision system, ways of data retrieving and testing; testing of cable insulation and ground leakage flow from power panel ; the gathering and counting of alarm information in jointed station and locomotive; the operation of replay; other operating functions	重点、难点：信号集中监测系统操作主界面，调阅数据和测试数据方法 Key points and difficulties: the main operating interface of signal centralized supervision system, ways of data retrieving and testing	4
10		3.2 信号集中监测设备案例分析 Case study of signal centralized supervision equipments	交流、直流转辙机动作电流曲线分析；轨道电路电压曲线分析；轨道电路典型故障案例分析 The analysis of action current curves in DC/AC switch machine; the analysis of voltage curves in track circuit; the typical fault case analysis of track circuit	重点、难点：交流、直流转辙机动作电流曲线分析；轨道电路电压曲线分析；掌握轨道电路典型故障案例分析 Key points and difficulties: the analysis of action current curves in DC/AC switch machine; the analysis of voltage curves in track circuit; the typical fault case analysis of track circuit	4
11	项目4：课程实验 Item 4: experiment	4.1 实验一　道岔控制电路监测项目测量实验 The measuring experiment of switch-controlled circuit supervision	道岔监测内容与采集点位置；道岔启动电路电压测量方法；道岔表示电压测量方法及在不同故障情况下的电压分布；根据所测数据对道岔控制电路故障原因进行分析 Contents and acquisition position of switch supervision; the measuring approaches of voltage in switch starting circuit; the measuring ways of switch indicated voltage and voltage distribution under different fault cases; to analyze the reasons of the breakdowns in switch controlled circuit according to the measured data	重点、难点：根据所测数据对道岔控制电路故障原因进行分析 Key points and difficulties: to analyze the reasons of the breakdowns in switch controlled circuit according to the measured data	4

续表

序号 No.	项目（模块） Items	任务（单元） Tasks	教学内容 Teaching contents	重点、难点、考核点 Key points, difficulties and evaluation points	学时 Hours
12		4.2 实验二 TJWX-2010信号微机监测系统的操作使用 Operation of TJWX-2010 signal microcomputer supervision system	JWX-2010 信号集中监测车站子系统软件的使用方法、调阅信号设备信息数据的方法、信号集中监测分析和处理信号设备故障信息的方法 The application method of subsystem software of TJWX-2010 signal centralized supervision station, the methods of browsing the information data of signal equipments, the analysis and fault-handling ways of signal equipments in TJWX-2010 signal centralized supervision	重点、难点：JWX-2010 信号集中监测分析和处理信号设备故障信息的方法 Key points and difficulties: the analysis and fault-handling ways of signal equipments in TJWX-2010 signal centralized supervision	4

说明：本课程标准适用于 40～48 学时的"铁路信号集中监测系统运用与维护"课程的教学，表 3 中的学时为建议和参考学时，实际教学内容和课时可结合课程标准，根据教学的专业和课时进行选择和调整。

Notes: this curriculum standard applies to the teaching of Operation and Maintenance Railway Signal Central Supervision System, accounting for 40—48 teaching periods. The teaching hours in table 3 are arranged for reference, the actual teaching contents and periods can be adjusted according to the major and practical teaching hours.

三、课程考核 Course Assessment

（1）课程考核分为总结性评价和过程性评价，关注学生个体差异。

Course assessment consists of summative evaluation and process evaluation, focusing on students' individual difference.

（2）总结性评价包括标准化试题的闭卷考试。

The summative evaluation includes standardized test.

（3）过程性评价指使用铁道信号自动控制专业教学资源库开展线上线、下混合式教学，由线上成绩、线下成绩、线上作业和线上考试组成。对项目中的平时作业、基本实践技能进行考核。考核内容可以根据实践教学设备的变化进行相应的调整。

Process evaluation is composed of online and off-line performance, online assignment and online test by using the online and off-line blended teaching through teaching resources database of railway signalling automatic control major. The usual performance and awareness in different items are also evaluated. Assessment contents can be ajusted according to the practical situation.

（4）课程考核比例：过程性评价占 30%，总结性评价占 70%。

The proportion of course assessment: process evaluation 30%, while summative assessment accounts for 70%.

四、实施要求 Implementation Requirements

1. 授课教师基本要求 Basic Requirements for Teachers

（1）具备铁道信号专业或相关专业岗位工作经历，大学本科及以上学历，具有高等学校教师资格证书。

Work experiences related to railway signalling major or relevant major, bachelor degree and above, with the teacher certificate of higher education.

（2）具备相应技术职称或本专业三级及以上职业资格证书。

With relevant technical titles or professional vocational qualification certificate of level-3and above.

（3）具有“双师型”教师证书。

With the certificate of dual qualified teacher.

（4）具备开发职业课程、组织与实施教学的能力。

Ability to develop vocational course and organize and implement teaching.

（5）专业教师每两年到现场实践锻炼应不少于两个月。

No less than two months' field practice every two years.

2. 教学方法和策略 Teaching Methods and Strategies

（1）教学方法 Teaching methods。

主要采用项目化教学法、情景教学法和工作过程导向教学法。将铁路运营企业铁路信号集中监测系统运用与维护的任务作为代表性的项目，理论知识的教学紧密围绕技能训练开展，应用大量的视频和图片，通过对比、举例、通俗的比喻等方法使学生更好地理解和掌握相关知识，运用多媒体教学手段化解教学难点。

Project method, situational teaching method and work process-oriented teaching method are adopted. With the assignments of operation and maintenance of railway signal central supervision system in railway operation as the representative project, teaching of theoretical knowledge revolves around the skill training. Through the methods of comparison, illustrations and common metaphor, plenty of videos and pictures are applied to make students better understand and master related knowledge. Multi-media teaching approaches are adopted to resolve difficulties in teaching.

（2）教学策略 Teaching strategies。

教学过程中采用铁道信号自动控制专业教学资源库实现混合式教学，如轨道电路监测设备维护、信号机监测设备维护、道岔转辙机监测设备维护等操作内容，可在专业教学资源库预先给学生操作视频或微课来学习，然后课堂上通过讲解和实操提醒注意事项。理论知识点也可以通过专业教学资源库的课程组课、在线答疑、网络考试、作业布置和修改等功能实现混合式教学。

The blended teaching through teaching resources database of railway signalling automatic control major is adopted during teaching process. Parts of the operating contents, such as maintenance of track circuit supervision devices, signal supervision devices and switch machine supervision devices can be studied in advance through operation videos or micro-lectures in the database. In-class explanation and reminding on operation are followed afterwards. Blending learning can be achieved through the use of re-mixing the courses, FAQ, online testing, assigning and correcting homework in the resources database.

在实践教学环节，采用企业实地考察，请企业专家、技术能手来给学生授课，让学生清楚企业的工作流程、岗位职责要求和企业岗位工作的其他纪律规定。

As to the practical teaching aspect, field investigation is adopted. Enterprise experts and technical experts are invited to lecture in order to make students be clear about the workflows, requirements of job description and work disciplines and rules of posts.

第三章　专业主干课程 Main Courses

第一节　“高铁道岔转辙设备维护实训”课程标准

Curriculum Standard for Maintenance Training of High-speed Railway Switch Equipment

一、课程性质 Nature of the Course

1. 课程类型、课程功能 Types and Functions

本课程是铁道信号自动控制专业的主干课，共计 24 课时，1.5 学分；是学生在学习了“电子技术基础”“电路分析基础”“铁路信号基础设备维护”“铁路车站自动控制系统维护”等课程，掌握了铁路道岔转辙设备的结构组成、工作原理，具备了电路分析、故障处理能力的基础上，开设的一门实践课。其功能是对接铁道信号自动控制专业人才培养目标，面向铁路企业，从事铁路信号设备的安装调试、维修养护工作岗位，培养信号设备的维护与检修、故障信息的收集、分析与处理能力，并为胜任铁路信号工工作岗位打下坚实的基础。

This course is the main course for the railway signalling automatic control majors, including 24 lessons and 1.5 credits. It is a practice course opened to the students who have learned the courses of The Basis of Electronic Technology, The Basis of Circuit Analysis, Maintenance of Basic Railway Signaling Equipment, Maintenance of Railway Station Automatic Control System, etc., and have mastered the structure and working principle of railway switch equipment with certain capabilities as circuit analysis and fault handling. Its function is to realize the training objective of railway signaling automatic control specialists and workers engaging in the installation, debugging, maintenance of railway signal equipment in the railway industries, to foster the ability of signal equipment maintenance, fault information collection, analysis and processing, and lay a solid foundation for the competent railway signal workers.

2. 课程功能定位 Orientation of the Function

表 1　课程功能定位分析

Table 1　Analysis of the Orientation of the Function

对接的工作岗位 Jobs	对接培养的职业岗位能力 Abilities
高速铁路现场信号设备维修岗位 Field work of signal equipment maintenance for high speed railway	按照中国铁路总公司最新颁布的《铁路信号维护规则》对高速铁路道岔转辙设备进行维护的能力 To maintain the switch equipment for high speed railway in accordance to the latest *Railway Signaling Maintenance Rules* issued by China Railway Corporation

二、课程目标与内容 Objective and content

1. 课程总目标 General Objective

通过故障分析与查找练习，掌握交流转辙机控制电路的动作程序，理解电路故障现象，分析故障原因及正确操作仪器仪表，完成电路故障判断，提高处理故障的能力。

Through the fault analysis and searching practice, to master the action procedure of the control circuit of the AC switches, to learn the circuit fault phenomenon and analyze the fault causes, to operate the instrument correctly and circuit fault diagnosis, so as to improve the fault handling abilities.

2. 课程具体目标 Specific Objectives

表 2　课程教学目标与内容 1

Table 2　Teaching Objectives and Content 1

序号 No.	毕业要求指标点 Index point of graduation requirement	知识目标 Knowledge goals	技能目标 Skill goals	素质目标 Quality goals	教学内容 Teaching contents
1	掌握交流转辙机控制电路故障处理 Master the troubleshooting of control circuit in AC switch machines	掌握交流转辙机启动电路动作顺序，根据故障现象进行分析及查找 Master the starting sequence of AC switch machines; analyse and find the cause based on the faults	能根据故障现象，分析处理交流转辙机启动电路故障 Be able to analyze and handle the starting circuit fault of AC switch machine according to the faults	具备较强的专业技能、安全责任意识 Have strong professional skills and responsibility awareness	交流转辙机启动电路故障分析及查找 Fault analysis and troubleshooting of starting circuit in AC switch machines
2		掌握交流转辙机表示电路工作原理，根据故障现象进行分析及查找 Master the working principle of the indication circuit of the AC switch machine; analyze and find out the faults	能根据故障现象，分析处理交流转辙机表示电路故障 Analyze and deal with the indication circuit fault of AC switch machine according to the fault phenomenon	具备较强的专业技能、安全责任意识 Have strong professional skills and responsibility awareness	交流转辙机表示电路故障分析及查找 Faul analysis and troublesooting of indication circuit in AC switch machines
3		全面了解交流转辙机单元控制电路动作顺序、工作原理，根据故障现象进行分析及查找 To learn the action sequence and working principle of the control circuit in the AC switch machine unit; analyze and find out the faults	能根据故障现象，分析处理交流转辙机单元控制电路故障 Analyze and deal with the circuit fault of AC switch machine according to the fault phenomenon	具备较强的专业技能、安全责任意识 Have strong professional skills and responsibility awareness	交流转辙机单元控制电路故障查找考核 Assessment of troubleshooting of control circuit in AC switch machine unit

表 3　课程教学目标与内容 2

Table 3　Teaching Objectives and Contents 2

序号 No.	项目（模块） Items	任务（单元） Tasks	教学内容 Teaching content	重点、难点 Key points and difficulties	学时 Hours
1	交流转辙机单元控制电路故障查找实训 Practical training on fault finding of unit control circuit of AC switch machine	1.1 交流转辙机启动电路 Starting circuit of AC switch machine	交流转辙机启动电路故障分析及查找 Fault analysis and trouble shooting of starting circuit in AC switch machine	重点：交流转辙机启动电路故障分析 Key points: fault analysis of starting circuit in AC switch machine 难点：交流转辙机启动电路故障查找 Difficulties: fault finding of starting circuit in AC switch machine	12

续表

序号 No.	项目（模块） Items	任务（单元） Tasks	教学内容 Teaching content	重点、难点 Key points and difficulties	学时 Hours
2		1.2 交流转辙机表示电路 Indication circuit of AC switch machine	交流转辙机表示电路故障分析及查找 Fault analysis and troubleshooting of indication circuit in AC switch machine	重点：交流转辙机表示电路故障分析 Key points: Fault analysis of indication circuit in AC switch machine 难点：交流转辙机表示电路故障查找 Difficulties: Fault analysis of indication circuit in AC switch machine	12

三、课程考核 Course Assessment

（1）课程考核分为总结性评价和过程性评价，关注学生个体差异。

Course assessment consists of summative evaluation and process evaluation, focusing on students' individual differences.

（2）总结性评价为技能考试。

The summative evaluation is the skills test.

（3）过程性评价指使用铁道信号自动控制专业教学资源库开展线上线、下混合式教学，由线上成绩、线下成绩、线上作业和线上考试组成。对项目中的实践技能进行考核，考核内容可以根据实践教学设备的变化进行相应的调整。

Process evaluation is composed of online and off-line performance, online assignment and online test by using the online and off-line blended teaching through teaching resources database of railway signaling automatic control major. The usual performance and awareness in different modules are also evaluated. Assessment contents can be adjusted according to the practical situation.

（4）课程考核比例：过程性评价占 40%，总结性评价占 60%。

The proportion of course assessment: process evaluation accounts for 40%, summative assessment accounts for 60%.

四、实施要求 Implementation Requirements

1. 授课教师基本要求 Basic requirements for Teachers

（1）具备铁道信号专业或相关专业岗位工作经历，大学本科及以上学历，具有高等学校教师资格证书。

Work experiences related to railway signalling major or relevant post, bachelor degree and above, with the teacher certificate of higher education.

（2）具备相应技术职称或本专业三级及以上职业资格证书。

Provided relevant technical titles or professional qualification certificates of level-3 and above.

（3）具有“双师型”教师证书。

With the teacher certificate of dual qualifications.

（4）具备开发职业课程、组织与实施教学的能力。

Ability to develop vocational course, organize and implement teaching.

（5）专业教师每两年到现场实践锻炼应不少于两个月。

No less than two months' field practice every two years for the professional staff.

2. 教学方法和策略 Teaching Methods and Strategies

（1）教学方法 Teaching Methods。

主要采用项目化教学法、情景教学法和工作过程导向教学法。将高速铁路道岔转辙设备维护的任务作为代表性的项目，实践教学紧密围绕技能训练开展，应用大量的视频和图片，通过对比、举例、通俗的比喻等方法使学生更好地理解和掌握相关知识，运用多媒体教学手段化解教学难点。

Project teaching method, situational teaching method, and work process-oriented teaching method are adopted. The task of high-speed railway switch equipment maintenance is listed as the typical project, practical learning performs closely around skill training. A great number of videos and pictures were used to enable students to better understand and master relevant knowledge through comparison, examples, popular metaphors, and solve teaching difficulties by applying the multimedia teaching method.

（2）教学策略 Teaching strategies。

教学过程中采用铁道信号自动控制专业教学资源库实现混合式教学，可以利用专业教学资源库预先给学生操作视频或微课学习。在教学过程中尽可能设置与高速铁路道岔转辙设备实际维护工作一致的作业分工、作业内容、作业步骤及要求。充分利用校内实训室等教学资源，根据每个学习任务的实际情况，在教学过程中采用小组合作、学生独立实操演练、技术比武等教学形式。

The blended teaching through the teaching resources database for railway signaling automatic control major is adopted during the process, and the students is advised to study the operation video and micro-lecture in advance. Set up the work division, work content, work steps and requirements which are consistent with the actual maintenance of high-speed railway switch equipment as far as possible. Make full use of the training room and other teaching resources in the school, and adopt the teaching methods such as group cooperation, students' independent practice and technical competition in the teaching process according to the actual situation of each learning task.

在实践教学环节，采用企业实地考察，请企业专家、技术能手给学生授课，让学生清楚企业的工作流程、岗位职责要求和企业岗位工作的其他纪律规定。

As to the practical teaching aspect, field investigation is adopted. Enterprise experts and technical experts are invited to lecture in order to make students be clear about the workflows, requirements of job description and work disciplines and rules of posts.

第二节 “铁路信号电源设备维护”课程标准

Curriculum Standard for Railway Signal Power Equipment Maintenance

一、课程性质 Nature of the Course

1. 课程类型、课程功能 Types and Functions

本课程是铁道信号自动控制专业的主干课，共计 36 课时，2.0 学分；是学生在学习了“电路分析基础”“铁道概论”“电子技术基础”等课程，具备了一定的电路知识与操作能力的基础上，开设的一门理论+实践课。其功能是对接铁道信号自动控制专业人才培养目标，面向车站与区间信号设备维修信号工工作岗位，培养学生关于电信号设备的供电概况的认识、日常维护、设备检修和故障分析处理的能力，并为其后续专业核心课程的学习奠定基础。

This course is the main course for the railway signaling automatic control majors, including 36 lessons and 2.0 credits. It is an integration of theory and practice, which is opened to the students who have already learned the courses of The Basis Circuit Analysis, An Introduce to the Railway, and The Basis of Electric Technology etc., and have certain circuit knowledge and operational capabilities.

Its function is to realize the training objective of railway signaling automatic control specialists and workers, to train the students' ability of overview, daily maintenance, equipment repairs, fault analysis and handling of power supply of electric signal equipment for the post of signal equipment maintenance in stations or sections, and lay a solid foundation for follow-up study of specialized courses.

2. 课程功能定位 Orientation of the Function

表 1　课程功能定位分析

Table 1　Analysis of the Orientation of the Function

对接的工作岗位 Jobs	对接培养的职业岗位能力 Abilities
车站与区间信号设备维修信号工 Signalman for station and section signal equipment maintenance	按照中国铁路总公司最新颁布的《铁路信号维护规则》对铁路信号电源设备进行维护的能力 To maintain the power supply equipment for railway signaling in accordance to the latest *Railway Signalling Maintenance Rules* issued by China Railway Corporation

二、课程目标与内容 Objective and Content

1. 课程总目标 General Objectives

本课程的目标是让学生了解铁路信号设备的供电概况，并通过变压器、电机与电器、交流稳压器等的结构、功能，进一步认识开关电源与信号电源屏的电路工作原理，熟练掌握大、小型继电电源屏的使用、施工和维修等知识，初步具备处理信号供电设备故障的能力。同时培养学生热爱铁路信号事业，为深入学习其他专业课程和进行专业技能训练以及日后走上工作岗位奠定坚实的思想基础和技术基础。

The purpose of this course is to enable students to understand the general situation of power supply for railway signal equipment, further understand the circuit working principle of switching power supply and signaling power supply panel through the structure and function of transformer, motor and electric appliance, AC voltage regulator, etc., master the use, construction and maintenance of large and small relay power supply panels, and initially have the ability to handle the failure of signal power supply equipment. Meanwhile build up the passions for the work in railway signaling, and lay a solid ideological and technical foundation for further study of other professional courses, professional skills training and future work.

2. 课程具体目标 Specific Objectives

具体描述课程的内容及学生应达到的知识目标、技能目标、素质目标，在进行目标表述时应以学生作为行为主体来表述。

Specifically describe the content of the course and the knowledge goals, skill goals and quality goals that students should achieve, and the description should be embodied on students' focus.

序号 No.	毕业要求指标点 Index point of graduation requirement	知识目标 Knowledge goals	技能目标 Ability goals	素质目标 Quality goals	教学内容 Teaching contents
1	铁路信号认知 Recognition of railway signal	了解铁路信号供电的基本要求和概况、铁路电源屏的发展 Understand the basic requirements and general situation of railway signal power supply, learn the development of railway power supply panel	认识铁路信号电源屏系统的结构、铁路信号供电概况 Understand the structure of railway signal power supply panel system and the general situation of railway signal power supply	激发学习电源设备维护的浓厚兴趣，培养良好的学习习惯 Stimulate strong interest in learning power equipment maintenance and cultivate good learning habits	1. 铁路信号供电基本要求认知 Recognition of the basic requirement for railway signal power supply 2. 信号设备供电概况认知 General overviews of power supply in signalling equipment 3. 信号电源屏发展认知 The developing of signalling power supply panel
2	掌握信号电源主要部件维护 Master the maintenance of main components of signal power supply	了解变压器、三相变压器的分类、作用、结构、额定值、运行特性；了解互感器的分类；理解电流互感器的结构、工作原理和使用注意事项；低压电器控制与保护设备电器；了解异步电动机、交流稳压器相关内容 Understand the classification, function, structure, rating and operation characteristics of transformer and three-phase transformer; understand the classification of transformer; understand the structure, working principle and cautions of current transformer; low voltage electrical control and protection equipment; understand the relevant contents of asynchronous motor and AC voltage regulator	了解主要部件的相关内容，能够在一定程度上对存在的问题加以分析并解决 Understand the relevant contents of main components, and analyze and solve the existing problems to a certain extent	提高学生分析问题和解决问题的能力 Improve students' ability to analyze and solve problems	1. 变压器的认知与维护 Recognition and maintenance of transformer 2. 铁磁变频器的认知与维护 Recognition and maintenance of ferromagnetic frequency converter 3. 低压电器的认知与维护 Recognition and maintenance of low voltage electrical appliances 4. 三相异步电动机的认知与维护 Recognition and maintenance of three phase asynchronous motor 5. 交流稳压器的认知与维护 Recognition and maintenance of AC voltage regulator

续表

序号 No.	毕业要求指标点 Index point of graduation requirement	知识目标 Knowledge goals	技能目标 Ability goals	素质目标 Quality goals	教学内容 Teaching contents
3	理解开关电源认知 Understand the recognition of switching power supply	了解开关电源的组成、作用、分类、功能，了解开关电源相关技术知识 Understand the composition, usage, classification and function of switching power supply, and know the relevant technical knowledge of switching power supply	学习电源设备组成所需要的多种技术支持，了解该技术和工作原理 Learn the various technical support required by the composition of power supply equipment and understand the working principle of the technology	提高逻辑思维分析能力，提升学习能力 Improve the ability of critical thinking and learning	1. 开关电源认知与维护 Recognition and maintenance of switching power supply 2. 逆变器认知与维护 Recognition and maintenance of converter 3. 脉宽调制技术认知与维护 Recognition and maintenance of PWM technology 4. 软启动技术认知 Recognition of soft start technology 5. 功率因数校正认知 Power factor correction recognition 6. 直流变换器认知 DC converter recognition 7. 并联均流技术认知 Recognition of parallel current sharing technology
4	理解UPS认知与维护 Understanding of UPS recognition and maintenance	了解蓄电池的结构、分类及功能；UPS供电系统的结构组成、发展趋势、功能特点 Understand the structure, classification and function of battery; learn the structure, trend and functional characteristics of UPS power supply system	能够认识UPS结构、组成 Be able to know UPS structure and composition	培养学生对仪器仪表及其操作的职业素质感情和职业道德 Cultivate students' passions and professional ethics for the vocational quality of instruments and their operation	1. 蓄电池认知与维护 Recognition and maintenance of battery 2. UPS认知与维护 Recognition and maintenance of UPS
5	掌握信号电源屏维护 Master the maintenance of signal power supply panel	了解信号电源屏的技术条件，掌握大站电源屏，了解计算机联锁电源屏、25Hz电源屏、交流转辙机电源屏、驼峰电源屏及其日常维护 Learn technical conditions of signal power supply panel, learn the power supply panel of large station; Learn computer interlocking power supply panel, 25Hz power supply panel, AC switch machine power supply panel, hump power supply panel and their daily maintenance	正确认识普通电源屏的内部结构、工作原理、不同电源屏之间的区别 Correctly understand the internal structure, working principle of common power supply panel and differences between different power supply panels	培养学生整体和局部的辩证唯物主义思想；养成认真细致、实事求是、积极探索的科学态度和工作作风 Cultivate students' dialectical materialism as a whole and as a part, and develop a scientific attitude and work style that are conscientious, meticulous, practical and realistic, and active in exploration	1、信号电源屏技术条件认知 Recognition of signal Power Screen technical condition 2. 大站电源屏认知 Recognition of power supply panel of large station 3. 计算机联锁电源屏认知 Recognition of computer interlocking power supply panel 4. 25Hz电源屏认知 Recognition of 25Hz power supply panel 5. 交流转辙机电源屏认知 Recognition of power supply panel in AC switch machine 6. 驼峰电源屏认知 Recognition of hump power supply panel 7. 电源屏日常维护 Routine maintenance of power supply panel

序号 No.	毕业要求指标点 Index point of graduation requirement	知识目标 Knowledge goals	技能目标 Ability goals	素质目标 Quality goals	教学内容 Teaching contents
6	理解信号智能电源屏维护 Understand the maintenance of signal intelligent power supply panel	了解信号智能电源屏的相关内容，PZG、PKX、PDZG、PMZG系列智能电源屏的电路结构、工作原理及维护 Learn the relevant contents of signal intelligent power supply panel, circuit structure, working principle and maintenance of PZG, PKX, PDZG and PMZG series intelligent power supply panel	掌握智能电源屏的结构、工作原理，能够做到简单维护和应急处理 Master the structure and working principle of intelligent power supply panel, and be able to conduct simple maintenance and emergency treatment	培养学生操作仪器仪表的熟练度 Cultivate students' proficiency in instruments	1. 信号智能电源屏的认知 Recognition of signal intelligent power supply panel 2. PZG、PKX 系列信号智能电源屏维护 Maintenance of PZG and PKX series signal intelligent power supply panel 3. PDZG 系列信号智能电源屏维护 Maintenance of PDZG series signal intelligent power supply panel 4. PMZG 系列铁路信号智能电源屏维护 Maintenance of PMZG series railway signal intelligent power supply panel

表 2　课程教学目标与内容 1

Table 2　Teaching Objectives and Contents 1

序号 No.	项目（模块） Items	任务（单元） Tasks	教学内容 Teaching contents	重点、难点 Key points and difficulties	学时 Hours
1	项目 1：铁路信号供电认知 Item 1: recognition of railway signal power supply	1.1 铁路信号供电基本要求认知 Recognition of basic requirements of railway signal power supply	了解铁路信号供电的基本要求 Understand the basic requirements of railway signal power supply	重点：铁路信号供电的三大基本要求 Key points: three basic requirements of railway signal power supply	1
2		1.2 信号设备供电概况认知 General knowledge of signal equipment power supply	了解铁路信号供电概况 Understanding of the general situation of railway signal power supply	重点：懂得信号电源对信号设备的重要性 Key points: learned the importance of signal power supply for signal equipment	1
3		1.3 信号电源屏发展认知 Recognition of signal power supply panel development	铁路电源屏的发展认知 Recognition of railway power supply panel development	重点：信号电源屏发展历程 Key points: the development history of signal power supply panel	1
4	项目 2：信号电源主要部件维护 Item 2: maintenance of main components of signal power supply	2.1 变压器的认知与维护 Recognition and maintenance of transformer	了解变压器、三相变压器的分类、作用、结构、额定值、运行特性；了解互感器的分类；理解电流互感器的结构、工作原理和使用注意事项	重点：变压器的结构、工作原理、运行特性和绕组的同极性端；三相变压器的绕组的连接方式；电流互感器的工作原理 Key points: structure, working principle, operation characteristics and the same polarity end of winding of transformer; connection mode of three-phase transformer winding; working principle of current transformer	4

续表

序号 No.	项目（模块）Items	任务（单元）Tasks	教学内容 Teaching contents	重点、难点 Key points and difficulties	学时 Hours
4	项目 2：信号电源主要部件维护 Item 2: maintenance of main components of signal power supply	2.1 变压器的认知与维护 Recognition and maintenance of transformer	Understand the classification, function, structure, rating and operation characteristics of transformer and three-phase transformer; understand the classification of transformer; understand the structure, working principle and precautions of current transformer	难点：变压器的运行特性和绕组的统计性端；三相变压器的绕组的连接方式；电流互感器的工作原理 Difficulties: operation characteristics of transformer and statistical end of winding of transformer; connection mode of winding of three-phase transformer; working principle of current transformer	
5		2.2 铁磁变频器的认知与维护 Recognition and maintenance of ferromagnetic frequency converter	了解铁磁变频器的分类、结构以及工作原理 Understand the classification, structure and working principle of ferromagnetic frequency converter	重点：铁磁变频器的工作原理 Key points: the working principle of ferromagnetic frequency converter 难点：参数激励振荡 Difficulties: parametric excited oscillation	1
6		2.3 低压电器的认知与维护 Recognition and maintenance of low voltage electrical appliances	低压电器控制与保护设备电器的结构、原理、参数 Low voltage electrical appliances control, and the structure, principle and parameters of the protection of electrical applionces	重点：交流接触器的结构、原理和参数 Key points: the structure, principle and parameters of AC contactor 难点：交流接触器的原理 Difficulties: the principle of AC contactor	2
7		2.4 三相异步电动机的认知与维护 Recognition and maintenance of three phase asynchronous motor	了解异步电动机的结构原理、分类、应用及工作原理 Understand the structure, classification, application and working principle of asynchronous motor	重点：异步电动机的结构、旋转磁场以及异步电动机的工作原理 Key points: structure of asynchronous motor, rotating magnetic field and working principle of asynchronous motor 难点：旋转磁场的产生 Difficulties: generation of rotating magnetic field	4
8		2.5 交流稳压器的认知与维护 Recognition and maintenance of AC voltage regulator	了解交流稳压器的认知与维护 Understand the recognition and maintenance of AC voltage regulator	重点：交流稳压器的种类、结构、原理 Key points: type, structure and principle of AC voltage regulator 难点：交流稳压器稳压过程 Difficulties: voltage stabilization process of AC voltage regulator	4

续表

序号 No.	项目（模块） Items	任务（单元） Tasks	教学内容 Teaching contents	重点、难点 Key points and difficulties	学时 Hours
9	项目3：开关电源认知 Item 3: recognition of switching power supply	3.1 开关电源认知与维护 Recognition and maintenance of switching power supply	了解开关电源的组成、作用、分类、功能 Understand the composition, function, classification and function of switching power supply	重点：开关电源的组成、分类 Key points: composition and classification of switching power supply 难点：开关电源的组成 Difficulties: the composition of switching power supply	4
10		3.2 逆变器认知与维护 Inverter's recognition and maintenance	了解逆变器的组成以及工作原理 Understand the composition and working principle of inverter	重点：逆变器的组成及工作原理 Key points: the composition and working principle of inverter 难点：逆变器的工作原理 Difficulties: the working principle of inverter	
11		3.3 脉宽调制技术认知与维护 Recognition and maintenance of PWM technology	了解脉宽调制技术的相关内容 Understand the related content of PWM technology	重点：脉宽调制技术的原理 Key points: principle of PWM technology 难点：脉宽调制技术的原理 Difficulties: principle of PWM technology	
12		3.4 软启动技术认知 Recognition of soft start technology	理解软启动技术的相关知识 Understand the knowledge of soft start technology	重点：软启动技术原理 Key points: principle of soft start technology 难点：软启动技术原理 Difficulties: principle of soft start technology	2
13		3.5 功率因数校正认知 Recognition of power factor correction	理解功率因数校正知识 Understand the power factor correction	重点：功率因数校正的原理 Key points: principle of power factor correction 难点：功率因数校正的原理 Difficulties: principle of power factor correction	
14		3.6 直流变换器认知 Recognition of DC converter	了解直流变换器的组成、分类、工作原理 Understand the composition, classification and working principle of DC converter	重点：直流变换器的分类、工作原理 Key points: the classification and working principle of DC converter 难点：直流变换器的工作原理 Difficulties: working principle of DC converter	
15		3.7 并联均流技术认知 Recognition of parallel current sharing technology	了解并联均流技术的内容、基本方法 Understand the contents and basic methods of parallel current sharing technology	重难点：并联均流的基本方法 Key point and difficulties: basic method of parallel current sharing	
16	项目4：UPS认知与维护 Item 4: recognition and maintenance of UPS	4.1 蓄电池认知与维护 Recognition and maintenance of battery	了解蓄电池的结构、分类及功能 Understand the structure, classification and function of battery	重点：蓄电池的结构与原理 Key points: structure and principle of battery 难点：蓄电池的原理 Difficulties: the principle of battery	2

续表

序号 No.	项目（模块） Items	任务（单元） Tasks	教学内容 Teaching contents	重点、难点 Key points and difficulties	学时 Hours
17	项目4：UPS认知与维护 Item 4: recognition and maintenance of UPS	4.2 UPS认知与维护 Recognition and maintenance of UPS	UPS供电系统的结构组成、发展趋势、功能特点 The structure, development trend and functional characteristics of UPS power supply system	重点：在线式UPS的概念、功能、分类 Key points: the concept, function and composition of online UPS 难点：在线式UPS的原理、组成 Difficulties: principle and composition of online UPS	2
18	项目5：信号电源屏维护 Item 5: maintenance of signal power supply panel	5.1 信号电源屏技术条件认知 Recognition of the technical conditions of signal power supply panel	了解信号电源屏的技术条件 Understand the technical conditions of signal power supply panel	重点：技术条件 Key points: technical conditions	6
19		5.2 大站电源屏认知 Recognition of power supply panel of large station	掌握转换屏、交流屏、直流屏和调压屏的结构、电路工作原理 Master the structure and circuit working principle of conversion panel, AC panel, DC panel and voltage regulating panel	重点：相关电源屏工作原理 Key points: the working principle of relevant power supply panel 难点：工作原理 Difficulties: the working principle	
20		5.3 计算机联锁电源屏认知 Recognition of computer interlocking power supply panel	计算机联锁电源屏认知 Recognition of computer interlocking power supply panel	重点：电路结构、工作原理 Key points: the circuit structure and working principle 难点：工作原理 Difficulties: the working principle	4
21		5.4 25Hz电源屏认知 Recognition of 25Hz power supply panel	25Hz电源屏认知 Recognition of 25Hz power supply panel	重点：电路结构、工作原理 Key points: circuit structure and working principle 难点：工作原理 Difficulties: working principle	
22		5.5 交流转辙机电源屏认知 Recognition of power supply panel of AC switch machine	交流转辙机电源屏认知 Recognition of power supply panel of AC switch machine	重点：电路结构、工作原理 Key points: the circuit structure and working principle 难点：工作原理 Difficulties: the working principle	
23		5.6 驼峰电源屏认知 Recognition of hump power supply panel	驼峰电源屏认知 Recognition of hump power supply panel	重点：电路结构、工作原理 Key points: the circuit structure and working principle 难点：工作原理 Difficulties: the working principle	
24		5.7 电源屏日常维护 Routine maintenance of power supply panel	了解电源屏施工、日常检查和测试工作等相关知识 Knowledge of power supply panel construction, daily inspection and testing	重点：判断故障点，处理和解决各种故障 Key points: judge the fault point, handle and solve various faults 难点：判断故障点 Difficulties: judge the fault point	

续表

序号 No.	项目（模块） Items	任务（单元） Tasks	教学内容 Teaching contents	重点、难点 Key points and difficulties	学时 Hours
25	项目6：信号智能电源屏维护 Item 6: maintenance of signal intelligent power supply panel	6.1 信号智能电源屏的认知 Recognition of signal intelligent power supply panel	分析原有信号电源屏存在的问题，了解信号智能电源屏的特点 Analyze the existing problems of the original signal power supply panel, and understand the features of the signal intelligent power supply panel	重点：信号智能电源屏的特点 Key points: the features of signal intelligent power supply panel	2
26		6.2 PZG、PKX 系列信号智能电源屏维护 Maintenance of PZG and PKX series signal intelligent power supply panel	认知 PZG、PKX 系列信号智能电源屏的结构和工作原理 Understand the structure and working principle of PZG and PKX series signal intelligent power supply panel	重点、难点：PZG、PKX 系列信号智能电源屏的结构和工作原理 Key points and difficulties: the structure and working principle of PZG and PKX series signal intelligent power supply panel	
27		6.3 PDZG 系列信号智能电源屏维护 Maintenance of PDZG series signal intelligent power supply panel	认知 PDZG 系列信号智能电源屏的结构和工作原理 Recognition of the structure and working principle of cognitive PDZG series signal intelligent power supply panel	重点、难点：PDZG 系列信号智能电源屏的结构和工作原理 Key points and difficulties: the structure and working principle of PDZG series signal intelligent power supply panel	2
28		6.4 PMZG 系列铁路信号智能电源屏维护 Maintenance of PMZG series railway signal intelligent power supply panel	认知 PMZG 系列信号智能电源屏的结构和工作原理 Recognition of the structure and working principle of PMZG series signal intelligent power supply panel	重点、难点：PMZG 系列信号智能电源屏的结构和工作原理 Key points and difficulties: the structure and working principle of PDZG series signal intelligent power supply panel	4

说明：本课程标准适用于 36～42 学时的“铁路信号电源设备维护”课程的教学，表 3 中的学时为建议和参考学时，实际教学内容和课时可结合课程标准，根据教学的专业和课时进行选择和调整。

Notes: this curriculum standard applies to the teaching of The Maitannence of Power Supply for Railway Signal, accounting for 36—42 teaching periods. The teaching hours in table 3 are arranged for reference, the actual teaching contents and periods can be adjusted according to the major and practical teaching hours.

三、课程考核 Course Assessment

（1）课程考核分为总结性评价和过程性评价，关注学生个体差异。

Course assessment consists of summative evaluation and process evaluation, focusing on students' individual difference

（2）总结性评价包括标准化试题的闭卷考试。

The summative evaluation includes standardized test.

（3）过程性评价指使用铁道信号自动控制专业教学资源库开展线上线、下混合式教学，由线上成绩、线下成绩、线上作业和线上考试组成。对项目中的平时作业、基本实践技能进行考核。考核内容可以根据实践教学设备的变化进行相应的调整。

Process evaluation is composed of online and off-line performance, online assignment and online test by using the online and off-line blended teaching through teaching resources database of railway signaling automatic control major. The usual performance and practical skills in different modules are also evaluated. Assessment contents can be adjusted according to the practical situation

（4）课程考核比例：过程性评价占 30%，总结性评价占 70%。

The proportion of course assessment: process evaluation accounts for 30%, summative assessment accounts for 70%.

四、实施要求 Implementation Requirements

1. 授课教师基本要求 Basic Requirements for Teachers

（1）具备铁道信号专业或相关专业岗位工作经历，大学本科及以上学历，具有高等学校教师资格证书。

Work experiences related to railway signaling major or relevant major, bachelor degree and above, with the teacher certificate of higher education.

（2）具备相应技术职称或本专业三级及以上职业资格证书。

With relevant technical titles or professional vocational qualification certificate of level-3 and above.

（3）具有“双师型”教师证书。

With the certificate of dual qualified teacher.

（4）具备开发职业课程、组织与实施教学的能力。

Ability to develop vocational course and organize and implement teaching.

（5）专业教师每两年到现场实践锻炼应不少于两个月。

No less than two months' field practice every two years.

2. 教学方法和策略 Teaching Methods and Strategies

（1）教学方法 Teaching Methods and Strategies。

本着“淡化理论、够用为度、培养技能、重在应用”的原则，课程注重培养学生分析和解决问题的能力以及对所学知识进行应用的能力。本课程主要推荐采用讲授教学法、讨论教学法、实验教学法、案例教学法、指导自学法等。

In line with the principle of “weaken the theories to be adequate for using, and emphasize applications when cultivate skills ”, the course focuses on cultivating students' ability to analyze and solve problems and to apply the knowledge they have learned. This course mainly recommends the use of lecture teaching method, discussion teaching method, experimental teaching method, case teaching method, self-study teaching method, etc.

（2）教学策略 Teaching strategies。

教学过程中采用铁道信号自动控制专业教学资源库实现混合式教学，可在专业教学资源库预先给学生操作视频或微课，然后课堂上通过讲解和实操提醒注意事项。理论知识点也可以通过专业教学资源库的课程组课、在线答疑、网络考试、作业布置和修改等功能实现混合式教学。

Blended teaching is adaptable in the teaching process by using teaching resource database for railway signal automatic control major. It is suggested to provide students with video or micro-learning in advance, then generates the precautions during the instruction and practice in class. Achieve blended teaching through the functions as course grouping, online problem solving, online testing, homework assigning and modifying in specialized teaching resource database.

在实践教学环节，采用企业实地考察，请企业专家、技术能手来给学生授课，让学生清楚企业的工作流程、岗位职责要求和企业岗位工作的其他纪律规定。

In the field practice, enterprise field visits are used, and enterprise experts and technical experts are invited to teach students, so that students can understand the company's workflow, job responsibilities and other disciplinary requirements.

第三节 “铁路行车调度集中系统维护”课程标准

Curriculum Standard for Railway CTC System Maintenance

一、课程性质 Nature of the Course

1. 课程类型、课程功能 Types and Functions

本课程是铁道信号自动控制专业的主干课，共计 28 课时，1.5 学分；是学生在学习了“铁道概论”“铁路信号基础设备维护”等课程，具备对铁路信号设备的基本认识能力的基础上，开设的一门理论+实践课。其功能是对接铁道信号自动控制专业人才培养目标，面向电子维护工区信号工岗位、电子设备综合工区信号工工作岗位，培养电子维护工区及设备综合工区信号工工作人员 TDCS、CTC 设备检修、维护及故障处理的能力，为其将来胜任铁路信号工工作岗位打下坚实的基础。

This is a main course for the railway signal automatic control major, including 28 lessons, 1.5 credits. It is an integration of theory and practice, and set up for the students who have learned the courses of An Introduction to Railway, Maintenance of Railway Signal Basic Equipment, etc. and have the basic understanding of railway signal equipment. Its function is to connect with the training objective of the railway signal automatic control specialist, and face to the position as electronic signal workers in the maintenance area and the electronic equipment comprehensive work area. Students shall be trained to have the ability of TDCS and CTC equipment overhaul, maintenance and fault handling, so as to lay a solid foundation to be qualified railway signal workers.

2. 课程功能定位 Orientation of the Function

表 1 课程功能定位分析

Table 1 Analysis of orientation of the Function

对接的工作岗位 Jobs	对接培养的职业岗位能力 Abilities
电子维护工区信号工岗位、电子设备综合工区信号工岗位 Signalman in electronic maintenance working area or electronic equipment complex processing area	按照中国铁路总公司最新颁布的《铁路信护号维规则》对铁路行车调度集中系统进行维护的能力 To maintain the CTC system on the railway in accordance to the latest *Railway Signaling Maintenance Rules* issued by China Railway Corporation

三、课程目标与内容 Objective and Content

1. 课程总目标 General Objectives

通过学习，使学生了解远程控制系统的基本原理、概念及组成，掌握铁路运输调度的组织管理、铁路运输调度指挥系统、铁路运输调度指挥系统应用情况，了解远动技术的网络结构、数据通信、总线控制、计算机网络等方面的知识。理解调度集中组织（CTC）系统的基本概念、系统功能、组成原理；了解系统的设计方法；重点掌握新一代分散自律调度集中系统的结构、基本特点及控制方式；熟知车站系统的设备组成；掌握新一代分散自律调度集中系统的功能和实际应用情况。了解铁路列车调度指挥系统（TDCS）总体目标、技术特点；掌握 TDCS 系统结构及功能，熟悉无线车次号校核系统的构成及功能。

Through learning, students can understand the basic principle, concept and composition of remote control system; grasp the organization and management of railway transportation dispatching, the railway transportation dispatching command system, the application of railway transportation dispatching command system; understand the network structure, data communication, bus control, computer network and other aspects of remote control technology. Understand the basic concept, systemic function and composition principle of CTC system; understand the design method of the system; focus on the structure, basic characteristics and control mode of the new generation of decentralized self-discipline centralized dispatching system; be familiar with the equipment composition of the station system; master the function and practical application of the new generation of decentralized self-discipline centralized dispatching system. Understand the overall objectives and technical characteristics of the railway train dispatching command system (TDCS); master the structure and functions of the TDCS system, and be familiar with the composition and functions of the wireless train number verification system

2. 课程具体目标 Specific Objectives

表 2 课程教学目标与内容 1

Table 2 Teaching Objectives and Contents 1

序号 No.	毕业要求指标点 Index point of graduation requirement	知识目标 Knowledge goals	技能目标 Ability goals	素质目标 Quality goals	教学内容 Teaching contents
1	远动系统认知及在铁路信号系统中的应用 The recognition of telecontrol system and its application in railway signal system	掌握远动系统的基本结构、概念、控制信息的发送方向。掌握 CTC、TDCS 级监测系统属于哪一类远动系统 Master the basic structure, concept and the sending direction of control information in telecontrol system; grabs the main idea of CTC and TDCS supervision system and their classification in telecontrol system	通过学习远动系统能分析我国主要的铁路信号系统属于远动系统 Able to analysize China's main railway signal system belongs to the telecontrol system after the study	培养学生对调度系统的兴趣，提高学生学习的热情 Cultivate students' passions in dispatching system and improve their enthusiasm for learning	熟悉远程控制系统的分类和作用 Familiar with the classification and function of remote control system 掌握遥控、遥信、遥测系统的概念和控制原理 Master the concept and control principle of remote control, remote signaling and telemetry system 掌握远程控制系统的基本组成 Master the basic composition of remote control system 远动系统在铁路信号控制系统中的实际应用 Application of telecontrol system in railway signal control system 掌握铁路运输调度指挥自动控制系统的概述 Master the overview of automatic control system of railway transportation command dispatching

序号 No.	毕业要求指标点 Index point of graduation requirement	知识目标 Knowledge goals	技能目标 Ability goals	素质目标 Quality goals	教学内容 Teaching contents
2	TDCS 系统结构及工作原理认知 Recognition of TDCS system structure and working principle	掌握 TDCS 的三层体网络系结构及各层间的关系，掌握核心层、区域层、接入层的功能 Master the three-layer network architecture of TDCS and the relationship between each layer, and master the functions of core layer, area layer and access layer	能够正确分析 TDCS 总体结构网络图及 TDCS 网络体系结构图 Correctly analyze TDCS overall structure network diagram and TDCS network architecture diagram	培养学生对于整个系统结构的分析能力 Cultivate students' ability to analyze the structure of the whole system	了解 TDCS 的发展方向、技术及功能特点 Understand the development direction, technology and functional characteristics of TDCS 掌握 TDCS 的整体结构和网络结构 Master the overall structure and network structure of TDCS 掌握 TDCS 网络特点及各个层的功能 Master the characteristics of TDCS network and the functions of each layer
	铁路总公司调度指挥中心 TDCS Train dispatching center of China Railway Corporation TDCS	掌握铁路局总公司调度指挥中心 TDCS 的网络结构、设备组成和主要功能。 Master the network structure, equipment composition and main functions of TDCS in the dispatching command center in the head office of Railway Bureau	能够正确分析铁路总公司调度指挥中心 TDCS 网络结构图，能够正确分析 TDCS 系统界面上的宏观显示信息 Correctly analyze the TDCS network structure diagram of the dispatching command center of the Railway Corporation and the macro displayed information on the TDCS system interface	培养学生网络结构分析能力及设备认知能力 Training students' ability of network structure analysis and equipment recognition	熟悉铁路局总公司调度指挥中心的 TDCS 的网络结构 Familiar with the TDCS network structure of the dispatching command center in the head office Bureau of the Railway 掌握铁路局总公司调度指挥中心的设备组成和主要功能 Master the equipment composition and main functions of the dispatching command center in the head office of the Railway Bureau.
	铁路局调度指挥中心 TDCS Dispatching command center of Railway Administrator TDCS	掌握铁路局调度指挥中心 TDCS 的网络结构、信息流程、设备组成和主要功能 Master the network structure, information flow, equipment composition and main functions of TDCS in the dispatching command center of Railway Bureau	能够正确分析铁路局调度指挥中心 TDCS 网络结构图，能够编写下达调度命令，分析列车自动追踪的原理 Correctly analyze the TDCS network structure diagram of the dispatching command center in Railway Bureau, compile and issue dispatching commands, and analyze the principle of automatic train tracking	培养学生网络结构分析能力及设备认知、操作能力 Cultivate students' ability of network structure analysis and equipment diagnostic and operation	熟悉铁路局调度所 TDCS 网络结构 Familiar with TDCS network structure in Railway Bureau 掌握铁路局调度所的 TDCS 整体结构及设备组成 Master the TDCS structure and equipment composition 掌握调度所 TDCS 的功能及信息流程 Master the function and massage process of TDCS

续表

序号 No.	毕业要求指标点 Index point of graduation requirement	知识目标 Knowledge goals	技能目标 Ability goals	素质目标 Quality goals	教学内容 Teaching contents
2	车站 TDCS Station's TDCS	掌握铁路局总车站 TDCS 的网络结构、设备组成和主要功能及车站 TDCS 与其他系统的接口 Master the network structure, equipment composition and main functions of railway station's TDCS and the interface between station's TDCS and other systems	能够正确分析车站 TDCS 网络结构图、设备连接图 Be able to correctly analyze the station's TDCS network structure's configuration and equipment connection diagram	培养学生网络结构分析能力及设备认知 Cultivate students' ability of network structure analysis and device recognition	熟悉车站 TDCS 网络结构 Familiar with station's TDCS network structure 掌握车站 TDCS 结构及设备组成 Grasp station's TDCS structure and equipment composition 掌握车站设备的功能 Grasp the function of station equipment 掌握 TDCS 系统与其他系统接口 Grasp the interfaces between TDCS system and other systems
	TDCS 设备认识及 TDCS 设备操作 The recognition and operation of TDCS facilities	掌握铁路 TDCS 系统体系结构和设备组成 Master the system structure and equipment composition of the railway TDCS system	掌握 TDCS 系统的基本操作 Master the basic operation of TDCS system	培养学生的职业素养及对设备的基本操作技能 Cultivate students' vocational qualities and basic operation skills of equipment	了解铁路列车调度指挥系统的框架结构 Understand the framework structure of train dispatching and command system 掌握 TDCS 系统的设备组成 Master the equipment composition of TDCS system 掌握 TDCS 系统的基本操作 Master the basic operation of TDCS system
3	CTC 系统认知及结构 CTC system recognition Be and structures	熟悉 CTC 系统的诞生、发展及现状，掌握 CTC 系统整体结构及各子系统的设备组成 familiar with the birth, development and current situation of CTC system; Understand the equipment composition of CTC system overall structure and subsystem	掌握传统 CTC 与分散自律 CTC 的区别，正确分析 CTC 系统整体构成图及网络子系统的网络基本连接图 Master the difference between traditional CTC and decentralized self-regulatory CTC, and correctly analyze the overall composition diagram of CTC system and the basic network connection diagram of the network subsystem	培养学生对 CTC 系统的兴趣、培养学生网络结构分析能力及设备认知能力 Cultivate students' interest in CTC system, foster the ability in network structure analysis and equipment recognition	了解分散自律调度集中系统 Understand the decentralized and autonomic CTC systems 了解分散自律调度集中系统的发展及现状 Understand the development and current situation of decentralized CTC autonomous system 熟悉 CTC 系统整体网络结构 Familiar with CTC system network structure 熟悉调度中心及车站子系统的设备组合 Familiar with the equipment combination of dispatching center and station subsystem 掌握 CTC 系统和 TDCS 的区别和联系 Master the difference and connection between CTC system and TDCS

续表

序号 No.	毕业要求指标点 Index point of graduation requirement	知识目标 Knowledge goals	技能目标 Ability goals	素质目标 Quality goals	教学内容 Teaching contents
3	CTC 系统调度中心子系统维护 CTC's subsystem maintenance	掌握 CTC 调度中心系统结构及设备组成 Master CTC's structure and equipment composition	能够正确分析 CTC 系统网络结构图，能够编写下达调度命令 Be able to correctly analyze CTC system network configuration, be able to write and issue dispatching commands	培养学生的职业素养、网络结构分析能力及设备操作能力 To cultivate students' vocational quality, network structure analysis ability and equipment operation ability	掌握 CTC 调度中心系统构成 Master the composition of CTC dispatching center system 了解 CTC 中心巡检、检修作业标准；掌握调度中心设备操作 Understand CTC centeral inspection and maintenance standards; Master the operation of dispatching center equipment
	CTC 车站子系统维护 CTC station's subsystem maintenance	掌握CTC车站子系统的结构，自律机板件的组成及功能 Master the structure of CTC station's subsystem, composition and the function of self-regulating machine	能够正确分析车站子系统结构图，能够掌握自律机指示灯的含义 Correctly analyze the station subsystem's configuration, grasp the meaning of the autonomous machine indicator light	培养学生职业素养、对 CTC 车站子系统结构分析能力及设备认知能力 Cultivate students' vocational quality and analysis of the structure of CTC station subsystem and recognition of equipment	掌握车站子系统设备构成； Master the structure of station's subsystem equipment 掌握自律机的组成，各板件的作用 Master the composition of the self-discipline machine and the function of each plate 了解 CTC 车站设备巡检、检修作业程序 Understand CTC's station equipment inspection and maintenance procedures
	CTC 系统功能和原理实现 CTC system's function and principle implementation	掌握CTC的控制模式、系统功能及自律控制原理 Master the CTC control module, function and self-regulating control principle	能够掌握CTC系统两种控制模式的转换方法，掌握列、调车作业流程 Master two control mode's conversion methods of CTC system, and master the operation procedure of shunting	培养学生职业素养及设备操作能力 Cultivate students' vocational quality and equipment operation ability	掌握 CTC 控制模式； Master CTC control mode 熟悉 CTC 系统的整体功能 Familiar with the overall function of CTC system 掌握 CTC 系统的行车指挥功能、调度集中功能、行车调度功能 Master CTC system's train traffic control, centralized dispatching and train dispatching function 掌握自律控制系统的基本原理 Grasp the basic principles of the self-regulating control system
	CTC 与其他系统的接口 CTC interface with other systems	CTC 与其他系统的接口方式及传输侧信息	能够通过所学的知识分析 CTC 系统与同他接口的系统间传输的主要信息	培养学生对系统整体认识的能力及联系其他系统的能力	掌握与计算机联锁、微机监测、列控中心的接口方式及传输的信息 Master the interface mode and transmitted information of interlocking, microcomputer supervision and control center with computer

序号 No.	毕业要求指标点 Index point of graduation requirement	知识目标 Knowledge goals	技能目标 Ability goals	素质目标 Quality goals	教学内容 Teaching contents
3	CTC 与其他系统的接口 CTC interface with other systems	The mode of CTC interface with other systems and transfer information	Analyze the main information transmitted between the CTC system and other system through the interfaces through the knowledge learned	Develop students' general ideas of the system and the ability to connect with other systems	熟悉 CTC 与调度命令无线上传系统、无线调车机车信号和调车监控等系统的接口方式及发送的信息 Familiar with CTC and dispatching command wireless upload system, interface mode and the sent massages of wireless shunting locomotive signal and shunting supervision system
	CTC 设备认识及相关操作 CTC equipment recognition and operation	了解铁路 CTC 系统体系结构和设备组成 Understand CTC systemic composition and facilities	掌握 CTC 系统的基本操作 Master the fundamental operation of CTC system	培养学生的职业素养及对设备的基本操作技能 Cultivate students' vocational quality and basic operational skills	了解铁路 CTC 系统体系结构和设备组成 Understand CTC system's architecture and composition in railway 掌握车站自律机的功能和结构 Master the function and structure of the station self-regulating machine 掌握 CTC 系统的基本操作 Master the basic operation of CTC system

表 3 课程教学目标与内容 2

Table 3 Teaching Objectives and Contents 2

序号 NO.	项目（模块） Items	任务（单元） Tasks	教学内容 Teaching contents	重点、难点 Key points and difficulties	学时 Hours
1	项目 1：远动系统认知 Item 1: Telomotor system recognition	1.1 远动控制系统的基本概念、远动系统在铁路信号控制系统中的实际应用 The basic concept of telomotor; the practical application of remote control system in railway signal control system	熟悉远程控制系统的分类和作用 Familiar with the classification and function of remote control system 掌握遥控、遥信、遥测系统的概念和控制原理 Master system concept and control principle of remote control, remote massage, telemeter 掌握 TDCS、CTC 是哪种远动系统 Know well about TDCS and CTC	重点：遥控、遥信、遥测系统控制原理及基本组成 Key points: control principle and basic composition of remote control, remote massage and telemeter system 难点：遥测、遥信系统的区别 Difficulties: the difference of remote control and remote massage system	2
2		1.2 铁路运输调度指挥系统概述 Introduction of railway transportation dispatch and command system	掌握铁路运输调度指挥自动控制系统的概述 Overview of dispatching command automatic control system in railway transportation	重点：远动系统在铁路信号控制系统中的实际应用 Key points: the practical application of remote control system in railway signal control system	2

续表

序号 NO.	项目（模块） Items	任务（单元） Tasks	教学内容 Teaching contents	重点、难点 Key points and difficulties	学时 Hours
3	项目2：列车调度指挥系统（TDCS）维护 Item 2: Maintenance of train dispatching command system (TDCS)	2.1 TDCS系统结构及工作原理认知 Recognition of system structure and working principle in TDCS	了解TDCS的发展方向、技术及功能特点 Understand the development direction, technology and functional characteristics of TDCS 掌握TDCS的整体结构和网络结构 Master the overall structure and network structure of TDCS 掌握TDCS网络特点及各个层的功能 Master TDCS's network features and function of each layer	重点：TDCS整体结构和网络结构 Key points: overall structure and network structure of TDCS 难点：TDCS各层网络的功能。 Difficulties: the function of each layer's network TDCS	2
4		2.2 铁路总公司调度指挥中心TDCS TDCS of railway corporation	熟悉铁路局总公司调度指挥中心的TDCS的网络结构；掌握铁路局总公司调度指挥中心的设备组成和主要功能 Familiar with the network structure of TDCS in the dispatching command center of railway Bureau; Master the equipment composition and main functions of the dispatching command center of the Railway Bureau	重点：铁路局总公司调度指挥中心的TDCS的网络结构及设备组成 Key points: the TDCS network structure and equipment composition of the TDCS command center 难点：铁路局总公司调度指挥中心网络结构 Difficulties: the network structure of the dispatching center of the railway Bureau head office	4
5		2.3 铁路局调度指挥中心TDCS TDCS Control Center of Railway Bureau	熟悉铁路局调度所TDCS网络结构 Familiar with TDCS network structure of railway bureau 掌握铁路局调度所的TDCS整体结构及设备组成 Master the TDCS structure and equipment composition of Railway Bureau 掌握调度所TDCS的功能及信息流程 Master the function and information flow of TDCS	重点：调度所TDCS的功能及网络结构 Key points: the function and network structure of TDCS 难点：调度所TDCS的功能 Difficulties: the function of TDCS in shunting center	6
6		2.4 车站TDCS TDCS in the station	熟悉车站TDCS网络结构 Familiar with station's TDCS network structure 掌握车站TDCS结构及设备组成 Master station's TDCS structure and equipment composition 掌握车站设备的功能 Master the function of station equipment 掌握TDCS系统与其他系统接口 Master the interface between TDCS system and other systems	重点：车站TDCS网络结构及设备组成 Key points: station's TDCS network structure and composition 难点：车站分机采集处理设备 Difficulties: acquisition and processing equipment of station extension	4

续表

序号 NO.	项目（模块） Items	任务（单元） Tasks	教学内容 Teaching contents	重点、难点 Key points and difficulties	学时 Hours
7	项目 2：列车调度指挥系统（TDCS）维护 Item 2: Maintenance of train dispatching command system (TDCS)	2.5 TDCS 设备认识及 TDCS 设备操作 The recognition and operation of TDCS equipment	了解铁路列车调度指挥系统的框架结构，掌握 TDCS 系统的设备组成，掌握 TDCS 系统的基本操作 Understand the framework of railway train dispatching and command system; Master the composition of TDCS system; Master the basic operation of TDCS system	重点：TDCS 系统的基本操作 Key points: basic operation of TDCS system	4
8	项目 3：调度集中（CTC）系统维护 Item 3: CTC system maintenance	3.1 CTC 系统认知及系统结构 The recognition of CTC and its structure	了解分散自律调度集中的系统；了解分散自律调度集中系统的发展及现状。 熟悉 CTC 系统整体网络结构；熟悉调度中心及车站子系统的设备组合 Understand the dispatching and self-regulation centralized system, and their developments and situations, be familiar with the network structure of CTC system and the constitution of subsystems	重点：分散自律调度集中的系统；CTC 系统整体网络结构，CTC 系统和 TDCS 的区别和联系 Key points: dispatching and self-regulation centralized system; The overall network structure of CTC system, the difference and connection between CTC system and TDCS 难点：CTC 系统整体网络结构 Difficulties: the overall network structure of the CTC system	2
9		3.2 CTC 系统调度中心子系统维护 Maintenance of CTC dispatching center's subsystem	掌握 CTC 调度中心系统构成 Master the structure of CTC dispatching center system 了解 CTC 中心巡检、检修作业标准 Understand the inspection and maintenance standards of CTC's central 掌握调度中心设备操作 Master the operation of dispatching center equipment	重点：掌握调度中心设备操作 Key points: master the operation of equipment in dispatching center 难点：掌握调度中心设备操作 Difficulties: master the operation of equipment in dispatching center	2
10		3.3 CTC 车站子系统维护 Maintenance of CTC's station subsystem	掌握车站子系统设备构成；掌握自律机的组成，各板件的作用 Master the structure of station subsystem equipment; Master the composition of the self - discipline machine and the role of each plate 了解 CTC 车站设备巡检、检修作业程序 Understand the inspection and maintenance procedures of CTC station equipment	重点：车站子系统设备构成 Key points: station subsystem equipment composition 难点：自律机的组成，各板件的作用 Difficulties: the composition of the self-discipline machine, the function of each board	2

续表

序号 NO.	项目（模块） Items	任务（单元） Tasks	教学内容 Teaching contents	重点、难点 Key points and difficulties	学时 Hours
11					
12		3.4 CTC 系统功能和原理实现 Realization of CTC's function and principle	掌握 CTC 控制模式 Master CTC control mode 熟悉 CTC 系统的整体功能 Familiar with the overall function of the CTC system 掌握 CTC 系统的行车指挥功能、调度集中功能、行车调度功能 Master the of driving command, centralized dispatching and driving dispatching functions of the CTC system 掌握自律控制系统的基本原理 Master the basic principles of the self-discipline control system	重点：CTC 控制模式及功能 Key points: CTC control mode and function 难点:自律控制系统基本原理 Difficulties: the basic principles of self-discipline control system	4
13		3.5 CTC 与其他系统的接口 Interfaces between CTC and other systems	掌握与计算机联锁、微机监测、列控中心的接口方式及传输的信息 Master the interface mode and transmitted information of microcomputer monitoring and column control center interlocked with computer 熟悉 CTC 与调度命令无线上传系统、无线调车机车信号和调车监控等系统的接口方式及发送的信息	重点：CTC 与系统的接口方式及传输的信息 Key points: the interface mode between CTC and the system and the information transmitted 难点：CTC 与其他系统之间输出的主要信息 Difficulties: main information output between CTC and other systems	4
14		3.6 CTC 设备认识及相关操作 CTC recognition and operation	了解铁路 CTC 系统体系结构和设备组成；掌握车站自律机的功能和结构 Understand railway CTC system architecture and equipment composition; Master the function and structure of the station self-discipline machine 掌握 CTC 系统的基本操作 Master the basic operation of CTC system	重点：CTC 系统设备组成及模拟操作 Key points: CTC system equipment composition and simulation 难点：CTC 系统的模拟操作 Difficulties: simulation of CTC system	4

说明：本课程标准适用于 28～36 学时的“铁路行车调度集中系统维护”课程的教学，表 3 中的学时为建议和参考学时，实际教学内容和课时可结合课程标准，根据教学的专业和课时进行选择和调整。

Notes: this curriculum standard applies to the teaching of The Maintenance of Centralized Traffic Control System, accounting for 28—36 teaching periods. The teaching hours in table 3 are arranged for reference, the actual teaching contents and periods can be adjusted according to the major and practical teaching hours.

四、课程考核 Course Assessment

（1）课程考核分为总结性评价和过程性评价，关注学生个体差异。

Course assessment consists of summative evaluation and process evaluation, focusing on students' individual difference.

（2）总结性评价包括标准化试题的闭卷考试。

The summative evaluation includes standardized test.

（3）过程性评价指使用铁道信号自动控制专业教学资源库开展线上、线下混合式教学，由线上成绩、线下成绩、线上作业和线上考试组成。对项目中的实践技能进行考核，考核内容可以根据实践教学设备的变化进行相应的调整。

Process evaluation is composed of online and off-line performance, online assignment and online test by using the online and off-line blended teaching through teaching resources database of railway signaling automatic control major. The usual performance and awareness in different modules are also evaluated. Assessment contents can be adjusted according to the practical situation.

（4）课程考核比例：过程性评价占 50%，总结性评价占 50%。

The proportion of course assessment: process evaluation accounts for 50%, while summative assessment accounts for 50%.

五、实施要求

1. 授课教师基本要求 Basic Requirements for Teachers

（1）具备铁道信号专业或相关专业岗位工作经历，大学本科及以上学历，具有高等学校教师资格证书。

Work experiences related to railway signaling major or relevant major, bachelor degree and above, with the teacher certificate of higher education.

（2）具备相应技术职称或本专业三级及以上职业资格证书。

With relevant technical titles or professional vocational qualification certificate of level-3 and above.

（3）具有“双师型”教师证书。

With the certificate of dual qualified teacher.

（4）具备开发职业课程、组织与实施教学的能力。

Ability to develop vocational course and organize and implement teaching.

（5）专业教师每两年到现场实践锻炼应不少于两个月。

No less than two months' field practice every two years.

2. 教学方法和策略 Teaching Methods and Strategies

（1）教学方法 Teaching methods。

本着“淡化理论、够用为度、培养技能、重在应用”的原则，课程注重培养学生分析和解决问题的能力以及对所学知识进行应用的能力。本课程主要推荐采用讲授教学法、讨论教学法、实验教学法、案例教学法、指导自学法等。

In line with the principle of “weaken the theories to be adequate for using, and emphasize of applications when cultivate skills ”, the course focuses on cultivating students' ability to analyze and solve problems and to apply the knowledge they have learned. This course mainly recommends the use of lecture teaching method, discussion teaching method, experimental teaching method, case teaching method, self-study teaching method, etc.

（2）教学策略 Teaching strategies。

教学过程中可采用铁道信号自动控制专业教学资源库实现混合式教学，可在专业教学资源库预先给学生操作视频或微课，然后课堂上通过讲解和实操提醒注意事项，理论知识点也可以通过专业教学资源库的课程组课、在线答疑、网络考试、作业布置和修改等功能实现混合式教学。

The blended teaching through teaching resources database of railway signaling automatic control major is adopted during the process. t is suggested to provide students with video or micro-learning in advance, then generates the precautions during the instruction and practice in the class. Achieve blend teaching through the functions of course grouping, online question answering, online examination, assignment and modification of professional teaching resource database.

在实践教学环节，采用企业实地考察，请企业专家、技术能手来给学生授课，让学生清楚企业的工作流程、岗位职责要求和企业岗位工作的其他纪律规定。

In the field practice, enterprise field visits are used, and enterprise experts and technical experts are invited to teach students, so that students can understand the company's workflow, job responsibilities and other disciplinary requirements.

第四节 “铁路信号中的通信技术应用”课程标准

Curriculum Standard for Communication Technology Application in Railway Signal

一、课程性质 Nature of the Course

1. 课程类型、课程功能 Types and Functions

本课程是铁道信号自动控制专业的主干课，共计 36 课时，2.0 学分；是学生在学习了“电路分析基础”“铁道概论”“电子技术基础”“铁路信号基础设备维护”等课程，具备铁道信号系统知识的基础上，开设的一门理论+实践课。其功能是对接铁道信号自动控制专业人才培养目标，面向车站与区间信号设备维修信号工工作岗位，培养学生关于电信号设备的供电概况的认识、日常维护、设备检修和故障分析处理的能力，并为后续“铁路行车调度集中系统维护”“铁路信号集中监测系统运用与维护”等课程的学习奠定基础。

This course is the main course for the railway signal automatic control major, including 36 hours, 2.0 credits. It is an integration of theory and practice for the students who have learned the courses of the Basis of Circuit Analysis, Introduction to Railway, Basic of Electronic Technology, Maintenance of Railway Signal Basic Equipment, etc. and have the basic knowledge of railway signal system. Its function is to connect with the objectives of railway signal automatic control specialized training, such as maintenance of signal equipment in station and section, and trains students with the knowledge of electric signal equipment and the ability for daily maintenance, apparatus maintenance and fault analysis and processing, and lay the foundation for the subsequent courses such as Maintenance of Railway Train Dispatching Centralized System and Operation and Maintenance of Railway Signal Centralized Monitoring System.

2. 课程功能定位 Orientation of the Function

表 1　课程功能定位分析

Table 1　Analysis of the Function

对接的工作岗位 Jobs	对接培养的职业岗位能力 Abilities
车站与区间信号设备维修信号工、电子与电气设备检修信号工、机车信号设备维修信号工 Signalman in station or section for signal equipment maintenance, for electronic and electrical equipment maintenance, for locomotive signal device maintenance	按照中国铁路总公司最新颁布的《铁路信号维护规则》对铁路信号中的子系统通信进行维护的能力 Ability to maintain the subsystem's communication in railway signals in accordance with the latest *Rules for Railway Signal Maintenance* promulgated by China Railway Corporation

二、课程目标与内容 Course Objective and Content

1. 课程总目标 General Objectives

通过本课程的学习将要达到的主要目的是，使学生了解通信技术在铁路信号系统中的应用，掌握通信技术的一些基本概念和应用方法。主要任务是通过学习能够使学生在已有的知识基础上，对通信技术在铁路信号系统中的应用从整体上有一个较清晰的全面、系统的了解。

The purpose of this course is to enable students to understand the application of communication technology into railway signal systems, and to master some basic concepts and application methods of communication technology. The main task is to enable students to have a clear, comprehensive and systematic understanding of the application of communication technology in railway signal systems based on the existing knowledge

2. 课程具体目标 Specific Objectives

具体表述课程的内容及学生应达到的知识目标、技能目标、素质目标，在进行目标表述时应以学生作为行为主体来表述。

Describe the content of the course and the knowledge goals, skill goals, and quality goals that the students should achieve, the students should be the main body of behavior in the process.

表 2　课程教学目标与内容 1

Table 2　Teaching Objectives and Contents 1

序号 NO.	毕业要求指标点 Index points for graduation requirements	知识目标 Knowledge goals	技能目标 Ability goals	素质目标 Quality goals	教学内容 Teaching contents
1	信号设备组成及铁路信号中的通信技术发展 The composition of signal equipment and the development of communication technology in railway signals	了解铁路信号的发展和组成 Understand the development and composition of railway signals	熟知信号中通信技术的基本知识 Familiar with the basic knowledge of communication technology in signals	1. 对通信相关新知识能触类旁通 Comprehend the new knowledge related to communication by analogy 2. 培养学生独立解决问题的能力 Develop students' ability to solve problems independently	铁路信号系统的发展和组成 Development and composition of railway signal system
2		了解铁路信号系统的构成 Understand the composition of the railway signaling system			现代铁路信号系统的组成 Composition of modern railway signaling system

续表

序号 NO.	毕业要求指标点 Index points for graduation requirements	知识目标 Knowledge goals	技能目标 Ability goals	素质目标 Quality goals	教学内容 Teaching contents
3	信号设备组成及铁路信号中的通信技术发展 The composition of signal equipment and the development of communication technology in railway signals	理解通信技术在铁路信号中的应用形式 Understand the application forms of communication technology in railway signals			通信技术在铁路信号中的应用 Application of communication technology in railway signal
4		理解数据通信的基本概念 Understand the basic concepts of data communication	熟知数据通信与网络基础 Familiar with data communication and network bases		数据通信及其系统 Data communication and its system
5	数据通信与网络基础 Data communication and network foundation	掌握通信网的网络拓扑结构 Master the network topology of the communication network			数据通信网的拓扑 Topology of data communication network
6		了解数据通信网的网络体系结构 Understand the network architecture of the data communication network			数据通信网的体系结构 Data communication network architecture
7	现场设备通信技术 Field device communication technology	了解异步和同步通信格式、协议，掌握串行通信在铁路信号设备中的应用 Understand the asynchronous and synchronous communication formats and protocols, and master the application of serial communication in railway signal equipment	熟知现场设备通信技术 Familiar with field device communication technology	3. 培养学生的团队协作精神 Cultivate students' teamwork spirit 4. 较强的动手意识 Strong hands-on consciousness 5. 表达能力 Expression ability	串行通信技术 Serial communication technology
8		理解 CAN 总线技术、ProfiBus 总线技术 Understand CAN bus technology, ProfiBus technology			现场总线技术 Field bus line technology
9		理解各种列车通信网络 Understand various train communication networks			列车通信网络 Train communication network
10		掌握计算机网络的基本概念 Master the basic concepts of computer networks			计算机网络基础 Computer network foundation
11	IP 网络技术 IP network technology	掌握 TCP/IP 协议的基础 Master the foundation of TCP/IP protocol	熟知现场设备通信技术 Familiar with field device communication technology		TCP/IP 协议 TCP/IP protocol
12		了解 IP 广域网技术 Understand IP WAN technology			IP 广域网技术 IP WAN technology

续表

序号 NO.	毕业要求指标点 Index points for graduation requirements	知识目标 Knowledge goals	技能目标 Ability goals	素质目标 Quality goals	教学内容 Teaching contents
13	IP 网络技术 IP network technology	理解 IP 网络在铁路信号中应用 Understand the application of IP network in railway signals	熟知现场设备通信技术 Familiar with field device communication technology		IP 网络在铁路信号中的应用 Application of IP network in railway signal
14	列车移动通信技术 Train movement communication technology	理解铁路无线通信的基本概念 Understand the basic concepts of railway wireless communication			铁路无线通信概述 Overview of railway wireless communication
15		理解列车移动通信原理 Understand the principles of train movement communication			列车移动通信原理 Train movement communication principle
16		理解 GSM-R 系统 Understand GSM-R system			GSM-R 系统 GSM-R system
17		理解基于 GSM-R 的列车运行控制系统 Understand train operation control system based on GSM-R			基于 GSM-R 的列车运行控制系统 Train operation control system based on GSM-R
18		了解 GSM-R 在信号中的应用 Understand the application of GSM-R in signaling			GSM-R 在信号中的应用实例 Application example of GSM-R in signaling

表 3　课程教学安排 2

Table 3　Teaching Arrangement 2

序号 NO.	项目（模块） Items	任务（单元） Tasks	教学内容 Teaching contents	重点、难点 Key points and difficulties	学时 Hours
1	项目 1：信号设备组成及铁路信号中的通信技术发展 Item 1: composition of signaling equipment and development of communication technology in railway signals	1.1 铁路信号系统的发展和组成 Development and composition of railway signal system	了解铁路信号的发展和组成 Understand the development and composition of railway signals	重点、难点：铁路信号系统的组成 Key points and difficulties: the composition of the railway signal system	2
2		1.2 通信技术在铁路信号中的应用形式 Application mode of communication technology in railway signal	理解通信技术在铁路信号中的应用形式 Understand the application of communication technology in railway signals	重点：通用异步串行通信技术、现场总线技术、车地通信技术 Key points: universal asynchronous serial communication technology, field bus technology, vehicle-ground communication technology 难点：通用异步串行通信技术、现场总线技术 Difficulties: universal asynchronous serial communication technology, field bus technology	2

续表

序号 NO.	项目（模块） Items	任务（单元） Tasks	教学内容 Teaching contents	重点、难点 Key points and difficulties	学时 Hours
3	项目 2：数据通信与网络基础 Item 2: data communication and network foundation	2.1 数据通信及其系统 Data communication and its system	理解数据通信基本概念 Understand the basic concepts of data communication	重点：数据通信的基本概念 Key points: basic concepts of data communication 难点：通信系统模型 Difficulties: communication system model	2
4		2.2 数据通信网的拓扑、传输介质 Topology and transmission medium of data communication network	掌握通信网的网络拓扑结构、传输介质 Master the network topology structure and transmission medium of the communication network	重点、难点：网络拓扑结构 Key points and difficulties: network topology structure	2
5		2.3 数据通信网的交换技术和网络体系结构 Exchange technology and network architecture of the data communication network	了解数据通信网的交换技术和网络体系结构 Understand the switching technology and network architecture of the data communication network	重点：三种交换技术、osi 网络体系结构 Key points: three switching technologies, osi network architecture 难点：分组交换 Difficulties: packet switching	6
6	项目 3：现场设备通信技术 Item 3: field device communication technology	3.1 串行通信技术 Serial communication technology	了解异步和同步通信格式、协议，掌握串行通信在铁路信号设备中的应用 Understand the asynchronous and synchronous communication formats and protocols, and master the application of serial communication in railway signal equipment	重点、难点：异步和同步通信格式、协议 Key points and difficulties: asynchronous and synchronous communication formats and protocols	2
7		3.2 现场总线技术 Field bus technology	理解 CAN 总线技术、ProfiBus 总线技术 Understand CAN bus technology, ProfiBus technology	重点、难点：CAN 总线技术、Profibus 总线 Key points and difficulties: CAN bus technology, Profibus bus	2
8		3.3 列车通信网络 Vehicle communication network	理解各种列车通信网络 Understand various train communication networks	重点、难点：各种列车通信网络 Key points and difficulties: various train communication networks	6
9	项目 4：IP 网络技术 Item 4: IP network technology	4.1 计算机网络基础 Computer network foundation	掌握计算机网络的基本概念 Master the basic concepts of computer network	重点：计算机网络的定义 Key points: definition of computer network 难点：计算机网络的分类 Difficulties: classification of computer network	2
10		4.2 TCP/IP 协议 TCP/IP protocol	掌握 TCP/IP 协议的基础 Master the foundation of TCP/IP protocol	重点：TCP/IP 协议的主要内容、IP 地址及其分类 Key points: main content of TCP/IP protocol, IP address and its classification 难点：TCP/IP 协议的工作原理、IP 地址及其分类 Difficulties: the working principle, IP address and classification of TCP/IP protocol	2

序号 NO.	项目（模块）Items	任务（单元）Tasks	教学内容 Teaching contents	重点、难点 Key points and difficulties	学时 Hours
11	项目 4：IP 网络技术 Item 4: IP network technology	4.3 IP 局域网、IP 广域网技术 IP LAN network, IP WAN technology	了解 IP 局域网、IP 广域网技术 Understand IP LAN network, IP WAN technology	重点、难点：IP 局域网技术、IP 广域网技术 Key points and difficulties: IP LAN technology, IP WAN technology	2
12		4.4 IP 网络在铁路信号中的应用 Application of IP network in railway signal	理解 IP 网络在铁路信号中应用 Understand the application of IP network in railway signal	重点：IP 网络在铁路信号中的应用、信号安全数据网 Key points: application of IP network in railway signal, signal safety data network 难点：信号安全数据网 Difficulties: signal security data network	2
13	项目 5：列车移动通信技术 Item 5: Train movement communication technology	5.1 铁路无线通信概述 Overview of railway wireless communication	理解铁路无线通信的基本概念 Understand the basic concepts of railway wireless communication	重点、难点：铁路无线通信 Key points and difficulties: railway wireless communication	2
14		5.2 列车移动通信原理 Train movement communication principle	理解列车移动通信原理 Understand the principles of train movement communication	重点、难点：多址连接技术、大区制与小区制 Key points and difficulties: multi-access technology, large-area system and community system	2
15		5.3 GSM-R 系统 GSM-R system	理解 GSM-R 系统 Understand GSM-R system	重点：GSM-R 集群调度业务、特殊业务 Key points: GSM-R cluster dispatching service, special service 难点：GSM-R 系统构成 Difficulties: GSM-R system structure	2
16		5.4 基于 GSM-R 的列车运行控制系统 Train operation control system based on GSM-R	理解基于 GSM-R 的列车运行控制系统 Understand the train operation control system based on GSM-R	重点、难点：GSM-R 组网方案 Key points and difficulties: GSM-R networking solution	2

说明：本课程标准适用于 32～40 学时的“铁路信号中的通信技术应用”课程的教学，表 3 中的学时为建议和参考学时，实际教学内容和课时可结合课程标准，根据教学的专业和课时进行选择和调整。

Notes: this curriculum standard applies to the teaching of The Application of Communication Technology in Railway Signal, accounting for 32—40 teaching periods. The teaching hours in table 3 are arranged for reference, the actual teaching contents and periods can be adjusted according to the major and practical teaching hours.

三、课程考核 Course Assessment

（1）课程考核分为总结性评价和过程性评价，关注学生个体差异。

Course assessment consists of summative evaluation and process evaluation, focusing on Students' individual difference.

（2）总结性评价包括标准化试题的闭卷考试。

The summative evaluation includes standardized test.

（3）过程性评价指使用铁道信号自动控制专业教学资源库开展线上、线下混合式教学，由线上成绩、线下成绩、线上作业和线上考试组成。对项目中的平时作业、基本实践技能进行考核。考核内容可以根据实践教学设备的变化进行相应的调整。

Process evaluation is composed of online and off-line performance, online assignment and online test by using the online and off-line blended teaching through teaching resources database of railway signaling automatic control major. The usual performance and basic practical skills are also evaluated. Assessment contents can be adjusted according to the practical situation.

（4）课程考核比例：过程性评价占 30%，总结性评价占 70%。

The proportion of course assessment: process evaluation accounts for 30%, while summative assessment accounts for 70%.

四、实施要求 Implementation Requirements

1. 授课教师基本要求 Basic Requirements for Teachers

（1）具备铁道信号专业或相关专业岗位工作经历，大学本科及以上学历，具有高等学校教师资格证书。

Work experiences related to railway signaling major or relevant major, bachelor degree and above, with the teacher certificate of higher education.

（2）具备相应技术职称或本专业三级及以上职业资格证书。

With relevant technical titles or professional vocational qualification certificate of level-3 and above.

（3）具有“双师型”教师证书。

With the certificate of dual qualified teacher.

（4）具备开发职业课程、组织与实施教学的能力。

Ability to develop vocational course and organize and implement teaching.

（5）专业教师每两年到现场实践锻炼应不少于两个月。

No less than two months' field practice every two years.

2. 教学方法和策略 Teaching Methods and Strategies

（1）教学方法 Teaching methods。

本着“淡化理论、够用为度、培养技能、重在应用”的原则，课程注重培养学生分析和解决问题的能力以及对所学知识进行应用的能力。本课程主要推荐采用讲授教学法、讨论教学法、实验教学法、案例教学法、指导自学法等。

In line with the principle of “weaken the theories to be adequate for using, and emphasize the applications when cultivate skills”, the course focuses on cultivating students' ability to analyze and solve problems and to apply the knowledge they have learned. This course mainly recommends the use of lecture teaching method, discussion teaching method, experimental teaching method, case teaching method, self-study teaching method, etc.

（2）教学策略 Teaching strategies。

教学过程中采用铁道信号自动控制专业教学资源库实现混合式教学，可在专业教学资源库预先给学生操作视频或微课，然后课堂上通过讲解和实操提醒注意事项。理论知识点也可以通过专业教学资源库的课程组课、在线答疑、网络考试、作业布置和修改等功能实现混合式教学。

Blend teaching is adaptable in the teaching process by using to teaching resource database of railway signal automatic control major. It is suggested to provide students with video or micro-learning in advance, then generates the precautions during the instruction and practice in the class. Achieve blend teaching through the functions of course grouping, online question answering, online examination, assignment and modification of professional teaching resource database.

在实践教学环节，采用企业实地考察，请企业专家、技术能手来给学生授课，让学生清楚企业的工作流程、岗位职责要求和企业岗位工作的其他纪律规定。

In the field practice, enterprise field visits are used, and enterprise experts and technical experts are invited to teach students, so that students can understand the company's workflow, job responsibilities and other disciplinary requirements

第五节 “铁路信号基础设备维护实训”课程标准

Curriculum Standard for Maintenance Training of Railway Infrastructure

一、课程性质 Nature of Course

1. 课程类型、课程功能 Types and Functions

本课程是铁道信号自动控制专业的主干课，共计 24 课时，1.5 学分；是学生在学习了“电子技术基础”“电路分析基础”“铁路信号基础设备维护”等课程，掌握了铁路道岔转辙设备的结构组成、工作原理，具备了电路分析、故障处理能力的基础上，开设的一门实践课。其功能是对接铁道信号自动控制专业人才培养目标，面向铁路企业，从事铁路信号设备的安装调试、维修养护工作岗位，培养信号设备的维护与检修、故障信息的收集、分析与处理能力，并为后续“铁路车站自动控制系统维护实训”“铁路信号设计与施工实训”“信号工技能鉴定实训”等课程的学习奠定基础。

This course is the main course for the railway signal automatic control major, induding 48 hours, 3 credits. It is a piratical course for the students who have learned The Basis of Electronic Technology, The Basis of Circuit Analysis, Railway Signaling Basic Equipment Maintenance etc., and have certain knowledge of the composition and working principle of railway switches, and the ability of circuit analysis, troubleshooting. Its function is to connect with the training goals of railway signal professionals with the ability to test, overhaul and troubleshoot in locks and computer interlocking equipment, and lay the foundation for the subsequent learning of Training of Railway Signal Design and Construction, Signalman Skills Identification Training and other courses.

2. 课程功能定位 Orientation of the Function

表 1　课程功能定位分析

Table 1　Analysis of Orientation of the Function

对接的工作岗位 Jobs	对接培养的职业岗位能力 Abilities
车站与区间信号设备维修信号工岗位 Signalman for signal equipment maintenance in station or section	按照中国铁路总公司最新颁布的《铁路信号维护规则》对车站、区间、驼峰信号设备进行准确认知及测量的能力 Accurately recognize and measure station, section, and hump signal facilities in accordance with the latest *Rules for Railway Signal Maintenance* issued by China Railway Corporation
信号工程施工岗位 Signal engineering construction	能按照铁路信号工程施工技术及工艺标准对相关信号设备进行施工、安装的能力 Construct and install related signal facilities in accordance with railway signal engineering construction technology and process standards

二、课程目标与内容 Objective and Content

1. 课程总目标 General Objectives

让学生掌握 ZD6-A 型电动转辙机牵引道岔的机械调整等铁路基本技能。通过本课程的学习，理论联系实际，加强学生动手能力训练的同时，培养学生分析问题和解决问题的能力。为学生进一步学习后续课程和专业知识，奠定坚实的基础。

Enable students to master the basic railway skills such as the mechanical adjustment of ZD6-A electric traction switch. Through the study, the theory is combined with practice, and the training of students' practical ability is strengthened, and the students' ability to analyze and solve problems is cultivated. To lay a solid foundation for students to further study the follow-up courses and professional knowledge.

2. 课程具体目标 Specific Objectives

表 2　课程教学目标与内容

Table 2　Teaching Objectives and Content

序号 No.	毕业要求指标点 Index point of graduation requirement	知识目标 Knowledge goals	技能目标 Skill goals	素质目标 Quality goals	教学内容 Teaching contents
1	形成信号工职场工作的基本工作规范；按标准对 ZD6-A 型电动转辙机牵引道岔进行机械调整 Develop the basic work specification for signalman in the workplace; mechanical adjustment of traction switch of the ZD6-A electric switch motor according to the standard	ZD6-A 型电动转辙机牵引道岔密贴调整方法 Stick adjustment method of traction turnout of ZD6-A electric switch motor	ZD6-A 型电动转辙机牵引道岔定位、反位密贴调整 Positioning of traction turnout and stick adjustment of anti-position of traction turnout of ZD6-A electric switch motor	1. 熟悉现场工作的环境与工作要求 Familiar with the environment and requirements of on-site work 2. 培养分析与解决问题的能力 Develop the ability to analyze and solve problems	ZD6-A 型电动转辙机牵引道岔密贴调整实践训练 Practical training of the stick adjustment of traction turnouts of ZD6-A electric switch motor
2		ZD6-A 型电动转辙机牵引道岔表示调整方法 ZD6-A electric traction switch indication adjustment method	ZD6-A 型电动转辙机牵引道岔定位、反位表示调整 ZD6-A electric traction switch positioning, reverse position indication adjustment		ZD6-A 型电动转辙机牵引道岔表示调整实践训练 Practical training of the indication adjustment of traction turnouts of ZD6-A electric switch motor

表 3　课程教学安排

Table 3　teaching arrangement

序号 NO.	项目（模块） Items	任务（单元） Tasks	教学内容 Teaching content	重点、难点 Key points and difficulties	学时 Hours
1	ZD6-A 型电动转辙机牵引道岔机械调整 Mechanical adjustment of traction switch of ZD6-A electric switch motor	1.1 ZD6-A 型电动转辙机牵引道岔密贴调整 ZD6-A electric traction turnout stick adjustment	ZD6-A 型电动转辙机牵引道岔密贴调整实践训练 Practical training of the stick adjustment of traction turnouts of ZD6-A electric switch motor	重点、难点：ZD6-A 型电动转辙机牵引道岔密贴调整方法 Key points and difficulties: traction turnout stick adjustment method of ZD6-A electric switch motor.	12
2		1.2 ZD6-A 型电动转辙机牵引道岔表示调整 ZD6-A electric traction switch indication adjustment	ZD6-A 型电动转辙机牵引道岔表示调整实践训练 Traction turnout indication adjustment practice training of ZD6-A electric switch motor	重点、难点：ZD6-A 型电动转辙机牵引道岔表示调整方法 Key points and difficulties: traction turnout indication adjustment method of ZD6-A electric switch motor	12

三、课程考核　Course Assessment

（1）课程考核分为总结性评价和过程性评价，关注学生个体差异。

Course assessment consists of summative evaluation and process evaluation，focusing on students' individual difference.

（2）总结性评价为技能考试。

The summative evaluation includes standardized test.

（3）过程性评价指使用铁道信号自动控制专业教学资源库开展线上线、下混合式教学，由线上成绩、线下成绩、线上作业和线上考试组成。对项目中的实践技能进行考核，考核内容可以根据实践教学设备的变化进行相应的调整。

Process evaluation is composed of online and off-line performance, online assignment and online test by using the online and off-line blended teaching through teaching resources database of railway signaling automatic control major. The usual performance and awareness in different modules are also evaluated. Assessment contents can be adjusted according to the practical situation.

（4）课程考核比例：过程性评价占 40%，总结性评价占 60%。

The proportion of course assessment: process evaluation accounts for 40%, while summative assessment 60%.

四、实施要求 Implementation Requirements

1. 授课教师基本要求 Basic Requirements for Teachers

（1）具备铁道信号专业或相关专业岗位工作经历，大学本科及以上学历，具有高等学校教师资格证书。

Work experiences related to railway signaling major or relevant major, bachelor degree and above, with the teacher certificate of higher education.

（2）具备相应技术职称或本专业三级及以上职业资格证书。

With relevant technical titles or professional vocational qualification certificate of level-3 and above.

（3）具有“双师型”教师证书。

With the certificate of dual qualified teacher.

（4）具备开发职业课程、组织与实施教学的能力。

Ability to develop vocational course and organize and implement teaching.

（5）专业教师每两年到现场实践锻炼应不少于两个月。

No less than two months' field practice every two years.

2. 教学方法和策略 Teaching Methods and Strategies

（1）教学方法 Teaching methods。

主要采用项目化教学法、情景教学法和工作过程导向教学法。将高速铁路道岔转辙设备维护的任务作为代表性的项目，实践学紧密围绕技能训练开展，应用大量的视频和图片，通过对比、举例、通俗的比喻等方法使学生更好地理解和掌握相关知识，运用多媒体教学手段化解教学难点。

Project teaching method, situational teaching method, and work process-oriented teaching method are adopted. The task of high-speed railway switch equipment maintenance is listed as the typical project, practical learning performs closely around skill training. Largen number of videos and pictures were used to enable students to better understand and master relevant knowledge through comparison, examples, popular metaphors, and teaching difficulties were solved by applying the multimedia teaching method.

（2）教学策略 Teaching strategies。

教学过程中采用铁道信号自动控制专业教学资源库实现混合式教学，可以在专业教学资源库预先给学生操作视频或微课。在教学过程中尽可能设置与铁路道岔转辙设备实际维护工作一致的作业分工、作业内容、作业步骤及要求。充分利用校内实训室等教学资源，根据每个学习任务的实际情况，确定在教学过程中采用小组合作、学生独立实操演练、技术比武等教学形式。

The blended instruction through teaching resources database of railway signaling automatic control major is adopted during teaching process, and the students is advised to study the operation video and micro-lecture previously. Set up the work division, work content, work steps and requirements consistent with the actual maintenance of high-speed railway switch equipment as far as possible. Make full use of the training room and other teaching resources in the school, and determine to adopt the teaching modules such as group cooperation, students' independent practice and technical competition in the teaching process according to the actual situation of each learning task.

在实践教学环节，采用企业实地考察，请企业专家、技术能手来给学生授课，让学生清楚企业的工作流程、岗位职责要求和企业岗位工作的其他纪律规定。

As to the practical teaching aspect, field investigation is adopted. Enterprise experts and technical experts are invited to lecture in order to make Students be clear about the workflows, requirements of job description and work disciplines and rules of posts.

第六节 “铁路车站自动控制系统维护实训”课程标准

Curriculum Standard for Maintenance Training of Train Station Automatic Control System

一、课程性质 Nature of Course

1. 课程类型、课程功能 Types and Functions

本课程是铁道信号自动控制专业的主干课，共计 48 课时，3 学分；是在学生学习了“铁路信号基础设备维护”“铁路车站自动控制系统维护”课程，具备信号继电器检修、信号机维护、轨道电路维护、转辙机维护、防雷及接地设置维护等能力的基础上，开设的一门实践课。其功能是对接铁路信号专业人才培养目标，面向信号工工作岗位，培养学生电气集中联锁和计算机联锁设备的测试、检修和故障处理能力，并为后续“铁路信号设计与施工实训”“信号工技能鉴定实训”等课程的学习奠定基础。

This course is the main course for the railway signal automatic control major, including 48 hours, 3 credits. It is a practical course for the students who have learned the Railway Signal Basic Equipment Maintenance, Railway Station Automatic Control System Maintenance courses, with the capabilities of signal relay maintenance, signal machine maintenance, track circuit maintenance, switch machine maintenance, lightning protection and grounding installation maintenance. Its function is to connect with the training objectives of railway signal professionals with the ability to test, overhaul and troubleshoot in locks and computer interlocking equipment, and lay the foundation for the subsequent learning of Railway Signal Design and Construction Training, Signalman Skills Appraisal Training and other courses.

2. 课程功能定位 Orientation of the Function

表 1 课程功能定位分析

Table 1 Analysis of the Orientation of the Function

对接的工作岗位 Jobs	对接培养的职业岗位能力 Abilities
车站、驼峰信号设备维修信号工岗位 Station and hump signal equipment maintenance signalman	按照中国铁路总公司最新颁布的《铁路信号维护规则》对车站、驼峰信号设备进行维护的能力 Be able to maintain stations' and humps' signal equipment in accordance with the latest *Railway Signal Maintenance Rules* issued by China Railway Corporation

二、课程目标与内容 Objective and Content

1. 课程总目标 General Objectives

能够对 6502 电气集中设备和计算机联锁设备进行操作；能够掌握四线制道岔、五线制道岔控制电路结构、工作原理和故障处理方法，具备四线制道岔、五线制道岔控制电路的故障处理能力；掌握进站信号机、出站信号机和调车信号机点灯电路的组成、工作原理和故障处理方法，具备标准化作业及常见故障处理能力；掌握计算机联锁系统的基本知识，典型计算机联锁系统的组成、工作原理和日常维护程序及标准，具备标准化作业及常见故障处理能力。

Capable of operating 6502 electrical centralized equipment and computer interlocking equipment; Capable of mastering the control circuit structure, working principle and fault handling methods of four-wire turnouts and five-wire turnouts, equipped with the ability of four-wire turnouts and five-wire turnout control circuits fault proussing; Master the composition, working principle and fault processing method of the lighting circuit of inbound signal, outbound signal and shunting signal, with standardized operations and common fault handling capabilities; Master the basic knowledge of computer interlocking system, constitution of typical computer interlocking system, working principle and daily maintenance procedures and standards of the interlocking system; Equipped with the ability of standardized operation and common fault handling.

2. 课程具体目标 Specific Objectives

表 2 课程教学目标与内容 1

Table 2 Teaching Objectives and Contents 1

序号 No.	毕业要求指标点 Index point of graduation requirement	知识目标 Knowledge goals	技能目标 Skill goals	素质目标 Quality goals	教学内容 Teaching contents
1	掌握车站联锁设备操纵使用 Master the operation of station interlocking equipment	熟练掌握车站联锁设备的操作使用方法 Familiar with the operation of station interlocking equipment	能够按照要求对车站联锁设备进行操作 To operate station interlocking equipment as required	强化学生的岗位职业能力 Strengthen students' specialized abilities	车站联锁设备的操纵使用训练 Operation training of station interlocking equipment
2	具备 6502 电路开路故障处理能力 Capable of handling 6502 open circuit faults	掌握 6502 电气集中选择组电路和执行组电路的动作原理 Master the operate principle of 6502 electrical centralized selection group circuit and execution group circuit	能处理 6502 电气集中电路的故障 Handle the failure of 6502 electrical centralized circuits	安全工作意识 Awareness of safety	6502电气集中 1-11 线网络电路开路故障处理训练 Training of 6502 electric ccentralized 1-11 line network open circuit fault processing
2	具备四线制转辙机道岔控制电路故障处理能力 Capable of handling the fault in the switch control circuit of the four-wire switch	熟练掌握四线制道岔控制电路结构、工作原理和故障处理方法 Proficient in the control circuit structure, working principle and fault treatment method of four-wire turnout	能处理四线制转辙机道岔控制电路故障 Deal with the fault of the switch control circuit of the four-wire switch	自主学习能力，团队协作意识 Self-learning ability, teamwork awareness	四线制道岔控制电路故障处理训练 Training of four-wire turnout control circuit fault handling
3	具备五线制转辙机道岔控制电路故障处理能力 Capable of handling the fault in the control circuit of five-wire switch motor switch	熟练掌握五线制道岔控制电路结构、工作原理和故障处理方法 Familiar with the control circuit structure, working principle and fault treatment method of five-wire turnout	能处理五线制转辙机道岔控制电路故障 Deal with the fault of the switch control circuit in the five-wire switch	自主学习能力，团队协作意识 Self-learning ability, teamwork awareness	五线制道岔控制电路故障处理训练 Training of fault handling for control circuit in five-wire turnout

续表

序号 No.	毕业要求指标点 Index point of graduation requirement	知识目标 Knowledge goals	技能目标 Skill goals	素质目标 Quality goals	教学内容 Teaching contents
4	具备信号机标准化作业及常见故障处理能力 Capable of standardized signal operating and common fault handling	熟练掌握进站、出站、调车信号机点灯电路的组成、工作原理和故障处理方法 Proficient in the composition, working principle and fault handling method of the lighting circuit of the inboard, outboard, and shunting signal	能进行标准化作业；能处理信号机常见故障 Carry out standardized operations; Handle common faults of signal machine	规范操作意识，细心，耐心 Standardized operation awareness, be careful and patient	信号点灯电路测试和常见故障处理训练 Training of signal lighting circuit test and common fault handling
5	具备计算机联锁系统标准化作业及常见故障处理能力 Ability to standardize the operation of the computer interlocking system and handle common fault	掌握 TYJL-ADX、DS6-K5B 型计算机联锁系统的设备维护常识与故障处理方法 Master the equipment maintenance knowledge and troubleshooting methods of TYJL-ADX, DS6-K5B computer interlocking system	能处理 TYJL-ADX、DS6-K5B 型计算机联锁系统的设备常见故障 Deal with the common faults of TYJL-ADX, DS6-K5B computer interlocking system	培养计算机联锁系统安全操作意识 Cultivate the consciousness of safe operation of computer interlocking system	TYJL-ADX、DS6-K5B 型计算机联锁系统的设备维护与故障处理训练 Training of equipment maintenance and troubleshooting of TYJL-ADX, DS6-K5B computer interlocking system

表 3　课程教学目标与内容 2

Table 3　Teaching Objectives and Contents 2

序号 No.	项目（模块） Items	任务（单元） Tasks	教学内容 Teaching contents	重点、难点 Key points and difficulties	学时 Hours
1	项目 1：车站联锁知识 Item 1: station interlocking knowledge	车站联锁设备的组成与功能、操纵使用 The composition, function and operation of station interlocking equipment	车站联锁设备的操纵使用训练 Operational training of station interlocking equipment	重点、难点：电气集中设备的操纵使用 Key points and difficulties: the operation and use of electrical centralized equipment	4
2	项目 2：6502 电气集中设备维护 Item 2: maintenance of 6502 electrical centralized equipment	1～11 线网络电路开路故障处理 Open circuit fault handling of 1～11 line network circuit	1～11 线网络网络电路开路故障处理训练 Open circuit fault handling training of 1~11 line network	重点、难点：1～11 线网络电路开路故障处理 Key points and difficulties: open circuit fault handling of 1~11 line network circuit	20
3	项目 3：道岔控制电路设备维护与故障处理 Item 3: maintenance and troubleshooting of turnout control circuit equipment	四线制道岔控制电路故障处理 Trouble-shooting of control circuit for four-wire turnout	四线制道岔控制电路故障处理训练 Training of four-wire turnout control circuit fault handling	重点、难点：四线制道岔控制电路故障处理 Key points and difficulties: fault handling of the four-wire turnout control circuit	8
4		五线制道岔控制电路故障处理 Handling of faults of control circuit for five-wire turnout	五线制道岔控制电路故障处理训练 Training of fault handling for control circuit of five-wire turnout	重点、难点：五线制道岔控制电路故障处理 Key points and difficulties: handling the fault of the five-wire turnout control circuit	8

序号 No.	项目（模块） Items	任务（单元） Tasks	教学内容 Teaching contents	重点、难点 Key points and difficulties	学时 Hours
5	项目 4: 信号机点灯电路故障处理 Item 4: fault handling of the signal lighting circuit	信号机点灯电路常见故障处理 Handling of the common faults of the lighting circuit of signal	信号机点灯电路常见故障分析处理训练 Analysis and training of the common faults of the signal light circuit	重点：信号点灯电路测试和常见故障的分析处理方法 Key points: signal lighting circuit test and common fault analysis and processing methods 难点：信号点灯电路测试和常见故障处理 Difficulties: signal lighting circuit test and common fault handling	4
6	项目 5: 计算机联锁设备维护 Item 5: maintenance of computer interlocking equipment	计算机联锁系统故障处理 Faults handling of computer interlocking system	TYJL-ADX、DS6-K5B 型计算机联锁故障处理训练 Training of fault handling of TYJL-ADX, DS6-K5B computer interlocking	重点、难点：TYJL-ADX、DS6-K5B 型计算机联锁故障处理 Key points and difficulties: TYJL-ADX, DS6-K5B computer interlocking fault handling	4

三、课程考核 Course Assessment

（1）课程考核分为总结性评价和过程性评价，关注学生个体差异。

Course assessment consists of summative evaluation and process evaluation, focusing on students' individual difference.

（2）总结性评价包括标准化试题的闭卷考试。

The summative evaluation includes standardized test.

（3）过程性评价指使用铁道信号自动控制专业教学资源库开展线上线、下混合式教学，由线上成绩、线下成绩、线上作业和线上考试组成。对项目中的实践技能进行考核，考核内容可以根据实践教学设备的变化进行相应的调整。

Process evaluation is composed of online and off-line performance, online assignment and online test by using the online and off-line blended teaching through teaching resources database of railway signaling automatic control major. The usual performance and awareness in different modules are also evaluated. Assessment contents can be adjusted according to the practical situation

（4）课程考核比例：过程性评价占 50%，总结性评价占 50%。

The proportion of course assessment: process evaluation accounts for 50%, summative assessment accounts for 50%.

四、实施要求 Implementation Requirements

1. 授课教师基本要求 Basic Requirements for Teachers

（1）具备铁道信号专业或相关专业岗位工作经历，大学本科及以上学历，具有高等学校教师资格证书。

Work experiences related to railway signaling major or relevant major, bachelor degree and above, with the teacher certificate of higher education.

（2）具备相应技术职称或本专业三级及以上职业资格证书。

With relevant technical titles or professional vocational qualification certificate of level-3 and above.

（3）具有“双师型”教师证书。

With the certificate of dual qualified teacher.

（4）具备开发职业课程、组织与实施教学的能力。

Ability to develop vocational course and organize and implement teaching.

（5）专业教师每两年到现场实践锻炼应不少于两个月。

No less than two months' field practice every two years.

2. 教学方法和策略 Teaching Methods and Strategies

（1）教学方法 Teaching methods。

主要采用项目化教学法、情景教学法和工作过程导向教学法。将高速铁路道岔转辙设备维护的任务作为代表性的项目，实践教学紧密围绕技能训练开展，应用大量的视频和图片，通过对比、举例、通俗的比喻等方法使学生更好地理解和掌握相关知识，运用多媒体教学手段化解教学难点。

Project teaching method, situational teaching method and work process-oriented teaching method are adopted. The task of high-speed railway switch equipment maintenance is listed as the typical project, practical learning performs closely around skill training. Large number of videos and pictures are used to enable students to better understand and master relevant knowledge through comparison, examples and popular metaphors. Teaching difficulties are solved by applying the multimedia teaching method.

（2）教学策略 Teaching strategies。

教学过程中采用铁道信号自动控制专业教学资源库实现混合式教学，可以在专业教学资源库预先给学生操作视频或微课。在教学过程中尽可能设置与铁路道岔转辙设备实际维护工作一致的作业分工、作业内容、作业步骤及要求。充分利用校内实训室等教学资源，根据每个学习任务的实际情况，确定在教学过程中采用小组合作、学生独立实操演练、技术比武等教学形式。

The blended instruction through teaching resources database of railway signaling automatic control major is adopted during teaching process, and the students is advised to study the operation video and micro-lecture in advance. Set up the work division, work content, work steps and requirements consistent with the actual maintenance of high-speed railway switch equipment as far as possible. Make full use of the training room and other teaching resources in the school, and determine to adopt the teaching modules such as group cooperation, students' independent practice and technical competition in the teaching process according to the actual situation of each learning task.

在实践教学环节，采用企业实地考察，请企业专家、技术能手来给学生授课，让学生清楚企业的工作流程、岗位职责要求和企业岗位工作的其他纪律规定。

As to the practical teaching aspect, field investigation is adopted. Enterprise experts and technical experts are invited to lecture in order to make Students be clear about the workflows, requirements of job description and work disciplines and rules of posts.

第七节 “铁路区间自动控制系统维护实训”课程标准

Curriculum Standard for Maintenance Training of Railway Sections Automatic Control System

一、课程性质 Nature of Course

1. 课程类型、课程功能 Types and Functions

本课程是铁道信号自动控制专业的主干课，共计 48 课时，3 学分；是学生在学习了“电子技术基础”“电路分析基础”“铁路信号基础设备维护”“铁路区间自动控制系统维护”等课程，掌握了铁路区间自动控制系统的结构组成、工作原理，具备了电路分析、故障处理能力的基础上，开设的一门实践课。其功能是对接铁道信号自动控制专业人才培养目标，面向铁路企业，从事车站与区间信号设备维修信号工、电子与电气设备检修信号工工作岗位，培养信号设备的维护与检修、故障信息的收集、分析与处理能力，并为后续“铁路信号设计与施工实训”“信号工技能鉴定实训”等课程的学习奠定基础。

This course is the main course of the railway signal automatic control majors, induding 24 lessons and 1.5 credits. It is a practical course opened to the students who have learned the courses of The Basis of Electronic Technology, The Basis of Circuit Analysis ,Basic Railway Signaling Equipment Maintenance, Maintenance of Railway Station Automatic Control System, etc., and have mastered the structure and working principle of railway switch equipment with the capabilities of circuit analysis and fault handling. Its function is to realize the training objective of railway signaling automatic control specialists and workers, such as signalman to maintain signal equipment, signalman to check the electric and electronic equipment in stations or sections, to foster the ability of signal equipment maintenance, fault information collection, analysis and processing, and lay a solid foundation for the study of Training of Railway Signal Design and Construction, Signalman Skill Appraisal Training.

2. 课程功能定位 Orientation of the Function

表 1 课程功能定位分析

Table 1 Analysis of the Orientation of the Function

对接的工作岗位 Jobs	对接培养的职业岗位能力 Abilities
车站与区间信号设备维修信号工、电子与电气设备检修信号工 Signalman of signaling equipment, electronic and electrical equipment in station or section	按照中国铁路总公司最新颁布的《铁路信号维护规则》对区间信号设备进行维护的能力 The ability to maintain the signal equipment in section in accordance to the latest *Railway Signaling Maintenance Rules* issued by China Railway Corporation

二、课程目标与内容 Objective and Content

1. 课程总目标 General Objectives

通过对 ZPW-2000A 移频自动闭塞设备故障的分析、查找以及处理等练习，使学生进一步具备以下能力：

Through the practices such as analysis, search and handling faults of ZPW-2000A frequency-shifting automatic blocking equipment, students are further equipped with the following abilities:

（1）熟知 ZPW-2000A 移频自动闭塞的设备组成和安装。

Familiar with the composition and installation of ZPW-2000A frequency-shifting automatic blocking equipment.

（2）看懂组合配线图、设备电路图，熟悉系统运用状态和设备正常工作的相关条件。

Understand the combination wiring diagram, equipment circuit diagram, familiar with the system operation status and the relevant conditions of the equipment's normal operation.

（3）熟悉组合侧面端子板及零层端子板的端子编号和应用；熟悉发送器、接收器、衰耗器的类型及设备底座板编号名称的意义和作用。

Familiar with the terminal number and application of the combined side terminal board and zero-layer terminal board, familiar with the types and meanings of the transmitter, receiver, attenuator and thier base board numbers and names.

（4）熟知 ZPW-2000A 移频自动闭塞系统技术条件、电气特性参数及工作原理，会查阅电路图和分析电路工作原理。

Familiar with the technical conditions, electrical characteristics and working principles of ZPW-2000A frequency-shifting automatic blocking system, and check the circuit diagram and analyze the working principle.

（5）牢记处理 ZPW-2000A 移频自动闭塞系统一般故障的流程，熟练掌握分析、查找一般故障的方法，具备符合现场岗位要求的技能水平。

Keep in mind the process of handling general failures of the ZPW-2000A frequency-shifting automatic blocking system, master the methods of analyzing and checking general failures, and have the skills that meet the requirements of on-site jobs.

（6）能够熟练使用常用工具和仪表，提高实际工作能力。

To use common tools and instruments proficiently to improve actual work ability.

2. 课程具体目标 Specific Objectives

表 2　课程教学目标与内容 1

Table 2　Teaching Objectives and Contents 1

序号 No.	毕业要求指标点 Index point of graduation requirement	知识目标 Knowledge goals	技能目标 Ability goals	素质目标 Quality goals	教学内容 Teaching contents
1	掌握 ZPW-2000A 轨道电路 Master ZPW-2000A track circuit	掌握客运专线 ZPW-2000A 轨道电路的特点、结构和工作原理 Master the characteristics, structure and working principle of ZPW-2000A track circuit in passenger dedicated line	能正确查找 ZPW-2000A 轨道电路的故障，描述其特点 Correctly find the fault of ZPW-2000A track circuit and describe the features	接受新知识的能力、举一反三的能力 Ability to accept new knowledge and make references	1. 使用 CD96-3Z 移频综合测试仪等仪表进行 ZPW-2000A 型无绝缘移频轨道电路的电气特性参数测试 Use the CD96-3Z frequency shift comprehensive tester and other instruments to test the electrical characteristics of the ZPW-2000A non-insulated frequency shift rail circuit

续表

序号 No.	毕业要求指标点 Index point of graduation requirement	知识目标 Knowledge goals	技能目标 Ability goals	素质目标 Quality goals	教学内容 Teaching contents
1	掌握 ZPW-2000A 轨道电路 Master ZPW-2000A track circuit	掌握客运专线 ZPW-2000A 轨道电路的特点、结构和工作原理 Master the characteristics, structure and working principle of ZPW-2000A track circuit in passenger dedicated line	能正确查找 ZPW-2000A 轨道电路的故障，描述其特点 Correctly find the fault of ZPW-2000A track circuit and describe the features	接受新知识的能力、举一反三的能力 Ability to accept new knowledge and make references	2. 熟读 ZPW-2000A 移频自动闭塞一般闭塞分区电路图(含通过信号机点灯电路)，熟知电路工作原理 Familiar with the circuit diagram of ZPW-2000A frequency-shifting automatic occlusion's general occlusion zone (including the lighting circuit through the signal), and be familiar with the working principle of the circuit 3. 懂得根据电路图分析、查找系统室内故障，具备快速、准确完成 ZPW-2000A 型移频自动闭塞常见故障的判断及处理的能力 Know how to analyze and find indoor faults in the system according to the circuit diagram, and have the ability to quickly and accurately complete the judgment and processing of common faults of ZPW-2000A frequency-shifting automatic block

表 3　课程教学目标与内容 2

Table 3　Teaching Objectives and Contents 2

序号 No.	项目（模块） Items	任务（单元） Tasks	教学内容 Teaching contents	重点、难点 Key points and difficulties	学时 Hours
1	铁路区间自动控制系统维护实训 Maintenance training for automatic control system of railway section	铁路区间自动控制系统维护实训 Maintenance training for automatic control system of railway section	1. 使用 CD96-3Z 移频综合测试仪等仪表进行 ZPW-2000A 型无绝缘移频轨道电路的电气特性参数测试 Use the CD96-3Z frequency shift comprehensive tester and other instruments to test the electrical characteristics of the ZPW-2000A non-insulated frequency shift rail circuit 2. 理解 ZPW-2000A 移频自动闭塞一般闭塞分区电路图（含通过信号机点灯电路），掌握电路工作原理 Understand the circuit diagram of general occlusion zone on ZPW-2000A frequency-shift automatic block (including the lighting circuit through the signaling), and master the working principle of the circuit 3. 掌握分析、查找系统室内故障的方法，具备快速、准确完成 ZPW-2000A 型移频自动闭塞常见故障的判断及处理的能力 Master the method of analyzing and finding indoor faults in the system, with the ability to quickly and accurately complete the judgment and processing of common faults in ZPW-2000A frequency-shifting automatic block	重点：ZPW-2000A 移频自动闭塞一般闭塞分区电路图；ZPW-2000A 型移频自动闭塞常见故障的判断及处理 Key points: ZPW-2000A frequency-shifting automatic block general block zoning circuit diagram; ZPW-2000A frequency-shifting automatic block common fault judging and handling 难点：ZPW-2000A 型移频自动闭塞常见故障的判断及处理 Difficulties: judging and handling of common faults of ZPW-2000A frequency-shift automatic block	48

三、课程考核 Course Assessment

（1）课程考核分为总结性评价和过程性评价，关注学生个体差异。

Course assessment consists of summative evaluation and process evaluation, focusing on students' individual differences.

（2）总结性评价为技能考试。

The summative evaluation tests the skills.

（3）过程性评价指使用铁道信号自动控制专业教学资源库开展线上、线下混合式教学，由线上成绩、线下成绩、线上作业和线上考试组成。对项目中的实践技能进行考核，考核内容可以根据实践教学设备的变化进行相应的调整。

Process evaluation is composed of online and off-line performance, online assignment and online test by using the online and off-line blended teaching through teaching resources database of railway signaling automatic control major. The usual performance and awareness in different modules are also evaluated. Assessment contents can be adjusted according to the practical situation.

（4）课程考核比例：过程性评价占 50%，总结性评价占 50%。

The proportion of course assessment: process evaluation accounts for 50%, while summative assessment accounts for 50%.

四、实施要求 Implementation Requirements

1. 授课教师基本要求 Basic Requirements for Teachers

（1）具备铁道信号专业或相关专业岗位工作经历，大学本科及以上学历，具有高等学校教师资格证书。

Work experiences related to railway signaling major or relevant post, bachelor degree and above, with the teacher certificate of higher education.

（2）具备相应技术职称或本专业三级及以上职业资格证书。

Provided relevant technical titles or professional qualification certificates of level-3 and above.

（3）具有“双师型”教师证书。

With the teacher certificate of dual qualifications.

（4）具备开发职业课程、组织与实施教学的能力。

Ability to develop vocational course, organize and implement teaching.

（5）专业教师每两年到现场实践锻炼应不少于两个月。

No less than two months' field practice every two years.

2. 教学方法和策略 Teaching Methods and Strategies

（1）教学方法 Teaching methods。

主要采用项目化教学法、情景教学法和工作过程导向教学法。将高速铁路道岔转辙设备维护的任务作为代表性的项目，实践教学紧密围绕技能训练开展，应用大量的视频和图片，通过对比、举例、通俗的比喻等方法使学生更好地理解和掌握相关知识，运用多媒体教学手段化解教学难点。

Project teaching method, situational teaching method and work process-oriented teaching method are adopted. The task of high-speed railway switch equipment maintenance is listed as the typical project, practical learning performs closely around skill training. Large number of videos and pictures are used to enable students to better understand and master relevant knowledge through comparison, examples and popular metaphors. Teaching difficulties are solved by applying the multimedia teaching method.

（2）教学策略 Teaching strategies。

教学过程中采用铁道信号自动控制专业教学资源库实现混合式教学，可以在专业教学资源库预先给学生操作视频或微课。在教学过程中尽可能设置与铁路道岔转辙设备实际维护工作一致的作业分工、作业内容、作业步骤及要求。充分利用校内实训室等教学资源，根据每个学习任务的实际情况，确定在教学过程中采用小组合作、学生独立实操演练、技术比武等教学形式。

The blended instruction through teaching resources database of railway signaling automatic control major is adopted during teaching process, and the students is advised to study the operation video and micro-lecture in advane. Set up the work division, work content, work steps and requirements consistent with the actual maintenance of high-speed railway switch equipment as far as possible. Make full use of the training room and other teaching resources in the school, and determine to adopt the teaching modules such as group cooperation, students' independent practice and technical competition in the teaching process according to the actual situation of each learning task.

在实践教学环节，采用企业实地考察，请企业专家、技术能手来给学生授课，让学生清楚企业的工作流程、岗位职责要求和企业岗位工作的其他纪律规定。

As to the practical teaching aspect, field investigation is adopted. Enterprise experts and technical experts are invited to lecture in order to make Students be clear about the workflows, requirements of job description and work disciplines and rules of posts.

第八节 “铁路信号设计与施工实训”课程标准

Curriculum Standard for Practical Training of the Railway Signal Design and Construction

一、课程的性质 Nature of the Course

1. 课程类型、课程功能 Types and Functions

本课程是铁道信号自动控制专业的主干课，共计 24 课时，1.5 学分；是学生在学习了“铁路信号基础设备维护”“铁路车站自动控制系统维护”“铁路区间自动控制系统维护”“铁路信号设计与施工”课程，具备了一定的铁路信号系统知识的基础上，开设的一门实践课。其功能是对接铁道信号自动控制专业人才培养目标，面向铁路信号工、信号工程施工、铁路信号设计研究员岗位，培养学生按照铁路信号施工设计标准进行相关设备的安装、调试的能力，为其胜任铁路信号工工作岗位打下坚实的基础。

It is a main course for the railway signal automatic control majors. Including 24 hours, 1.5 credits. As a practical course, it set for the students who have learned the course of Maintenance of Railway Signaling Basic Equipment, Automatic Control System Maintenance in Station, Automatic Control System Maintenance in Section, Design and Construction of Railway Signaling, and have basic knowledge of the railway signaling system. The function is to meet the training objective of workers of railway signal automatic control, such as railway signalman, signal engineering construction, railway signal designer or researcher, cultivate the capabilities to install and debug certain facilities under the norm of railway signal construction and design, and lay a solid foundation to be a qualified signalman in the railway.

2. 课程功能定位 Orientation of the Function

表 1 课程功能定位分析

Table 1 Analysis of the Orientation of the Function

对接的工作岗位 Jobs	对接培养的职业岗位能力 Abilities
铁路信号工、信号工程施工、铁路信号设计研究员岗位 Signalman, engineering construction, design and research engineer	能按照铁路信号工程施工技术及工艺标准对相关信号设备进行施工、安装的能力 Construct and install certain signal facilities under the norm of railway signal construction technology and skill

二、课程目标与内容 Objective and Content

1. 课程总目标 General Objectives

综合运用铁路信号的专业知识，解决铁路信号设备、产品等在工程设计、施工安装等方面的实际问题。培养学生掌握铁路信号工程设计的基本规范、规程，掌握铁路信号工程设备施工安装的基本工艺、基本流程等。

Use the specialized knowledge of railway signaling to deal with the issues like engineering design and construction in railway singnaling facilities or products; Train the students with the awearness of basic rules and regularities on railway signaling; Master the skills and fundamental procedures for the engineering construction and installation of railway signaling.

2. 课程具体目标 Specific Objectives

对铁路信号设备工程设计与施工全过程有一个比较系统的了解；能看懂实际站例的信号设备工程图纸；能进行信号设备施工的一般图纸设计；能进行坐标和电缆长度、芯线数计算；能处理施工中遇到一般故障和问题。

Have a systemic understanding of the whole process for railway signal engineering design and construction; Be able to interpret the engineering diagram of real stations, to design the diagram for the construction of signal facilities, to calculate the coordinate, length and cores of the cables, to deal with the faults and problems in the process of construction.

表 2 课程教学目标与内容 1

Table 2 Teaching Objectives and Contents 1

序号 NO.	毕业要求指标点 Index point of graduation requirement	知识目标 Knowledge goals	技能目标 Ability goals	素质目标 Quality goals	教学内容 Teaching contents
1	了解勘测调查的依据、内容和要求 Understand the basis, content and requirements of survey and investigation	掌握初步设计的任务及工作内容 Master the task and work content of preliminary design	依据任务书，能进行现场勘测，掌握现场设计所需资料收集 Carry out on-site surveys and master the data collection required for on-site design according to the mission	培养业务学习热情、积累现场维护知识 Foster learning enthusiasm and accumulate on-site maintenance knowledge	勘测调查 Survey and investigation

续表

序号 NO.	毕业要求指标点 Index point of graduation requirement	知识目标 Knowledge goals	技能目标 Ability goals	素质目标 Quality goals	教学内容 Teaching contents
2	掌握车站信号平面布置图的设计内容 Grasp the content of the station signal plan design	掌握车站信号设备平面布置图设计的原则、步骤和方法 Master the principles, steps and methods for designing the layout of station signal equipment	了解集中区的划分原则，信号机、轨道电路、道岔等信号设备位置的确定，理解信号机的布置方法、轨道区段的划分原则和方法 Understand the principle of dividing the concentration area, determine the location of signal equipment such as signals, track circuit, turnout, etc., understand the layout method of signal, the principle and method of dividing the track section	能根据车站信号设备平面布置图，准确确定各种信号设备设计的准确位置 Accurately determine the exact location of various signal equipment designed based on the layout of station signal equipment	车站信号设备平面布置图设计 Design of layout diagram for station signal equipment
3	掌握电缆径路图的设计内容 Master the content of the cable rout diagram design	掌握轨道区段设置、电缆芯数的计算、电缆箱盒选用 Master the setting of track sections, calculation of the number of cable cores and the selection of cable boxes	掌握坐标计算方法、电缆径路选择、电缆长度及芯线的确定方法 Master the methods of coordinate calculation, cable path selection, cable length and core wire determination	能独自完成车站电缆径路图设计 Complete the design of station cable rout diagram independently	车站电缆径路图设计 Design of station cable rout diagram
4	掌握车站信号平面图、双轨图及电缆径路图设计的内容 Grasp the content of the design of the station signal plan, double track diagram and cable route diagram	掌握车站信号平面图、双轨图及电缆径路图的设计方法 Grasp the design method of the station signal plan, double track diagram and cable rout diagram	掌握车站信号平面图、双轨图及电缆径路图设计的内容及标准 Grasp the content and standards for the design of the station signal plan, double track diagram and cable path diagram	能根据电缆径路图，完成电缆的敷设及设备的安装及导通 Complete cable laying and equipment installation and conduction according to the cable path diagram	平面图、双轨图及电缆径路图认知 The recognition of floor plan, double track diagram and cable path diagram
5	掌握室内设备布置图、组合排列表设计的内容 Master the content of indoor equipment layout and combination list design	掌握室内设备布置图、组合排列表设计的方法 Master the design method of indoor equipment layout and combined list	掌握室内设备布置的方法及组合的选用 Master the method and combination of indoor equipment layout	根据设计图，完成室内设备的安装 According to the designed diagram, complete the installation of indoor equipment	室内信号设备布置图及组合排列表 The layout and combination list for indoor signal equipment
6	掌握接口电路图设计的内容 Master the content of interface circuit design	掌握信号机、道岔及轨道电路接口电路的设计方法 Master the design method of interface circuit in signal controller, switchs and track circuit	掌握接口电路图设计的内容及方法 Master the content and methods of interface circuit diagram design	能看懂接口电路图的内容及一般故障的处理方法 Able to understand the content of the interface circuit diagram and the general troubleshooting methods	接口电路图的设计 The design of interface circuit diagram

续表

序号 NO.	毕业要求指标点 Index point of graduation requirement	知识目标 Knowledge goals	技能目标 Ability goals	素质目标 Quality goals	教学内容 Teaching contents
7	掌握信号机点灯电路图的设计内容 Master the content for the lighting circuit diagram design of the signal	掌握信号机点灯电路图的设计步骤和方法 Master the design steps and methods for the lighting circuit diagram of the signal	掌握进站、出站及调车等信号机点灯电路相对固定的定型图 Master the relatively fixed stereotypes of lighting circuit of signal lights such as inbound, outbound and shunting	掌握信号机点灯电路的工作原理及故障处理方法 Master the working principle and the troubleshooting methods of the lighting circuit of the signal machine	信号机点灯电路图设计 The design of signal lighting circuit
8	掌握道岔控制电路图的设计内容 Master the content of turnout control circuit diagram design	掌握道岔控制电路图的设计步骤和方法 Master the design steps and methods for turnout control circuit diagram	掌握单动、双动道岔控制电路相对固定的定型图 Master the relatively fixed stereotypes of single-action and double-action turnout control circuits	掌握道岔控制电路的工作原理及故障处理方法 Master the working principle and the troubleshooting methods of the switch control circuit	道岔控制电路图设计 The design of turnout control circuit
9	掌握轨道电路的设计原则、步骤和方法 Master the design principles, steps and methods of track circuits	掌握扼流变压器、25HZ轨道电路的设计原则及轨道电路组合类型的选用 Master the design principles of choke transformer and 25Hz track circuit, and the selection of track circuit combination	掌握轨道电路的工作原理 Master the working principle of the track circuit	掌握轨道电路的故障处理方法 Master the troubleshooting methods of the track circuit	轨道电路图设计 The design of track circuit diagram
10	掌握站内电码化电路设计内容 Master the content of the coded circuit design in the station	掌握站内电码化电路正线接车、正线发车、正线股道、侧线股道的设计方法 Master the design method of the main line pick-up, main line departure, main line strand and side line strand of the coded circuit in the station	掌握站内电码化电路的工作原理 Master the working principle of the coded circuit in the station	掌握站内电码化电路的故障处理方法 Master the troubleshooting methods of the coded circuits in the station	站内电码化电路图设计 The design of the coded circuit diagram in the station
11	掌握室内设备配线图表设计的内容 Master the content of indoor equipment wiring diagram design	掌握室内各种机柜配线图表设计的构成及方法 Master the structure and methods of wiring diagram design for various indoor cabinets	掌握室内设备配线图表的设备端子配线意义 Grasp the significance of terminal wiring in indoor equipment wiring diagrams	能根据室内设备配线图表完成设备端子间配线 Complete the wiring between equipment terminals according to the wiring diagram of indoor equipment	室内配线图表设计 The design of indoor wiring diagram

续表

序号 NO.	毕业要求指标点 Index point of graduation requirement	知识目标 Knowledge goals	技能目标 Ability goals	素质目标 Quality goals	教学内容 Teaching contents
12	掌握室外设备配线图表设计的内容 Master the content of outdoor equipment wiring diagram design	掌握室外设备配线图表设计的方法 Master the methods of wiring diagram design for outdoor equipment	掌握室外设备配线图表的设备端子配线意义 Grasp the significance of terminal wiring in outdoor equipment wiring diagrams	能根据室外设备配线图表完成设备端子间配线 Complete the wiring between equipment terminals according to the wiring diagram of outdoor equipment	室外配线图表设计 The design of outdoor wiring diagram
13	掌握区间信号设备平面布置图设计的内容 Grasp the content of the layout design of the section signal equipment	掌握区间信号设备平面布置图设计的原则、步骤和方法 Grasp the principles, steps and methods of layout design for section signal equipment	掌握区间信号设备的定位方法 Master the positioning method for the signal equipment in the section	根据区间信号设备平面布置图完成设备安装 Complete the installation of the equipment according to the layout of the signal equipment	区间信号平面布置图 Signal layout in section
14	掌握区间电缆径路图的设计内容 Grasp the content of the cable path diagram design in the section	掌握区间电缆使用原则、长度计算、芯数确定和方向盒型号的确定方法 Master the principles of using cable, calculating length, determining the number of cores and determining the model of direction box	掌握区间电缆的使用类型及设计标准 Grasp the use type and design standard of section's cable	能根据电缆径路图完成区间电缆敷设及设备安装 Able to complete the cable laying and equipment installation according to the cable path diagram	区间电缆径路图 Section's cable path diagram
15	掌握自动闭塞电路图的设计的内容 Master the content of automatic block circuit design	掌握自动闭塞电路图的设计步骤和方法 Master the steps and methods of automatic block circuit diagram design	了解自动闭塞分区电路、N+1 电路、站间联系电路、报警电路及区间信号采集电路的工作原理 Understand the working principle of automatic block circuit, N+1 circuit, inter-station connection circuit, alarm circuit and section signal acquisition circuit	能根据电路图完成自动闭塞电路设备的维修 Complete the maintenance of automatic block circuit equipment according to the circuit diagram	自动闭塞电路图 Automatic block circuit diagram
16	掌握自动闭塞室内设备配线图表设计的内容 Master the content of wiring diagram design for automatic block indoor equipment	掌握自动闭塞室内配线图表设计步骤和方法 Master the design steps and methods of automatic block indoor wiring diagram	掌握室内设备配线图表的设备端子及电源端子配线意义 Grasp the significance of equipment terminal and power terminal wiring on the indoor equipment wiring diagram	根据室内配线图表完成设备配线 Complete the equipment's wiring according to the indoor wiring diagram	自动闭塞室内配线图表设计 Design diagram of automatic block indoor wiring

续表

序号 NO.	毕业要求指标点 Index point of graduation requirement	知识目标 Knowledge goals	技能目标 Ability goals	素质目标 Quality goals	教学内容 Teaching contents
17	掌握室外设备配线图表设计的内容 Master the content of outdoor equipment wiring diagram design	掌握室外设备配线图表设计的步骤和方法 Master the design steps and methods of outdoor equipment wiring diagram	掌握室外设备配线图表的设备端子配线意义 Grasp the significance of equipment terminal wiring on the outdoor equipment wiring diagram	能根据室外设备配线图表完成设备端子间配线 Complete the wiring between the terminals of the equipment according to the wiring diagram for the outdoor equipment	自动闭塞室外配线图表设计 Design of automatic block outdoor wiring diagram
18	掌握6502电气集中工程图纸的全部内容 Master all the contents on 6502 electrical centralized engineering diagram	掌握工程图纸与实物的对应关系 Master the correspondence between engineering diagram and real object	掌握工程图纸设计内容及设备配线方法 Master the content of engineering diagrams design and methods for equipment wiring	能根据工程图进行设备安装及维修 To install and maintain equipment according to the engineering diagrams	6502电气集中工程图纸识图 Recognition of 6502 electrical centralized engineering diagram
19	掌握图纸设计内容及设备配线 Master the content of diagram design and equipment wiring	掌握工程图纸与实物的对应关系 Master the correspondence between engineering diagrams and real objects	进一步掌握室内设备配线图表的设备端子及电源端子配线意义 Further grasp the significance of equipment terminal and power terminal wiring on indoor equipment wiring diagram	进一步提高设备配线速度和质量 Further improve equipment's wiring speed and quality	室内设备配线图识读 Recognition of indoor equipment wiring diagram
20	掌握图纸设计内容及设备配线 Master the content of diagram design and equipment wiring	掌握工程图纸与实物的对应关系 Master the correspondence between engineering diagram and real object	进一步掌握室外设备配线图表的设备端子配线意义 Further grasp the significance of the terminal wiring on the outdoor equipment wiring diagram	进一步提高设备配线速度和质量 Further improve equipment's wiring speed and quality	室外设备配线图识读 Recognition of outdoor equipment wiring diagram

表3　课程教学目标与内容2

Table 3　Teaching Objectives and Contents 2

序号 No.	项目（模块） Items	任务（单元） Tasks	教学内容 Teaching contents	重点、难点 Key points and difficulties	学时 Hours
1	项目1：计算机联锁工程设计 Item 1: engineering design for computer interlocking	1.1 勘测调查 Survey and investigation	勘测调查的内容 The content of the survey and investigation	重点、难点：地形、地貌的确认 Key points and difficulties: confirm the topography and landform	2
2		1.2 车站信号设备平面布置图设计 Design of layout diagram of station signal equipment	车站信号设备平面布置图设计的原则、步骤和方法 Principles, steps and methods of designing the layout of station signal equipment	重点、难点：车站信号设备平面布置图设计的方法 Key points and difficulties: method for designing layout plan of station signal equipment	2
3		1.3 车站电缆径路图 Station cable rout diagram	车站电缆径路图设计的内容、步骤和方法 The content, steps and methods of station cable rout diagram design	重点、难点：坐标计算，电缆长度和芯线计算 Key points and difficulties: coordinate calculation, cable length and core calculation	8

续表

序号 No.	项目（模块） Items	任务（单元） Tasks	教学内容 Teaching contents	重点、难点 Key points and difficulties	学时 Hours
4	项目 1：计算机联锁工程设计 Item 1: engineering design for computer interlocking	1.4 平面图、双轨图及电缆径路图 Floor plan, double-track diagram and cable rout diagram	平面图、双轨图及电缆径路图认知 Recognition of floor plan, double track diagram and cable path diagram	重点、难点：电缆径路图的认知 Key points and difficulties: recognition of cable rout diagram	2
5		1.5 室内信号设备布置图及组合排列表 Indoor signal equipment layout diagram and combined list	室内信号设备布置图及组合排列表的设计方法 Design method of indoor signal equipment layout diagram and combined list	重点、难点：组合排列表的设计方法 Key points and difficulties: design method of combined list	2
6		1.6 接口电路图 Interface circuit diagram	接口电路图的设计内容和方法 The content and method of interface circuit diagram design	重点、难点：接口电路图的设计方法 Key points and difficulties: interface circuit diagram design method	2
7		1.7 信号机点灯电路图 Signal lighting circuit diagram	信号机点灯电路图的设计内容和方法 The design content and method of lighting circuit diagram of signal lighting	重点、难点：信号机点灯电路图的设计内容和方法 Key points and difficulties: The design content and method of lighting circuit diagram of signal lighting	2
8		1.8 道岔控制电路图 Turnout control circuit diagram	道岔控制电路图的设计内容和方法 The content and method of turnout control circuit diagram design	重点、难点：道岔控制电路图的设计方法 Key points and difficulties: the design method of turnout control circuit diagram	2
9		1.9 轨道电路图 Track circuit diagram	轨道电路图的设计内容和方法 The content and method of track circuit diagram design	重点、难点：轨道电路图的设计方法 Key points and difficulties: the method of track circuit diagram design	2
10		1.10 站内电码化电路图 Station coded circuit diagram	站内电码化电路图的设计内容和方法 The content and method of coded circuit diagram design in the station	重点、难点：站内电码化电路图的设计方法 Key points and difficulties: the method of coded circuit diagram design in the station	2
11		1.11 室内配线图表设计 Indoor wiring diagram design	室内配线图表的设计内容和方法 The content and method of indoor wiring diagram design	重点、难点：室内配线图表的设计方法 Key points and difficulties: the method of indoor wiring diagram design	4
12		1.12 室外配线图表设计 Outdoor wiring diagram design	室外配线图表的设计内容和方法 The content and method of outdoor wiring diagram design	重点、难点：室外配线图表的设计方法 Key points and difficulties: the method of outdoor wiring diagram design	4
13	项目 2：自动闭塞工程设计 Item 2: design of automatic block engineering	2.1 区间信号平面布置图 The section signal layout	区间信号平面布置图的设计内容和方法 The content and method of section signal layout design	重点、难点：区间信号平面布置图的设计方法 Key points and difficulties: the method of the layout plan design of the section signal	2

序号 No.	项目（模块） Items	任务（单元） Tasks	教学内容 Teaching contents	重点、难点 Key points and difficulties	学时 Hours
14	项目 2：自动闭塞工程设计 Item 2: design of automatic block engineering	2.2 区间电路径路图 The path diagram of section electrical circuit	区间电路径路图的设计内容和方法 The content and method of section electric path diagram design	重点、难点：区间电路径路图的设计方法 Key points and difficulties: the method of section electrical circuit diagram design	2
15		2.3 自动闭塞电路图 The automatic block circuit diagram	自动闭塞电路图的设计内容和方法 The content and method of automatic block circuit diagram design	重点、难点：自动闭塞电路图的设计方法 Key points and difficulties: the method of automatic block circuit diagram design	2
16		2.4 自动闭塞室内配线图表设计 Design of automatic block indoor wiring diagram	自动闭塞室内配线图表的设计内容和方法 The content and method of automatic block indoor wiring diagram design	重点、难点：自动闭塞室内配线图表的设计方法 Key points and difficulties: the method of automatic block indoor wiring diagram design	2
17		2.5 自动闭塞室外配线图表设计 Design of automatic block outdoor wiring diagram	自动闭塞室外配线图表的设计内容和方法 the content and method of automatic block outdoor wiring diagram design	重点、难点：自动闭塞室外配线图表的设计方法 Key points and difficulties: the method of automatic block outdoor wiring diagram design	2
18	项目 3：工程施工 Item 3: construction	3.1 6502 电气集中工程图纸识图 The recognition of 6502 electrical centralized engineering diagram	6502 电气集中工程图纸识图 The recognition of 6502 electrical centralized engineering diagram	重点、难点：工程图与现场实物核对 Key points and difficulties: checking of the engineering diagrams and on-site objects	4
19		3.2 室内设备配线图识读 The interpretation of wiring diagram for indoor equipment	室内设备配线图识读 The interpretation of wiring diagram for indoor equipment	重点、难点：现场配线核对 Key points and difficulties: check on-site wiring	2
20		3.3 室外设备配线图识读 The interpretation of wiring diagram for outdoor equipment	室外设备配线图识读 The interpretation of wiring diagram for outdoor equipment	重点、难点：现场配线核对 Key points and difficulties: check on-site wiring	4

三、课程考核 Course Assessment

（1）课程考核分为总结性评价和过程性评价，关注学生个体差异。

Course assessment consists of summative evaluation and process evaluation, focusing on students' individual differences.

（2）总结性评价为技能考试。

The summative evaluation tests the skills.

（3）过程性评价指使用铁道信号自动控制专业教学资源库开展线上、线下混合式教学，由线上成绩、线下成绩、线上作业和线上考试组成。对项目中的实践技能进行考核，考核内容可以根据实践教学设备的变化进行相应的调整。

Process evaluation is composed of online and off-line performance, online assignment and online test by using the online and off-line blended teaching through teaching resources database of railway signalling automatic control major. The usual performance and awareness in different modules are also evaluated. Assessment contents can be ajusted according to the practical situation.

（4）课程考核比例：过程性评价占 50%，总结性评价占 50%。

The proportion of course assessment: process evaluation accounts for 50%, summative assessment accounts for 50%.

四、实施要求 Implementation Requirements

1. 授课教师基本要求 Basic Requirements for Teachers

（1）具备铁道信号专业或相关专业岗位工作经历，大学本科及以上学历，具有高等学校教师资格证书。

Work experiences related to railway signaling major or relevant post, bachelor degree and above, with the teacher certificate in an institution of higher education.

（2）具备相应技术职称或本专业三级及以上职业资格证书。

Provided relevant technical titles or professional qualification certificates of level-3 and above.

（3）具有“双师型”教师证书。

With the teacher certificate of dual qualifications.

（4）具备开发职业课程、组织与实施教学的能力。

Ability to develop vocational course, organize and implement teaching.

（5）专业教师每两年到现场实践锻炼应不少于两个月。

No less than two months’ field practice every two years.

2. 教学方法和策略 Teaching Methods and Strategies

（1）教学方法 Teaching methods。

主要采用项目化教学法、情景教学法和工作过程导向教学法。将高速铁路道岔转辙设备维护的任务作为代表性的项目，实践教学紧密围绕技能训练开展，应用大量的视频和图片，通过对比、举例、通俗的比喻等方法使学生更好地理解和掌握相关知识，运用多媒体教学手段化解教学难点。

Project teaching method, situational teaching method and work process-oriented teaching method are adopted. The task of high-speed railway switch equipment maintenance is listed as the typical project, practical learning performs closely around skill training. Large number of videos and pictures are used to enable students to better understand and master relevant knowledge through comparison, examples, popular metaphors. Teaching difficulties are solved by applying the multimedia teaching method.

（2）教学策略 teaching strategies。

教学过程中采用铁道信号自动控制专业教学资源库实现混合式教学，可以在专业教学资源库预先给学生操作视频或微课。在教学过程中尽可能设置与铁路道岔转辙设备实际维护工作一致的作业分工、作业内容、作业步骤及要求。充分利用校内实训室等教学资源，根据每个学习任务的实际情况，确定在教学过程中采用小组合作、学生独立实操演练、技术比武等教学形式。

In the teaching resources database for railway signaling automatic control major, the blended teaching is adopted during the process, where the students could learn in advance through operating videos or micro-lectures. The division, content, procedure and requirement of works assigned should be consistence to the actual maintenance of rail switch equipment as much as possible. Make full use of the teaching resource in the school such as the training rooms, and adopt the teaching mode such as group study, independent practice, skill contest in concordance to the real tasks.

在实践教学环节，采用企业实地考察，请企业专家、技术能手来给学生授课，让学生清楚企业的工作流程、岗位职责要求和企业岗位工作的其他纪律规定。

As to the practical teaching aspect, field investigation is adopted. Enterprise experts and technical experts are invited to lecture in order to make Students be clear about the workflows, requirements of job description and work disciplines and rules of posts.

第九节 “信号工技能鉴定实训”课程标准

Curriculum Standard for Practical Training of Signalman Skill Appraisal

一、课程性质 Nature of the Course

1. 课程类型、课程功能 Types and Functions

本课程是铁道信号自动控制专业的主干课，共计 140 课时，7.5 学分；是学生在学习了铁道信号自动控制专业的所有核心课程与主干课程，具备了一定的铁路信号系统知识的基础上，开设的一门实践课。其功能是对接铁道信号自动控制专业人才培养目标，面向车站与区间信号设备维修信号工工作岗位。本课程是对学生两年来专业学习的综合检验，是学生获取中级信号工职业资格证书的保证，为胜任铁路信号工工作打下坚实的基础。

This course is the main course for the railway signal automatic control major, including 140 hours, 7.5 credits. It is set for the students who has already learned all the core courses and the main courses, and have the basic knowledge of railway singling system. Its function is to connect the training objectives with railway signal professionals, such as the position to repair the signal equipment on stations or sections. It is a comprehensive test for their two years specialized studies, a promise to the intermediate professional qualification certificate for signalman, and a solid basis for the position on the railway signaling.

2. 课程功能定位 Orientation of the Function

表 1 课程功能定位分析

Table 1 Analysis of the Orientation of the Function

对接的工作岗位 Jobs	对接培养的职业岗位能力 Skills
车站与区间信号设备维修信号工 Signal equipment maintenance in station and section	按照中国铁路总公司最新颁布的《铁路信号维护规则》对车站信号设备进行维护的能力 Be able to maintain stations' signal equipment in accordance with the latest *Railway Signal Maintenance Rules* issued by China Railway Corporation

二、课程目标与内容 Objective and Contents

1. 课程总目标 General Objectives

通过培训，使学生进一步熟悉继电电路的特点与配线，进一步熟悉铁道信号基本理论知识；熟悉ZD6电动转辙机的结构、动作原理，掌握ZD6电动转辙机的机械调整、电气特性测试及开路故障查找技能；掌握6502电气集中设备的原理、操作使用及1～8网络线开路故障处理的基本技能；学会信号设备室内外开路故障范围的判断及处理方法。达到对现场信号一般检维修人员岗位的工作要求。

Through the training, students are further familiar with the characteristics and wiring of relay circuits, and have the basic theoretical knowledge of railway signals; They are familiar with the structure and operating principle of ZD6 electric switch machine, and master the mechanical adjustment, electrical characteristics test for ZD6 electric switch machine and the skills for checking fault in its open circuit; Master the principle, operation and use of 6502 electrical centralized equipment and the basic skills of fault handling in open circuit for 1—8 network lines; Learn the judgment and processing of indoor and outdoor open circuit fault in the range of signaling, meet the requirements of the general inspection and maintenance for signalman on-site.

2. 课程具体目标 Specific Objectives

表2　课程教学目标与内容1

Table 2　Teaching Objectives and Contents 1

序号 No.	毕业要求指标点 Index point of graduation requirement	知识目标 Knowledge goals	技能目标 Skills goals	素质目标 Quality goals	教学内容 Teaching contents
1	学会填写"行车设备检查登记簿" Learn to fill in the Register of Traffic Equipment Inspection	1. 了解"行车设备检查登记簿"填写内容 Understand the content of the Register of Traffic Equipment Inspection 2. 填写故障发生时间、设备名称、故障地点、故障现象 Fill in the time of failure, equipment, location and phenomenon 3. 填写车站每月（季）组织的设备联合检查的情况。 Fill in the monthly joint inspection of equipment at the station 4. 进行道岔缺口检查、轨道电路电压测试、主副灯丝转换试验、各部螺丝检查牢固等不影响设备正常使用的作业，需办理登、销记，车站值班员利用行车间隔安排	能判断车站设备正常状态，会故障状态的现象和故障修复时间填写"行车设备检查登记簿" Able to judge the normal state of the station's equipment, and fill in the Register of Traffic Equipment Inspection according to the fault state and repair time	提高学生的分析和解决问题能力 Improve students' ability to analyze and solve problems	根据知识目标列举的各种情况，按要求填写"行车设备检查登记簿" According to the various situations listed in the knowledge goals fill in the Register of Traffic Equipment Inspection in accordance with the requirements

续表

序号 No.	毕业要求指标点 Index point of graduation requirement	知识目标 Knowledge goals	技能目标 Skills goals	素质目标 Quality goals	教学内容 Teaching contents
1	学会填写“行车设备检查登记簿” Learn to fill in the Register of Traffic Equipment Inspection	Carry out check-in and check-out for operations that do not affect the normal use of equipment during the interval, such as inspection of turnout gaps, track circuit voltage test, main and auxiliary filament conversion test, and firm inspection of screws, etc. 5. 填写轨道电路分路不良等情况 Fill in the information such as bad track circuit shunt 6. 填写道岔手摇把等重要工具的使用情况 Fill in the information of the use of important tools such as turnout hand cranks			
2	熟练掌握道岔机械调整；Master the mechanical adjustment of turnout	1. 了解ZD6的作业内容、要求及标准 Understand the operation content, requirements and standards of ZD6 2. 掌握作业材料、工具的用途和使用方法 Master the usage of working materials and tools 3. 了解巡检和检修作业程序 Understand the inspection and maintenance procedures 4. 了解作业人员组成和分工，作业安全风险防控措施 Understand the constitution and division of workers, and prevent and control measures for operational safety risks 5. 重点掌握ZD6道岔进行机械调整 Focus on mastering mechanical adjustment of ZD6 turnout	能胜任检修过程中的各项工作。能说得清，做得好。特别是准确调整道岔的摩擦电流和密贴表示性能 Be competent for the work in the maintance process. Make sure well done, well said. correctly adjust the friction current and the stick contact indicator on turnout	培养学生理论联系实际的能力和动手能力 Cultivate students' ability to integrate theory with practice and hands-on ability	检修作业程序、训练道岔的摩擦电流和密贴表示调整训练 Training of overhaul operation procedures and indication adjustment between the friction current and stick contact on turnout
3	熟练掌握电动转辙机的电气特性测试及故障处理 Proficiency in electrical characteristics testing and troubleshooting of electric switch machine	1. 掌握电动转辙机的电气特性测试 Master the electrical characteristics testing of electric switch machine 2. 掌握电动转辙机启动电路和表示电路的故障处理 Master the troubleshooting of starting circuit and indicating circuit of electric switch machine	能通过电气特性分析设备的状态 Analyze the status of equipment through electrical characteristics 能在规定的时间内处理电路的开路故障 Handle the open circuit faults within a specified time	培养学生职业水平和故障应急处理能力 Cultivate students' occupational level and emergency response ability	ZD6维护训练及电气特性测试、电路故障处理训练。 Training of ZD6 maintenance, electrical characteristics testing and circuit fault handling

续表

序号 No.	毕业要求指标点 Index point of graduation requirement	知识目标 Knowledge goals	技能目标 Skills goals	素质目标 Quality goals	教学内容 Teaching contents
4	熟练掌握 6502 电气集中电路的故障处理 Proficiency in troubleshooting of 6502 electrical centralized circuit	控制台各项操作方法、进路办理、图纸识读以及车站设备认知 Various operation methods of the console, route management, diagram interpretation and station equipment recognition	能通过操作方法、进路办理出现的现象分析设备的状态 Analyze the status of the equipment through the phenomenon generated by operation and access management 能在规定的时间内处理电路的开路故障 Handle open circuit faults within a specified time	培养学生逻辑思维和故障应急处理能力 Cultivate students' logical thinking and emergency response capabilities	控制台各项操作方法、进路办理、图纸识读以及车站设备认知训练 Training of various operation of the console, route management, diagram interpretation and station equipment recognition 电气集中网络电路开路故障处理训练 Training of open circuit fault handling for electrical centralized network
5	理论题库练习 Theoretical test bank exercises	全面了解和掌握铁路信号的相关知识，提高学生的理论水平 Fully understand and master the relevant knowledge of railway signals, to improve students' theoretical level	能通过智能考核系统平台的理论测试，并达到 70 分以上 Pass the theoretical test on the intelligent assessment system platform with more than 70 points	培养学生对作专业知识的熟悉程度 Cultivate students' familiarity with specialized knowledge	与其他实训项目平行开展教学和训练 Conduct teaching and training in parallel with other training programs

表 3　课程教学安排 2

Table 3　Course Arrangement 2

序号 No.	项目（模块） Items	任务（单元） Tasks	教学内容 Teaching content	重点、难点 Key points and difficulties	学时 Hours
1	项目 1：填写“行车设备检查登记簿” Item 1: fill in the Register of Driving Equipment Inspection	1.1 运统 46 介绍 Introduction to Yuntong 46	1. 运统 46 用途 The performance of Yuntong 46 2. 运统 46 表格栏目介绍 Introduction of Yuntong 46 forms and columns	重点：填写项目 Key points: fill in the project 难点：填写方法 Difficulties: fill in method	4
		1.2 运统 46 填写训练 Yuntong 46 registration training	运统 46 填写训练 Yuntong 46 registration training	重点：填写项目 Key points: fill in the project 难点：填写方法 Difficulties: fill in method	8
2	项目 2：道岔机械调整 Item 2: turnout mechanical adjustment	2.1 ZD6 日常维护及电气和机械特性测试训练 1ZD6 daily maintenance and training of electrical and mechanical characteristics test	1. 部件认知训练 Component recognition training 2. 检修过程对标训练 Benchmark training of the maintenance process 3. 电气特性测试训练 Electrical characteristic test training 4.机械特性测试训练 Mechanical characteristic test training	重点：机械特性测试 Key points: mechanical characteristic testing 难点：检修过程对标 Difficulties: benchmarking the maintenance process	12
		2.2 道岔密贴机械调整训练 Training of turnout sticking mechanical adjustment	1.工具材料运用训练 Tool and material application training 2.机械特性测试训练 Mechanical characteristic test training	重点：调整标准 Key points: the standard of adjusting 难点：调整方法 Difficulties: the adjusting method	12

续表

序号 No.	项目（模块） Items	任务（单元） Tasks	教学内容 Teaching content	重点、难点 Key points and difficulties	学时 Hours
2	项目 2：道岔机械调整 Item 2: turnout mechanical adjustment	2.3 道岔表示机械调整训练 Turnout indicator mechanical adjustment training	1.工具材料运用训练 Tool and material application training 2.机械特性测试训练 Mechanical characteristic test training		12
		2.4ZD6 道岔机械调整项目考核总结 Summary of assessment of ZD6 turnout mechanical adjustment project	按照信号工技能鉴定要求专项考核 Specialized assessment according to the requirements of signal technician skill appraisal		8
3	项目 3：电动转辙机的电气特性测试及故障处理 Item 3: electrical characteristics test and troubleshooting of electric switch machine	3.1 ZD6 图纸识读和设备认知 ZD6 diagram recognition and equipment recognition	ZD6 图纸识读和设备认知训练 Training of ZD6 diagram recognition and equipment recognition	重点：部件名称认知 Key points: identify the components 难点：部件作用 Difficulties: the role of components	12
		3.2 ZD6 继电器电路开路故障处理 Open circuit trouble shooting of ZD6 relay circuit	1DQJ/2DQJ 励磁电路故障查找训练 1DQJ/2DQJ excitation circuit trouble shooting training	重点：操作方式 Key points: operation mode 难点：查找方法 Difficulties: search method	12
		3.3 ZD6 启动电路开路故障处理 Open circuit trouble shooting of ZD6 start circuit	直流电机电路故障查找训练 Trouble shooting training fault DC motor circuit	重点：故障范围判断 Key points: judgment of fault range 难点：动态查找方法 Difficulties: dynamic search method	12
		3.4 ZD6 表示电路开路故障处理 Fault handling of ZD6 symbolic open circuit	表示继电器电路故障查找训练 Trouble shooting training of relay circuit indication	重点：故障范围判断 Key points: the judgment of fault range 难点：静态查找方法 Difficulties: static search method	12
		3.5 ZD6 单元电路项目考核总结 ZD6 unit circuit project assessment summary	按照信号工技能鉴定要求专项考核 Special assessment according to the requirements of signal technician skill appraisal	重点：故障点判断 Key points: judgment of the fault point 难点：查找方法 Difficulties: checking method	8
4	项目 4：6502 电气集中网络电路的故障处理； Item 4: troubleshooting of 6502 electrical centralized network circuit	4.1 6502 电气集中控制台各项操作 Operations of 6502 electric centralized control console	按钮和表示等用途和符号对照和进路（变通），重复开放信号等相关操作 Buttons and indications of other purposes and symbols comparison and access (alternative), Related operations as repeat the open signal	重点：按钮表示用途 Key points: the indicated purpose of buttons 难点：人工解锁 Difficulties: manual unlock	12
		4.2 6502 电气集中网络图纸识读和设备认知 Diagram interpretation and equipment recognition of 6502 electric centralized network	组合类型、网络结构 The type of combination and network structure 送电规律、动作程序 Power transmission regularities and action procedures	重点、难点：网络结构 Key points and difficulties: network structure	10

续表

序号 No.	项目（模块） Items	任务（单元） Tasks	教学内容 Teaching content	重点、难点 Key points and difficulties	学时 Hours
4	项目 4：6502 电气集中网络电路的故障处理； Item 4: troubleshooting of 6502 electrical centralized network circuit	4.3 选择组开路故障处理 Fault handling of selection group's open circuit	选择组继电器励磁电开路故障查找训练 Fault checking training of selection group relay excitation electric open circuit	重点：操作方式 Key points: operation mode 难点：查找方法 Difficulties: checking method	10
		4.4 执行组开路故障处理 Fault handling of execution group's open circuit	执行组继电器励磁电开路故障查找训练 Fault checking training of execution group relay excitation electric open circuit	重点：操作方式 Key points: operation mode 难点：查找方法 Difficulties: checking method	10
		4.5 6502 电气集中网络电路项目考核总结 Summary of 6502 electrical centralized network circuit project assessment	按照信号工技能鉴定要求专项考核 Special assessment according to the requirements of signal technician skill appraisal	重点：故障点判断 Key points: judgment of fault point 难点：查找方法 Difficulties: checking method	8
5	项目 5：理论题库练习 Item 5: theoretical test bank exercises	通过智能考核系统进行理论训练 Conduct theoretical training through the intelligent assessment system	通过智能考核系统平台的理论测试，并达到 70 分以上 Pass the theoretical test on the intelligent assessment system platform with more than 70 points	重点：信号中级工考试题库 Key points: signalman examination bank for intermediate engineer 难点：在教学中没有涉及的题目 Difficulties: topics not covered in teaching	6

三、课程考核 Course Assessment

（1）课程考核分为总结性评价和过程性评价，关注学生个体差异。

Course assessment consists of summative evaluation and process evaluation, focusing on students' individual differences.

（2）总结性评价为项目 1、项目 2、项目 3、项目 4 考核成绩的平均成绩。

The summative evaluation is the average scours of item 1 to 4.

（3）过程性评价指使用铁道信号自动控制专业教学资源库开展线上线、下混合式教学，由线上成绩、线下成绩、线上作业和线上考试组成。对项目中的实践技能进行考核，考核内容可以根据实践教学设备的变化进行相应的调整。

Process evaluation is composed of online and off-line performance, online assignment and online test by using the online and off-line blended teaching through teaching resources database of railway signaling automatic control major. The usual performance and awareness in different modules are also evaluated. Assessment contents can be adjusted according to the practical situation.

（4）课程考核比例：过程性评价占 50%，总结性评价占 50%。

The proportion of course assessment: process evaluation accounts for 50%, while summative assessment accounts for 50%.

四、实施要求 Implementation Requirements

1. 授课教师基本要求 Basic Requirements for Teachers

（1）具备铁道信号专业或相关专业岗位工作经历，大学本科及以上学历，具有高等学校教师资格证书。

Work experiences related to railway signaling major or relevant post, bachelor degree and above, with the teacher certificate of higher education.

（2）具备相应技术职称或本专业三级及以上职业资格证书。

Provided relevant technical titles or professional qualification certificates of level-3 and above.

（3）具有“双师型”教师证书。

With the teacher certificate of dual qualifications.

（4）具备开发职业课程、组织与实施教学的能力。

Ability to develop vocational course, organize and implement teaching.

（5）专业教师每两年到现场实践锻炼应不少于两个月。

No less than two months' field practice every two years

2. 教学方法和策略 Teaching Methods and Strategies

（1）教学方法 Teaching methods。

主要采用项目化教学法、情景教学法和工作过程导向教学法。将高速铁路道岔转辙设备维护的任务作为代表性的项目，实践教学紧密围绕技能训练开展，应用大量的视频和图片，通过对比、举例、通俗的比喻等方法使学生更好地理解和掌握相关知识，运用多媒体教学手段化解教学难点。

Project teaching method, situational teaching method, and work process-oriented teaching method are adopted. The task of high-speed railway switch equipment maintenance is listed as the typical project, practical learning performs closely around skill training. Large number of videos and pictures are used to enable students to better understand and master relevant knowledge through comparison, examples, popular metaphors. Teaching difficulties are solved by applying the multimedia teaching method.

（2）教学策略 Teaching strategies。

教学过程中采用铁道信号自动控制专业教学资源库实现混合式教学，可以在专业教学资源库预先给学生操作视频或微课。在教学过程中尽可能设置与铁路道岔转辙设备实际维护工作一致的作业分工、作业内容、作业步骤及要求。充分利用校内实训室等教学资源，根据每个学习任务的实际情况，确定在教学过程中采用小组合作、学生独立实操演练、技术比武等教学形式。

The blended teaching through teaching resources database of railway signaling automatic control major is adopted during teaching process, where the students could learn in advance through operation videos or micro-lectures. The division, content, procedure and requirement of works assigned should be consistence to the actual maintenance of rail switch equipment as much as possible. Make full use of the teaching resource in the school such as the training rooms, and adopt the teaching modes such as group study, independent practice, skill contest in concordance to the real tasks.

在实践教学环节，采用企业实地考察，请企业专家、技术能手来给学生授课，让学生清楚企业的工作流程、岗位职责要求和企业岗位工作的其他纪律规定。

As to the practical teaching aspect, field investigation is adopted. Enterprise experts and technical experts are invited to lecture in order to make Students be clear about the workflows, requirements of job description and work disciplines and rules of posts.

附录一

课程建设单位名单 The Authorized Institution

序号 NO.	单位名称 Names of Authorities
1	柳州铁道职业技术学院 Liuzhou Railway Technical Vocational College
2	中国铁路南宁局集团有限公司柳州电务段 Liuzhou Communication and Signal Division of Nanning Bureau in China Railway Corporation
3	中国铁路南宁局集团有限公司南宁电务段 Nanning Communication and Signal Division of Nanning Bureau in China Railway Corporation
4	广西沿海铁路股份有限公司钦州电务段 Qinzhou Communication and Signal Division of Guangxi Coastal Railway Co., Ltd.

附录二

铁道信号自动控制专业课程设置及学时学分分配表

Course Setting and Credit Allocation Table for Railway Signal Automatic Control Major

课程设置及学时学分分配表

铁道信号自动控制专业（三年制）

课程类型	序号	课程编码	课程名称	学分	考核方式	教学总学时	其中实践学时	开课时数	开课学期					
									1	2	3	4	5	6
									14/19	20/21	15/20	13/20	4/20	16
公共基础课	1	001001060	思想道德修养与法律基础	3.0	课内考试	48	12	4/10	4					
	2	001003080	毛泽东思想和中国特色社会主义理论体系概论	4.0	课内考试	64	8+8	4/14		4				
	3	001002020	形势与政策	1.0	考查	16		讲座	讲座					
	4	008005040	创业基础与就业指导	2.0	考查	32	8	8+4/2+4/2+4/2						
	5	009001010	安全教育	0.5	考查	10		讲座	讲座					
	6	010003040	大学生心理成长	2.0	考查	32		2/8+2/8		2				
	7	005001040	体育与健康	2.0	考查	24	22	2/12	2					
	8	005005040	体育专项选修 1	2.0	考查	28	26	2/14		2				
	9	005006040	体育专项选修 2	2.0	考查	28	26	2/14			2			
	10	005007040	体育专项选修 3	2.0	考查	28	26	2/14				2		
	11	003007080	公共英语	4.0	统一考试	52	14	4/13	4					
	12	003017060	铁道信号专业英语	3.0	课内考试	36	待订	3/12				3		
	13	502001060	计算机文化基础	3.0	考证	48	24	2/12		2				
	14	002001060	高等数学	3.0	统一考试	48		4/12	4					
	15	004004040	写作与沟通	2.0	课内考试	32		3/11				3		
	16	004001030	普通话	1.5	课内考试	24		2/12		2				
	17	011002040	军事训练	2.0	考查	112			2w					
	18	011001040	军事理论	2.0	考查	36		2/11+2/7	2					
	19	012001120	第二课堂	6.0					平台记录参与过程					
	20	007003080	公共选修课（见公共选修课手册）	4.0	考查	60		2/15+2/15						
	20	012002040	美育选修课（见公共选修课手册）	2.0	考查	30		2/15						
	21	007005020	劳动实践	1.0	考查	28		28/1			1w			
	公共基础课合计			54.0		816	174		16	12	2	8	0	0
专业（技能）课 专业基础课	1	102001090	电路分析基础	4.5	统一考试	72	12	6/12	6					
	2	102004100	电子技术基础	5.0	统一考试	84	16	6/14		6				
	3	102002030	铁道概论	1.5	课内考试	26	0	2/13	2					
	4	102098030	计算机辅助制图	1.5	考查	24	24	24/1					1w	
	5	102003030	电路认知与焊接实训	1.5	考查	24	24	24/1	1w					
	6	102034060	电工操作技能实训	3.0	课内考试	48	48	24/2			2w			
	7	102096060	单片机与传感器应用技术	3.0	课内考试	48	24	4/12			4			
	8	102010060	铁路安全规章	3.0	考查				第 4 学期录成绩					
	9	107013030	公关礼仪	1.5	考查	24		2/12	2					
	专业基础课合计			24.5		350	148		10	6	4	0	0	0

续表

课程类型		序号	课程编码	课程名称	学分	考核方式	教学总学时	其中实践学时	开课时数	开课学期					
										1	2	3	4	5	6
										14/19	20/21	15/20	13/20	4/20	16
专业（技能）课	专业核心课	1	102006100	铁路信号基础设备维护	5.0	统一考试	84	12	6/14		6				
		2	102011100	铁路车站自动控制系统维护	5.0	统一考试	84	18	6/14			6			
		3	102013070	铁路区间自动控制系统维护	3.5	统一考试	60	10	6/10			6			
		4	102064070	列车运行自动控制系统维护	3.5	统一考试	60	10	6/10				6		
		5	102021070	铁路信号设计与施工	3.5	统一考试	60	6	6/10				6		
		6	102067050	铁路信号集中监测系统运用与维护	2.5	统一考试	40	12	4/11				4		
		专业核心课合计			23.0		388	68		0	6	12	16	0	0
	专业主干课	1	102088030	高铁道岔转辙设备维护实训	1.5	课内考试	24	24	24/1			24			
		2	102014040	铁路信号电源设备维护	2.0	统一考试	36	8	6/6			6			
		3	102012030	铁路行车调度集中系统维护	1.5	课内考试	28	4	4/7			4			
		4	102017040	铁路信号中的通信技术应用	2.0	课内考试	36	8	6/6			6			
		5	102022030	信号规章与业务管理	1.5	考查	24	12	24/1					1w	
		6	102056030	铁路信号基础设备维护实训	1.5	课内考试	24	24	24/1		1w				
		7	102077060	铁路区间自动控制系统维护实训	3.0	课内考试	48	48	24/2			2w			
		8	102076060	铁路车站自动控制系统维护实训	3.0	课内考试	48	48	24/2				2w		
		9	102103030	铁路信号设计与施工实训	1.5	考查	24	24	24/1					1w	
		10	102057150	信号工技能鉴定实训	7.5	课内考试	140	140	28/5				5w		
		11	102097090	供电工综合实训	4.5	考查	72	72	24/3					3w	
		12	102027120	毕业设计	6.0	考查	96	96	24/4					4w	
		13	102100320	实习	16.0	考查	448	448	28/16						16w
		专业主干课合计			51.5		1048	956		0	0	30	0	0	0
	专业限选课	1	102054030	创业规划与实践	1.5	考查	24	24	24/1					1w	
		2	102095060	创新设计与实践	3.0	课内考试	48	48	24/2					2w	
		3	304098030	铁路线路构造与维护	1.5	课内考试	28	6	4/7		4				
		4	302045030	桥隧构造与维护	1.5	课内考试	28	6	4/7		4				
		5	201065030	电力线路维护	1.5	课内考试	28	6	4/7				4		
		6	201069060	接触网维护	3.0	课内考试	48	48	24/2					2w	
		7	102082020	人工智能概论	1.0	讲座	16	0						讲座	
		专业限选课合计			13		220	138		0	4	0	4	0	0
总合计					166.0		2822	1484	学期总课时	503	481	492	496	392	458
									周总课时	26	28	48	28	0	0
说明					每学期有一周机动和一周考试（前四学期），第五学期有一周机动。铁道类专业需开设“××规章”课程，不单独安排课内学时，在2、3、4学期组织学生进行考查，学生通过考查即可获得相应学分					毕业方式					
										××综合实践或毕业设计					